RESEARCH AND EVALUATION FOR BUSY PRACTITIONERS

A time-saving guide

Helen Kara

First published in Great Britain in 2012 by

The Policy Press
University of Bristol
Fourth Floor
Beacon House
Queen's Road
Bristol BS8 1QU
UK
Tel +44 (0)117 331 4054
Fax +44 (0)117 331 4093
e-mail tpp-info@bristol.ac.uk
www.policypress.co.uk

North American office:
The Policy Press
c/o The University of Chicago Press
1427 East 60th Street
Chicago, IL 60637, USA
t: +1 773 702 7700
f: +1 773-702-9756
e:sales@press.uchicago.edu
www.press.uchicago.edu

British Library Cataloguing in Publication Data
A catalogue record for this book is available from the British Library.

Library of Congress Cataloging-in-Publication Data
A catalog record for this book has been requested.

ISBN 978 1 44730 115 8 paperback
ISBN 978 1 44730 116 5 hardcover

Cover design by Qube Design Associates, Bristol
Front cover: image kindly supplied by www.istock.com
Printed and bound in Great Britain by Hobbs, Southampton
The Policy Press uses environmentally responsible print partners

To my parents, Julie and Mark Miller, who taught me to read, write and think, gave me a love of learning, and encouraged me even when my choices were different from their own.

Contents

List of figures, tables and boxes

Figures

Tables

Boxes

About the author

Dr Helen Kara has been an independent social researcher and writer since 1999. Her background is in social care and the third sector, and she works with third sector organisations and social care and health partnerships. While working full time, she obtained both her MSc in Social Research Methods and her PhD. She is a Director of We Research It Ltd and a member of the Social Research Association, the UK Evaluation Society, and the SROI Network. Helen is also an Associate Research Fellow of the Third Sector Research Centre at Birmingham University. She teaches research methods to practitioners and students, and loves to demystify the processes of writing and research.

For further information about this book please visit www.policypress.co.uk/resources/kara

You can find the author on Twitter: @helen_kara

Acknowledgements

There may be only one name on the spine, but it takes more than a single person to make a book. In fact, it takes more than just people. For example, this book would never have been written without Montezuma's organic chilli chocolate to keep my brain on fire, and the Co-op's Fairtrade wines to damp it down when necessary.

My family have to be supportive, because it's in the job descriptions for Mother, Father, Sister, Brother-in-Law and Nephew: that's Julie Miller, Mark Miller, Ros Hodge, Carl Hodge, and Jamie Round, respectively. Talking of families, my out-laws – the Holmeses, Mengells and Parrishes – aren't a bad bunch either.

A number of people have helped this book along in ways that surpass the bounds of friendship. These are: Debi Alper, Jenny Beattie, Pam Carter, Zoë Clarke, Su Connan, Anne Cummins, Mike Cummins, Nick Dixon, Leigh Forbes, Anjali Gupta, Radhika Holmström, Helen Hunt, Denyse Kirkby, Jenny Maltby, Rachel McAllister, Lucy Pickering, Wayne Thexton and Katy Vigurs.

Writing can be a solitary process, but my friends on Twitter alleviated my solitude, usually by taking the mick. The enchanting illustrations are by Carol Burns; I would encourage you to see more of her excellent artwork at www.etsy.com/shop/ArtsAutobiographical. Martin Holmes of the University of Victoria, Canada, gave me great advice on referencing when we met in Paris. My colleagues at Katharine House Hospice in Stafford have delighted me with their interest in, and support for, my writing life. The technical aspects of this book would have been woeful without the help of Nik Holmes from Creative Technology. Enthusiasm for this project from curators at the British Library was heartening, particularly Simone Bacchini, Jennie Grimshaw, and John Kaye, whose input on Chapters 6 and 8 was invaluable.

At The Policy Press, Karen Bowler, Kathryn King, Dave Worth, Laura Vickers and Claire Harper were kind, supportive, and on the ball. Hawk-eyed and knowledgeable copy editor, Judith Oppenheimer, saved me from many blunders. I owe a big debt of gratitude to five anonymous referees of the proposal for this book; without your helpful and constructive suggestions, this would have been a much feebler tome. I owe another big debt of gratitude to the 20 anonymous people who gave their time and expertise in interviews for this book; your input has strengthened it enormously. But the biggest thanks of all, for his constant love and support, goes to my beloved Nik.

All the mistakes are, of course, mine. So are most of the good parts.

ONE

Introduction

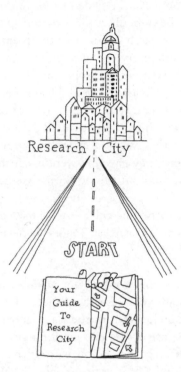

Introduction

This book is for practitioners in public services. 'Public services' are services run by society for society, such as health, social care, criminal justice, and education services from pre-school to university. Some public services are paid for by the state from our taxes, and others are run as charities, businesses, or social enterprises. 'Practitioners' are people who work in one of these services, whether they are paid or unpaid. Practitioners may also be users of the services in which they work and/or of other public services.

In the current climate, more and more practitioners are being required to do research on top of their main jobs. This may be workplace research, such as evaluation of a service or intervention, a service-user satisfaction survey, a skills audit, or training needs analysis. Or it may be academic research such as a diploma, a Master's degree, or a PhD, for the practitioner's professional development. The differences between workplace and academic research are not as pronounced as you may think. Good-quality research demands most of the same approaches and techniques, regardless of context. Where there is a difference, this will be described and discussed.

I have worked alongside practitioners as an independent researcher in public services since the late 1990s. After a while, practitioners began to ask my advice about their own research projects. I decided to write this book because I have seen at first hand some of the difficulties practitioners encounter when they are faced with the need to do research. As part of the preparation for writing this book, I conducted 20 in-depth interviews with public service practitioners. These practitioners had a wide range of roles (see Appendix 1) and they all had experience of doing research on top of a main job. Some also had experience of doing research as service users, or of supporting service users or other practitioners through the research process. I asked them how they managed to do research on top of their main jobs, and what advice they would give others who found themselves in a similar position. The insights they gave me were invaluable. Quotes from their interviews can be found throughout this book in boxes, like this:

> I think, obviously naïvely, where's the book that will tell me what to do? It doesn't exist because it's more complex than that. There's no one book that will say, "If you want to research this, do this."

As this interviewee suggests, this book is not an instruction manual that will lead you step by step through your research project. That's because there is no such book. Writing a comprehensive instruction manual for research would be as impossible as writing an instruction manual for a city. You have to find your own way through your research, just as you would have to find your own way around an unfamiliar city, and this is your guidebook. Within these pages you will find much useful advice about places to go – and places to avoid. Then it's up to you whether you go to the recommended places, or the dangerous places; the risk is yours. Think about it, though. Careful use of a guidebook can help to increase enjoyment and reduce stress when you are in an unfamiliar place. Similarly, this book is designed to help maximise enjoyment and minimise stress as you navigate through your research project.

Being a researcher

While you are conducting research, you are a researcher (Davies, 2007: 6). It doesn't matter whether you are a novice or experienced; whether your project is one of many in your life, or the only piece of research you ever carry out. While you are doing your project, you have the identity of 'researcher' to add to all your other identities: friend, colleague, sibling, parent, service user, and so on. You already know what those identities mean and how they interact. For example, you might be more likely to talk about your emotional problems to a family member than to a colleague. You will probably respond lovingly if a child wakes you in the night because they had a bad dream, but you might be less sympathetic if you were woken for the same reason by a friend.

Some common qualities of researchers are:

determined	creative	thoughtful
intelligent	tenacious	organised
reflective	empathic	meticulous
conscientious	thorough	analytical
self-aware	assertive	honest

> From a personal point of view, I want to do it to the best of my ability. I have had comments like, "Just do enough to pass." I think, "Yes, I will," but I can't. It's not who I am.

Researchers also need to be skilled in reading, writing, thinking, generating ideas, making connections, dealing with people, negotiating, balancing competing needs, and managing setbacks.

This may look terribly daunting. I include it here because I think it's easier to find your way if you know where you're going. All identities are learned. You will have had experience of this during your life: perhaps you learned to be a university student, or a parent, or a sportsperson. So you can learn to be a researcher – and, like all identities, you learn it on the job.

All identities overlap and interact with each other. Nobody is 'just a shop assistant' or 'only a student'. We all manage multiple identities all the time. Nevertheless, adding a new identity to our portfolio can be a stressful process. Most research-methods textbooks are written as if the research process exists in a bubble, separate from everything else. My intention is not to criticise research-methods textbooks, or the wider body of research-methods literature, much of which is very useful. I have drawn on a considerable amount of that literature, and I certainly couldn't have written this book without learning a great deal from those who have gone before me. My aim is to acknowledge that research is part of life in all its messy complexity, and to demonstrate ways of managing the research process in its wider context.

One key research skill is communication. Fortunately, public service practitioners usually have good communication skills. However, embarking on research can leave you feeling like a bumbling amateur. I think this is because you're working from an unfamiliar identity – that of researcher – and you're putting other people into unfamiliar identities of their own, such as research participant, before you have acquired the skills to help this along.

> For people who haven't got a lot of experience in doing research, it gets very difficult when you're learning on the job, in front of your colleagues, in a whole new sphere of skills that you haven't actually got, so you feel well outside of your comfort zone even though you're a very experienced practitioner. People feel very exposed and

unsure, and that gets very difficult for a lot of practitioners who are very experienced to understand that they've got to go through that learning process.

Also, research inevitably includes a lot of 'first contacts', which are notoriously difficult for us humans who are predisposed to jump to conclusions (Kahneman, 2011: 83–4). Whatever your first impression of someone you meet during the research process – whether favourable or unfavourable – try to keep an open mind about that person, and remember how little you actually know about them. Where possible, take the time to find out more. Kahneman points out that we often operate as if what we see is all there is (2011: 85), and so are willing to reach a conclusion about someone's personality and potential on the basis of a very brief contact. In fact, people are astonishingly complex, and even a small investment of time and attention can often pay dividends.

Other key research skills, such as negotiation and time management, will be covered later in the book.

Why do practitioners do research?

We do research all the time, don't we? If you want to buy a product for work, say we need some marketing materials produced, I'm not going to go with the first company, I'll go with the company that gives the best product at the best price. That's research.

Why are you doing research? Because you've been told to? To earn money? To please your manager? To improve your CV or help you get a qualification? To increase knowledge, improve practice, or influence policy? For some other reason? Or for two or more of these reasons, combined?

One reason may be that the requirement for research to be conducted within public services appears to be increasing. I have observed this in recent years, as an independent researcher working with practitioners in a range of public services, and ten of the 20 interviewees for this book – from across the sectors – also said that this was their experience.

Due to the worldwide economic downturn, there is less money to outsource research, so it has become part of the main job for more people. There are also positive reasons for the increase. One interviewee from the health sector was eloquent about this:

Some reasons I can think of are:

1. Health professionals such as nurses access education at degree level and above now, which has changed in the last few years. This has increased the body of literature regarding nursing, midwifery and health visitors generated by those professionals.

2. Education at these levels creates more academically confident professionals who understand, can contribute to and can critique and apply research. They understand the benefit of research and how it can benefit patient care in a way that was not there previously.

3. Extended roles for nurses, midwives and health visitors have been developed over recent years, such as prescribing, which was traditionally the stronghold of the medical profession. The ability to manage complex issues and to make clear decisions requires higher-level skills.

4. The NHS is required to make best use of resources and deliver best-possible outcomes for patients – evidence base is needed to inform this.

5. Patients are able to access information such as through the Web and health professionals need to be able to demonstrate that the treatments they offer are the best available in terms of safety and efficacy – this can be shown through research evidence.

Another interviewee, from the criminal justice system, said an increase hadn't happened yet in the UK, but they could see it coming:

> This whole research thing, it's something that is ripe for expansion. In America there's research and development departments in some police forces. There is in Australia, Australians in some respects are quite far ahead of the British in terms of establishing a police research culture. In Britain, there's one or two research and development type departments but they're few and far between. I think if the police had the capacity to do their own research, the database that they have, if they had the ability to use academic analysis on their material, they would, I'm certain be able to reduce crime quite significantly because they have the data that people would just love to get access to, but because it's confidential you can't.

As these interview extracts indicate, practitioners in public services are ideally placed to conduct research that will improve those services. This applies whether research done by practitioners is conducted entirely in the workplace or is for an academic qualification. In some countries, and in some disciplines, research skills are a requirement for career progression at certain levels. For example, in New Zealand, social workers have to demonstrate that they can do a piece of evaluation or research before they can progress to senior clinician status. However, as the interviews for this book showed, public service workers are often required to do research with little or no training or support.

> I know people who think research is just about going in and talking to people, and don't understand even that you shouldn't ask leading questions. There is something to having done your background research before you've done the research. It's not

true that anyone can do it. I don't think you necessarily need formal qualifications, but to have read something about it, or done a training course, you would probably reap the rewards.

Formal training is seen as helpful, but difficult to access, for a number of reasons: budget restrictions, lack of local courses, lack of courses in the subject area, and insufficient understanding of training needs.

I don't think there's enough training courses available in this area. I don't think people understand, really, that things like training audits, skills audits, evaluation, all fall under research.

I don't know of any training for evaluation. I'm sure it's there, but there's nothing in our induction about it. It's almost like you pick it up by osmosis or something.

One interviewee had some advice for those starting a job involving research when they had no experience of research.

You need to set aside a day of your induction, sit with your line manager, or ideally your head of department, and get them to show you what evaluations they've done, how they do it, and what they expect of you. So you're really seeing either a benchmark you're working towards, or the style of working practice.

This book will explain the fundamental principles and practices of research in public services. It won't provide everything you need — no book can do that — but it will give you a good grounding in the subject, as well as lots of practical advice about how to manage the research process in tandem with the rest of your life, and tips to save you time and stress. Here's an example:

 *Back-up everything you produce on a computer, every single day.*

Some of the tips in the book, like this one, may at first sight seem to add extra work to your load. Think, though: is it worth saving less than a minute of your time each day to risk losing days or weeks or months of work? If you don't already have a back-up strategy, there are many ways you can do this. You can transfer your work to a memory stick or a CD, set up a free e-mail address via one of the many providers such as Yahoo! and send your work to it, or use a free cloud-based service such as Dropbox, iCloud or Skydrive (see Appendix 3 for more information about working 'in the cloud'). Any of these processes will take only a few minutes to set up initially, and just a few seconds to use each day. You should of course keep your back-up somewhere away from your main data store; there's not much point backing up onto a memory stick that you then put in the same bag as your laptop. Also, you need to consider the wisdom of using cloud-based services for people's personal data that should be kept confidential. But between all the options, if you take a little time to think it through, you should be able to set up an easy-to-use system that will protect you against time-consuming and stressful data loss.

While you're working on a computer, get into the habit of pressing Ctrl+S (on a PC) or Apple+S (on a Mac) every few minutes. This will save your latest work against computer crashes, power cuts, or accidents.

Insider and outsider research

'Insider' and 'outsider' are opposites, but presenting them in this dichotomous way conceals the fact that they're actually two ends of a spectrum. If you're a practitioner conducting research within the service you help to run, or a service user researching the service you use, you're definitely an insider. But when are you an outsider? When you've stopped working in, or using, a service? If so, do you become an outsider straight away, or only after a period of time? Or are you only, really, an outsider if you've never worked in, or used, that service? In which case, can anyone ever conduct outsider research on primary healthcare or school education? Conversely, how much research does an outsider have to do within a particular organisation before they become an insider?

There are pros and cons to both insider and outsider research (Robson, 2011: 403–4). A comparison is set out in Table 1.1 (and I am indebted to Robson for many of the points made here).

As you can see, neither insider nor outsider research is 'best'. The answer to the question of which approach should be used depends on the nature of the research to be conducted.

Table 1.1: Comparing insider and outsider research

Insider research	Outsider research
Insider researchers have expert knowledge of their service that will help to inform the research.	Outsider researchers have to spend time learning about the service.
Insider researchers know where to go for help and information within their organisation.	Outsider researchers have to spend time getting to know the people and politics of the organisation.
Insider researchers may be attached to a particular view of their service.	Outsider researchers bring a fresh, independent view to the research.
Insider researchers may have more credibility with their colleagues and service users than an external stranger (although the reverse can also be true).	Outsider researchers have to build relationships and develop trust with service staff, volunteers, and users.
Insider researchers may have difficulty in challenging the practice of their colleagues, or their own practice, even where research findings demonstrate that change is needed.	Outsider researchers usually find it easier to challenge practice where necessary.
Insider researchers are likely to have full access to confidential information.	Outsider researchers may not have full access to confidential information.
Organisations may be more willing to facilitate insider researchers' access to potential participants.	Outsider researchers may find it more difficult to gain access to potential participants.
Some participants will give fuller and more honest information to insider researchers whom they already know and trust.	Some participants will give fuller and more honest information to outsider researchers who they believe will maintain their anonymity.
Insider researchers are well placed to oversee implementation of the research findings or recommendations.	Outsider researchers have to let go of the research when it is finished, and leave the organisation to implement its findings or recommendations.
Research done by an insider, with the full involvement of service users and colleagues, can greatly improve the working practices of the organisation.	Research done by an outsider can become the focus of organisational discontent, at worst leading to the outsider researcher's becoming a scapegoat.

Doing research

For a long time, writers on research have acknowledged that participating in research – say by completing a questionnaire, or taking part in an interview – may not be someone's top priority. Interviewees were also aware of this:

> It's OK doing research but if you can't get anyone to take part in it and you've got very low sample numbers it almost becomes pointless. It's never anyone's priority, it's only the priority of the person conducting it, never the recipient's.

I'd go further. I think it's essential to acknowledge that there are times when conducting research isn't even a researcher's top priority. There are times when looking after a sick child, a night out with friends, visiting a bereaved relative, or going on holiday with your partner will come first. And quite right too.

There is an art in balancing research with the rest of your life. Everyone will differ in the extent to which they prioritise research. I prioritise it highly, because I love research and have made it both career and hobby since the late 1990s. For some people, research is a full-time job, or full-time study, and most people in either of these situations do not have difficulty finding time for their research. But for many people it is a part-time occupation, and for some people very part time. For example, someone who has been forced to do a service evaluation – by a manager whom they don't like, with no training or support, when they are sure they already know what the findings will be – is not likely to prioritise their research very highly at all.

Whether research is a high or low priority for you, and whatever your other commitments, this book will help you find ways to fit research into your life. And it is important to balance research with the rest of your life, or there can be long-lasting consequences, as these interviewees found after neglecting friends and family in favour of research.

> I did not spend the time I should have with them and I know I lost lots of contact with relatives and friends which I miss now that I am semi-retired and have the time.

> I do feel that I probably lost a little bit of my social circle because I wasn't as accessible, I wasn't the party animal I had been. Now I'm trying to make up for it!

> Some friendships have been sacrificed, and relationships have been sacrificed. Some people need you to make that time and if you're not there to make that time, well, I'm OK with that. I think from an impact point of view, I've perhaps been more absent than other friends, but the people who have persevered, we've perhaps got a deeper relationship.

Although, as the last interviewee hinted, there can also be positive consequences for family and friends from spending time on your research:

> I think if it had an impact, it was a positive one. My son has a great intellect but really struggles with his dyslexia, he struggles with getting things on paper. He learned perseverance. I think some of my women friends would say it's a bit inspiring to see one of your friends doing that, and they've gone on and retrained and changed what they do.

Several interviewees suggested that you should think through your plans at the earliest possible opportunity, and talk them over with people you trust.

> Do what we all teach, that is, your research into what impact this work will have on your personal and professional life. Then plan accordingly and do not take too much on board as it could impact on your health, etcetera. People should seek others out who have done what they are proposing and sit down and talk to them about the ups and downs.

> Get some good sounding-board people – they don't have to be researchers, but people you can talk to about the project, people you feel comfortable talking to about things.

Just as identities overlap and interact, so do the component parts of the research process. This book is written, like most books on research, as if there are separate and discrete parts of the process: background reading, data collection, data analysis, writing up. Here is some of the reality:

- Reading in various forms is likely to occur throughout the research (Hart, 2001: 7).
- Notes from your reading may be coded and analysed in the same way as primary data.
- Documents may be categorised as background reading, or secondary data, or both.
- Writing is an essential part of data analysis in particular, whether it be qualitative or quantitative, and of the whole research process in general (Rapley, 2011: 286).

These are just a few examples of the ways in which research processes interact and overlap. It is necessary to separate them for the purposes of discussion and teaching, but in reality, they are inextricable parts of a whole.

Nevertheless, there are transition points in research projects, and it is these transition points that some researchers find hardest to handle.

> I finished gathering the raw data, and it sat there and looked at me for about three weeks before I actually did anything with it. Then I did a few graphs and tables …

Even after years of experience, I still procrastinate when faced with the blank page on which I need to start writing a research report. But these days I know that it is the constants of reading, writing, and thinking that will carry me through the bumpier stages of the research process. So I read some of the notes I've written, and think about what I want to say, until I'm ready to start. Other people use different techniques, such as this interviewee:

> I've got a studying CD that involves quite a bit of Frank Zappa. It makes me laugh, it makes me relax, then I can get started. I need to find a way to relax. Music is my medicine.

Whatever works for you is fine. But if you don't yet know what works for you, I recommend experimenting with reading, writing, and thinking.

Reading, writing, and thinking permeate the research process (Hart, 2001: 8), and thinking is the most important of the three. Your thinking, like everyone else's, develops and moves on day by day. The fact that your brain is your most useful research tool is particularly helpful for busy practitioners, because you can think about your research when you don't have time to do any of your other research work. You can make progress with your thinking in the shower, on the bus, at the supermarket – any time you have to be doing something that doesn't require much of your brainpower. As a researcher, your brain is your greatest asset, both for conducting the research itself, and for working out the best ways to manage the research process in the context of the rest of your life.

The other thing it's important to say at this early stage is that there is no such thing as perfect research or evaluation. Yes, the standards are high, and with good reason. Research should be rigorous, ethical, and robust; researchers should be thorough and conscientious. If you don't yet have a good understanding of the reasons for this, you will by the time you've finished reading this book. But research and evaluation are never perfect, and can never be perfect, because they are conducted by, with, and for people just like us with all our conflicts and inadequacies. Planning and carrying out research or evaluation to a high standard, in the real world, is an enormous challenge – and can also be a source of great joy.

Structure of this book

Chapter Two gives an overview of research. It introduces quantitative, qualitative, mixed-method and value-based approaches to research, and research ethics. The role of service users is discussed, as are the links between research, theory, and practice.

Chapter Three looks at how to choose a research topic and refine it into a research question. Research methods are introduced, and advice is given on how to write a research proposal or plan.

Chapter Four discusses ways to manage the research process in the context of the rest of your life. Planning, organisation, and time management are discussed in detail, and there is a lot of advice from practitioners who are experienced in research. The pros and cons of receiving support for research from employers are outlined. The need to reward yourself, and look after yourself, as you do research, is emphasised. There is a summary of what works – and what doesn't work – in managing research.

Chapter Five describes the similarities and differences between document reviews for workplace research and literature reviews for academic research. Information is given about how to conduct document reviews and literature reviews, together with advice on record keeping, critical and strategic reading, finding open access materials, using libraries, and making notes.

Chapter Six explains the advantages and disadvantages of working with secondary data, and shows how to find secondary data on the World Wide Web. Chapter Seven covers a range of ways of collecting quantitative and qualitative primary data. Chapter Eight outlines some ways of preparing, coding, analysing, and synthesising quantitative and qualitative data.

Chapter Nine begins by identifying and dispelling some myths about the writing process. Then there is a full discussion of how to write research, with advice on how to structure, edit, and polish your writing. The chapter explains how to avoid plagiarism and how to cite other people's work.

Chapter Ten looks at how to disseminate research, why dissemination is important, and the potential barriers to this process. The advantages and disadvantages of different methods of dissemination are outlined. The similarities and differences of workplace and academic research are discussed, as are the ethics of dissemination.

Chapter Eleven concludes the book with a summary of the key points made in the earlier chapters. There is also a bibliography containing references, some of which were cited in the text and some of which will be of use to readers.

TWO

Overview of research

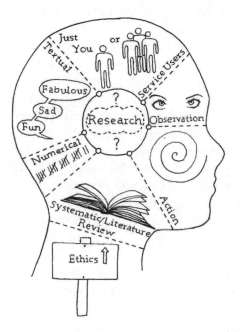

Introduction

As a whole, research is complicated. There's no point pretending it's easy and straightforward. It is hard to do your own research well, and it can be difficult to understand other people's research.

The good news is that research can be broken down into component parts that are much easier to understand. As you become familiar with each piece of the jigsaw, you will begin to see how they can fit together to create a whole picture. This will make it easier for you to plan and carry out research. It will also help you to assess research done by other people.

This chapter will introduce you to some of these component parts.

Quantitative or qualitative research?

In the simplest terms, quantitative research deals with numerical data, that is, things you can count or measure. Qualitative research deals with textual data, that is, words, and other forms of data such as pictures, sound, or multimedia.

Looked at another way, the two approaches can be held to express different philosophies or standpoints (Langdridge and Hagger-Johnson, 2009: 13). Classic quantitative research follows the more traditionally scientific or 'positivist' approach where a hypothesis is formulated, with a defined 'independent variable' whose variation can affect a 'dependent variable' or outcome. The questions are: 'What? How much, how many?' So a hypothesis might be that the amount of homework (independent variable) given to school pupils will affect their class test results (dependent variable). Numerical data about amounts of homework given, and test results achieved, would be collected and analysed using recognised statistical tests to produce numerical results.

Qualitative research, on the other hand, aims to provide an understanding of why things are as they are. Classic qualitative research follows a 'constructivist' approach where it is held that understanding is constructed by researchers and research participants together. The questions are: 'How? Why?' So a qualitative researcher who is interested in finding out about the factors affecting school pupils' class test results would be likely to ask pupils, teachers, and parents or carers for their views, probably through interviews and/or group discussions. The resulting textual data would be coded, and analysed using the researcher's own judgement.

These are very superficial descriptions of extremely complex fields. They make it look as if quantitative and qualitative approaches to research are very different from each other and completely incompatible. Researchers in one field will often trivialise or, at worst, demonise researchers in the other field.

> When I was doing my PhD I went and saw someone who was a supervisor for quantitative research. I said I was using phenomenology, and he said, "Well that's not really research is it?"

However, a closer look will show that quantitative and qualitative research are surprisingly similar. Both are created by a researcher's judgement. Qualitative researchers often aim to record their judgements and present them alongside their findings, so as to allow readers to make their own assessment of the quality of the research. Quantitative research is often presented as though the researcher's judgements are irrelevant or even non-existent, with the quality of the research being defined by the method itself. However, quantitative researchers, like qualitative researchers, have to make judgements at every stage of the process, such as: how to word a hypothesis, which variable(s) to choose, which sampling methods to use, which statistical tests to apply, what is of relevance in the statistical test results, how to present findings. There is no research without judgement, assumption, and interpretation.

Whether you choose to use quantitative or qualitative methods should depend on your research topic and question(s). For example, if you are interested in the extent to which reduced funding for third sector health services increases demand on statutory health services, you would probably choose a quantitative method to help you answer your 'how much?' questions. If you are interested in the effects on a community of reduced funding for third sector health services, you would probably choose a qualitative method to investigate your 'how and why?'

questions. In either case, however, I would encourage you to consider whether there is scope for you to use both approaches together.

Quantitative and qualitative research methods are often complementary. For example, in the case of the school pupils and their test results mentioned earlier, the quantitative approach would give a useful overview of the topic, while the qualitative approach would fill in some detail. In visual terms, you could say that the quantitative approach provides the outline, while the qualitative approach colours it in. The researcher may have chosen the quantitative method because of strong suggestions from elsewhere (for example the literature, dissertation supervisors, or research commissioners) that the amount of homework given to school pupils is the most likely predictor of class test results. They may have chosen the qualitative part of the research because of their own suspicions that other factors may also be relevant. Using both methods in one research project is often known as 'mixed-method' research.

Quantitative, qualitative, and mixed-method research are discussed in more detail in Chapter Three.

Solo or collaborative research?

Some research projects are led or carried out by a single researcher, others are done in partnership. Working in partnership can bring great benefits, such as opportunities to learn from others and a shared workload. However, it also requires a high level of communication and management skills – perhaps even more than solo research, as these interviewees found:

> In the research I did most recently, one of the biggest problems we had was the timetable was too tight and the brief was not clear enough. I think that was because people weren't working together, there were too many cooks in the pot. People were making decisions who had no research experience. A lot of it went belly-up because of lack of communication between all the parties involved. The whole research project was delayed because some of the parameters weren't set out correctly at the beginning. It was all done in a rush really.

> If you're working in a group as well, don't trust that other people are going to do their job! You might want to make sure that whatever you've had your hands on, even if someone else is keeping the literature-search file, keep your own to keep track of what you've done. If they don't do it at least you've got your bit. Then that means you don't need to get quite so angry with somebody else, because you've got something. If your qualification is dependent on lazy-ass getting their act together, or someone who's just had a baby ... this is control freak speaking! But being a control freak is quite helpful in these circumstances.

Ideally, the choice about whether research is carried out by one person or several should be led by the research topic and questions (see Chapter Three for more on this). However, like these interviewees, there may be times where you have no choice about whether your research will be carried out by you alone or collaboratively. And 'collaboration' can mean working with other researchers, and/or other practitioners, and/or service users.

Involving service users in research

'Service users' is a generic term for the users of public services – that is, all of us. Other names may be used for service users, such as patients, students, pupils, parents, carers, offenders, or clients. Service users began to become involved in planning and delivering public services in the mid-1990s (Kemshall and Littlechild (2000: 7). In the UK, in the mid-2000s, it became mandatory for service users to be involved in training social workers (Branfield, 2009: ix). Some other examples of service-user involvement in the UK are:

- parents as school governors;
- pupils on school councils;
- health service users on primary care advisory groups;
- health service users in local involvement networks;
- health service users in hospital patient–advice and liaison services;
- offenders on prison councils;
- offenders in probation service user groups.

There are similar systems of involvement in the US, Canada, Australia, and New Zealand.

Active service users in the UK now have a saying, 'Nothing about us without us'. It is not surprising, in this context, that the 21st century has seen a significant increase in service-user involvement in research (Barber et al, 2011: 217). 'Involvement' denotes a higher level of involvement than 'participation', which may simply mean completing a questionnaire or taking part in an interview. Service users can be involved at all stages of research, from planning and design to dissemination and implementation of recommendations (Barber et al, 2011: 218). This has a range of positive effects, such as increasing access to participants, better-quality data, and more relevant findings (Barber et al, 2011: 218–19). It also has some less positive effects. For example, it takes more time to do research with the full involvement of inexperienced researchers, so it often costs more too (Barber et al, 2011: 219).

If you're intending to involve service users in your research, allow plenty of time to give them any support they may need to enable them to be fully involved.

One interviewee for this book had worked with service users throughout a project, which was a high priority for that researcher but also created a range of problems to overcome:

> If you're going to use lay researchers, the training is most important. Also commitment. I did have a problem where people didn't turn up, I'd have to cancel or reschedule meetings with interview candidates because people didn't turn up that day. Sometimes people would be unwell, or not come in because of a conflict of priorities. I think the hardest part was the fluidity of participants. Those who started the project weren't those who ended it. Some people were more interested in setting up, some in the interviews, some in the data analysis. A very fluid group of people, and that was quite difficult. If I went back again, I'd probably try to have a different regime. My feeling is that having casual labour doesn't work. I'd rather take on four workers for a 10-hours-a-week contract that they could declare at the benefit agency over the whole duration of the project. That would be a lot more solid. With the casual workers, that was like juggling with jelly. There is also the issue that people were doing it mainly for the money, the £10 or £20 per interview. I don't blame them, when you're on benefits, but the primary driver for them wasn't the research itself. Some people would do more than they were paid for, some would get up and walk out of the room literally as soon as they'd earned their £15.

While service users can be involved in any stage of a research project, it may not always be appropriate for service users to be involved at every stage of research controlled by a practitioner. Equally, it may not always be appropriate for practitioners to be involved in research controlled by service users (Turner and Beresford, 2005: xii). A third option is for research to be carried out in partnership between practitioners and service users (Fox et al, 2007: 133). As a practitioner, you can only define your research as 'user controlled' if you are also a user of the service concerned. If you are not a user of that service, you may be able to work in partnership with service users when doing workplace research such as evaluation, although this kind of partnership is often unequal (Fox et al, 2007: 145). For academic research leading to a qualification, you will probably need to control the research (because it would be your qualification), with service users as participants or involved to a comparatively small extent.

In considering whether and/or how to involve service users in your research project, you need to think through a whole range of questions. It's not possible to provide an exhaustive list that will cover any research project, but here are some examples to get you started.

1. How might service–user involvement benefit your research?
2. How might your research benefit any service users who choose to become involved?
3. What are the characteristics of the service users who might become involved? Are there particular needs or constraints for you to take into account? If so, what are these, and how might they affect users' involvement in your research?
4. To what extent would any service users involved in your research be representative of a wider group of service users? What would be the implications of this?
5. Might any of the service users have some research experience? If so, how might this help or hinder your research?
6. Is there a way in which you can reward service users for their involvement in your research?
7. What other ethical issues might you face in involving service users?
8. Can you make contingency plans in case service users change their minds about being involved?

For some people, involving service users and other participants is good, ethical research practice in itself, as long as the involvement is genuine and not tokenistic.

> Because I have certain principles about how to carry out research, I always enjoy working out how to value participants and make them feel as much an active part of the research as possible. I enjoy working with people. So you're not parachuting in and buggering off, they get something out of it. It's not always possible, but I like to get them involved in data analysis where I can.

The references cited in this section and listed in the bibliography at the end of this book should also be useful in helping you to think through this subject.

Value-based research

Traditionally, research has been carried out to answer questions and increase knowledge. Some workplace research, such as evaluation research, has an added purpose of making recommendations for future action.

> That's a big thing between uni and work: at uni you don't have to make recommendations, you just have to present your findings, but at work you have to make recommendations.

A third purpose of research can be to effect positive change. This kind of value-based research is sometimes spoken of as 'emancipatory research' because another of its aims is to empower research participants within the research process (Fox,

2007: 48). Emancipatory research includes a variety of broadly similar approaches, such as: action research, participatory appraisal, action learning sets, cooperative enquiry, and participatory action research (PAR). This section will look at the similarities and differences between action research and PAR.

Action research resists a clear definition (Whitelaw et al, 2003: 8–9) but, in essence, is an iterative process of reflection and problem solving in groups or communities. Problems addressed through action research are those that affect members of the group or community carrying out the research. The process of action research involves identifying a problem, collecting information about the problem, deciding how to solve the problem, trying out the solution, seeing if the solution works, and so on. On-going action research can be thought of as a spiral, rather than a cycle, because each iteration builds on the last.

PAR perhaps takes this a step further, as it 'aims to produce knowledge in an active partnership with those affected by that knowledge, for the express purpose of improving their social, educational, and material conditions' (Bhana, 2006: 430). PAR and its close relative, participatory appraisal, grew from work done by activists in South America and Africa. The differences between action research and PAR stem from their differing histories, but their use in practice has highlighted the many similarities they share (Bhana, 2006: 431).

Action research and PAR are both likely to draw on creative techniques for data gathering, which is often known, within these approaches, as 'data creation' or 'data construction'. Such techniques could include:

- Spidergram – everyone has a pen and access to a large sheet of paper where they can write or draw whatever they wish in response to a question or problem written in the middle of the paper.
- Timeline – everyone has a pen and access to a long sheet of paper with a defined timeline (which may extend into the past, or the future, or both) where they can write or draw whatever they wish about events, experiences, wishes, or plans at particular times or over given time periods.
- Map – everyone has a pen and access to a large sheet of paper with an outline map of a local area, where they can write or draw whatever they wish about specific locations on that map.
- Ranking matrix – people work together to define options, say for solving a problem, and then to define criteria for selecting an option, before ranking options against criteria to identify priorities for action.

Ranking matrices can be difficult to visualise, so here is an example. A small-town community wanted to solve the problem of young people having few activities available to them outside school and home. This problem led to groups of young people congregating in the town centre, which made older people perceive them as anti-social (even though they were in fact perfectly well behaved). When young people were asked what activities they would like, they came up with several options, but the town couldn't afford to provide them all, so a ranking matrix was used to prioritise the young people's ideas against available resources. People of all ages worked together to define criteria for selection, and the options and criteria were made into a matrix, as shown in Table 2.1.

Table 2.1: Ranking matrix

Options	Criteria for selection					
	Cost	Construction needed?	Accessibility (age, ability etc)	Staff needed?	Venue available?	Total
Skateboard park	5	5	1	0	1	12
Youth club with games	4	1	2	5	3	15
Cookery courses	3	1	1	3	1	9
Dance studio	2	1	4	4	4	15
Music club with DJ	2	1	3	4	4	14

The group decided to mark each cell from 1 to 5 on the basis of discussion, with the marks running from 5 for undesirable criteria (high cost, construction needed, low accessibility, staff needed, and no venue available), to 1 for their opposites. Scores would then be added together such that the maximum possible score would be 25 and the minimum would be 5, with the lowest-scoring option being the best. The outcome of the discussions was that cookery courses scored 9, the skateboard park scored 12, and the other options all scored more highly. (The cookery courses could be run by volunteers at a local school; the skateboard park would be expensive to build but would have minimal running costs and no staff requirements.) The group decided that cookery courses could start straight away. They would also begin raising funds to build the skateboard park, and would start work on the other options once funds for the skateboard park had been secured.

Some people find value-based research very appealing. It fits well with the ethos of some public services, such as education and community development, although less well with others, such as some parts of the health and criminal justice services. But value-based research does have disadvantages. It is time consuming, and in academic arenas value-based research is often regarded as less rigorous than more traditional approaches (Fox, 2007: 48). I would advise you to consider all the implications before committing yourself to value-based research.

Highly time-consuming methods

There are several methods in qualitative and quantitative research that are usually too time consuming for workplace, undergraduate, or initial postgraduate research. Some examples are: randomised controlled trials, systematic reviews, meta-analyses, participant observation, and ethnographies. These methods may be used at doctoral level but, even then, I'd encourage you only to use one of these methods if you're absolutely sure it's the best way to achieve your research aims.

Randomised controlled trials are experiments where participants are randomly allocated to an experimental group or a control group. These trials are often used in drug testing, where each person can be given pills but only those in the experimental group are given pills that actually contain a drug. People in the control group are given pills that look identical but contain a harmless substance such as sugar. These trials may be conducted 'double-blind', which means that even the person administering the medication doesn't know which of the participants are getting the drugs and which are getting the fake pills. This is regarded by some people as the 'gold standard' of all social research methods (Robson, 2011: 99). However, like all methods, it should not be used for its own sake, but only when it is likely to be the best way of answering the research question. Randomised controlled trials are difficult to set up and administer, and can have unique ethical problems. For example, sometimes drug trials have to be ended early if a drug proves to have unexpected and harmful side-effects, or if interim results show that people in the control group are suffering because they are lacking a drug being given to those in the experimental group.

A systematic review is, in theory, a review of all the research already conducted around a specific research question. The aim is to reduce bias (Petticrew and Roberts, 2005: 10) by establishing selection criteria for the inclusion of research in the review, such as methodological soundness (Petticrew and Roberts, 2005: 2). However, the selection criteria are defined by researchers and are therefore likely to carry biases of their own. For example, although a researcher may have the best intentions of including all methodologically sound research in their systematic review, different researchers will have different views of what constitutes 'methodologically sound'. For example, one researcher might think that sample size is an important criterion, so they decide to exclude any study with a sample size of less than 60 participants. Another researcher might think that sample size is just as important, but they decide to exclude any study with a sample size of less than 30 participants. The second researcher might further decide that the findings of studies with 31 to 99 participants will be considered as indicative rather than conclusive. This could mean that the first researcher leaves out several studies with 40–50 participants that have relevant results, while the second researcher doesn't give enough weight to studies with 80–90 participants.

A systematic review differs from a literature review because it is a review only of reported research, and doesn't include any other kinds of literature. (Literature reviews are discussed in more detail in Chapter Five.) The use of inclusion criteria is intended to make the review systematic, because the research reports are systematically assessed against the defined inclusion criteria to help the researcher decide whether or not they should be included. A meta-analysis is similar to a systematic review, but also includes a statistical summary of quantitative findings.

So far it all sounds reasonably straightforward. In practice, however, conducting a systematic review or a meta-analysis can be a real challenge. Jesson, Matheson and Lacey (2011: 3) suggest that a systematic review shouldn't be attempted until a researcher has become a competent reviewer of literature using more traditional methods. They comment that 'one value of traditional reviews is that they often provide insights that can be neglected or passed over in the steps towards exclusion and quality control that are required in the systematic review model' (Jesson, Matheson and Lacey, 2011: 15).

In conducting a systematic review or meta-analysis, the researcher may be faced with a huge amount of data to analyse: in some cases, many hundreds of research reports. Systematic reviews and meta-analyses are as subject to the constraints of time and budget as any other kind of research, and even generous allowances of both may not be enough. Then the application of the inclusion criteria may not be as easy as it looks. Not all research is clearly written, which can make it difficult to assess the quality of the method(s) used and the robustness of the conclusions drawn. Therefore, I would assert that systematic reviews and meta-analyses, however well intentioned, require as much use of judgement, assumption, and interpretation as any other type of social research.

This is not intended as a criticism of the systematic review or meta-analysis methods. These are worthwhile and useful exercises in some contexts, such as to assess the effectiveness of an intervention where a single study may not give the full picture, and so to increase the chances of knowledge gained from research being translated into practice (Jesson, Matheson and Lacey, 2011: 15). However, it is important to remember that there is no such thing as a perfect piece of research, and systematic review and meta-analysis are no exception. My primary aim here is to emphasise that systematic reviews and meta-analyses should not be undertaken lightly.

Ethnography and participant observation are two further techniques that should not be underestimated in terms of the time and effort needed to use them properly. Ethnography comes from the Greek words for 'people' and 'writing', and literally means 'writing about people'. Ethnographers often use the technique of participant observation, which involves living and/or working with people while observing their experiences. For example, Philippe Bourgois spent five years living with crack dealers in a deprived area of New York (Bourgois, 2002), and Nigel Rapport spent a year working as a hospital porter at a large hospital in Scotland (Rapport, 2008). Both men are in fact career academics and spent their time observing the people they were living and working with, and writing about those people. The techniques they used come from the discipline of social anthropology, and are widely used by anthropology doctoral students, who don't find them easy.[1] They are particularly difficult for novice researchers to undertake effectively (Davies, 2007: 168, 170).

---

[1] Dr Lucy Pickering, personal communication, 2011.

Social return on investment

Social return on investment (SRoI) is a value-based mixed-method approach to all-round assessment of the social, economic, and environmental return on investment. This encompasses a much broader conception of how change is created and what change is worth than does a simple financial return on financial investment, or even cost-benefit analysis.

SRoI was first conceived and used in the 1990s, and the worldwide SRoI Network was founded in 2006. Use of the approach has developed rapidly, to a point where it is now being promoted in legislation, such as in the 2012 Public Services (Social Value) Act in the UK. Like the methods above, SRoI can be time and resource intensive, particularly at the outset. But it also, potentially, has a lot to offer in providing a framework for how to think rigorously about the nature and quality of public services.

SRoI is based on seven principles:

1. Involve stakeholders.
2. Understand what changes.
3. Value the things that matter.
4. Only include what is material.
5. Do not over-claim.
6. Be transparent.
7. Verify the result.

I would argue that some of these principles should apply to any kind of research, particularly numbers 1, 5, 6, and 7. (These principles will be discussed in more detail elsewhere in this book.) It is perhaps within principles 2, 3, and 4 that the uniqueness of SRoI resides. These principles raise specific questions that provide a useful framework for thought.

Central SRoI questions include:

- Who changes as a result of the service being provided? Does the service create change for its users? What about their families? Do the staff or volunteers of the service experience change? What about professionals referring people into the service, or accepting referrals from the service? Are there other people who change as a result of the service?
- In what ways do these people change? How do they know? How can they communicate the change to us?
- How can we measure the change? What is the evidence for the change?
- What is the change worth? Can the people experiencing the change express its value? Are there financial proxies we can use to express the value of the change?
- Is any of the change due to other factors apart from the provision of the service? Would any of the change have happened if the service didn't exist?

Are there other ways the change could have been created even though the service does exist?

- Will the change persist beyond the point where someone stops using the service? If so, for how long?
- How much of the change is relevant? Can the service deliver outcomes that are: required (or, conversely, blocked) by policy; needed by stakeholders; valued by stakeholders' peers who experience similar change from other sources; demanded by social norms; and/or have beneficial financial impacts?
- How much of the change is significant? Is the quantity of change too low for it to be significant? Is too much of the change caused by other factors for it to be significant? Would too much of the change have happened anyway, for it to be significant, even if the service did not exist?

Doing a full SRoI project is a sizeable undertaking, particularly if you have no previous experience. The approach always uses both qualitative and quantitative data, and requires a completely different approach to data analysis from any other type of research. And there are no short cuts.

However, although SRoI takes a lot of time, energy, and money to learn and use initially, the SRoI principles and questions in themselves are a valuable free resource for social researchers. We can all benefit from considering these questions as part of any research project that focuses on the provision of public services. SRoI Network members have seen, in practice, that this process can improve the quality of service delivery, by its rigorous approach to identifying the actual change that really happens, rather than by trying to find a level of change that doesn't actually exist. Sadly, the latter approach is still all too common.

> It's a one-week project and we still have to evaluate in terms of how much this has influenced their lives, when we know that's all about the long-term relationship rather than the quick wham-bam. It's "Have we changed your life?" which sometimes the organisation thinks is possible when it's not.

Given the speed with which SRoI has developed, it is perhaps not surprising that some misconceptions about SRoI have also arisen. In particular, SRoI does not provide a basis for comparison between services or organisations, so it cannot be used as a short cut to decisions about the allocation of resources. SRoI produces the 'SRoI ratio', which, at its briefest, says something like, 'For every £1 invested in the work of Super Service, £4's worth of social value is created.' It is tempting for people to focus on this at the expense of the associated narrative about change and value. If Mega Service creates £3's worth of social value for every £1 invested, that does *not* mean that Mega Service is less valuable, overall, than Super Service. Each SRoI will have been conducted in the context of each individual service, so the results are applicable only to that service. (Comparison between one SRoI and another of the same service, conducted after a suitable interval, can, however, be very useful indeed.)

This section is unreferenced, as SRoI is so new that there is very little formal literature about the method. I'm grateful to several members of the SRoI Network for their input on the above paragraphs.

If you want to find out more about SRoI, search the World Wide Web.

Research ethics

Ethics can be defined as the rules of conduct for a particular activity. This is not specific to research: there are medical ethics, legal ethics, and sporting ethics, among many others. Many public services have their own code of ethics (or equivalent, for example code of conduct), but research ethics are different from service ethics (Fox et al, 2007: 104). Within research there are different ethical codes for different disciplines, such as psychological research, social research, and market research. These codes are broadly similar but with slightly different foci. Several are listed in the bibliography at the end of this book.

Seek out the ethical code that is closest to your profession or discipline and familiarise yourself with its content at an early stage.

Research ethics have learned a lot from medical ethics. The basic principle of medical ethics, 'first do no harm', is useful for social researchers to keep in mind (Kumar, 2005: 214). Ethical dilemmas from medicine also provide useful illustrations of the fact that sometimes it is not possible to balance all competing interests and do no harm. For example, if a pregnant woman is diagnosed with cancer, and will die without treatment, but her unborn baby will die if she has treatment, she has to decide whether to prioritise her own life or that of her foetus. Whichever decision she makes, some people will think she should have made the other choice.

Every researcher will encounter ethical dilemmas. These can be minimised through careful planning and good research practice, but they can't be eradicated. Luckily, they're not usually matters of life and death. But social research does have the capacity to do great harm, to individuals, groups, and society as a whole, if it is unethically managed.

Generally speaking, it is during the primary data collection phase of research that people are most conscious of the need to be careful not to do harm to others. But ethical considerations should underpin every stage of the research process (Robson, 2011: 199). To begin with, why are you doing the research? Is it for your own benefit, for kudos in the workplace or to gain a qualification, or does it have a wider purpose? For many practitioners, their research, like their work in general, needs to achieve something worthwhile.

> I didn't want to do research just for the sake of doing research, because I think that's unethical. Whoever you speak to in the community needs to benefit from the research you're going to do.

As you plan your research, you need to think through the ethical issues for each stage, and show that you have done this in your research proposal or plan (see Chapter Three for more information about these). It might seem that working with literature or documents doesn't require any ethical considerations. However, as a researcher you have a responsibility to read carefully and give a faithful representation of others' work. If you don't take the time and make the effort to gain a full understanding of each text, you may misrepresent the author's views, which could harm their professional reputation – and yours. This does not mean reading uncritically; it is essential to form your own opinion on the merit of what you read. There is more about this in Chapter Five.

Primary data collection is the stage where most people do consider ethical issues. Potential research participants must always be able to choose freely whether or not to take part in your research. This means they need full information about what you are doing, why you are doing it, what the extent of their involvement would be, how their data will be stored, and the outcomes you expect. Research participants are volunteers, although some researchers think that, for ethical reasons, they should be given a tangible thank you: perhaps a nice pen to keep after using it to fill in a questionnaire, or a gift voucher at the end of an interview or focus group. In any case, in accordance with good volunteer-management practice, research participants should not be out of pocket as a result of volunteering to take part, so any travel or other expenses they incur as a result of their participation should be reimbursed from the research budget.

Some research projects focus on vulnerable groups, such as those with mental health problems, people with learning disabilities, bereaved people, children, or homeless people. In these cases even more care needs to be taken to ensure that potential and actual participants are not harmed in the course of the research. Participants should be reassured that they can end their participation at any point if they wish, or withdraw their data at a later stage. You need to specify when they will no longer be able to do this, and I would suggest that this is the point at which you start analysing the data. Once the analysis is under way, it becomes more difficult to withdraw data fully because it will have contributed to your thinking.

Use of secondary data also involves ethical considerations. Statistics and other numerical data are often presented as though they are neutral, but they are not value free. Human beings have decided how to present the figures, what to include and what to leave out, and how to arrange the numbers they have included. Those human beings have their own agendas that may unconsciously – or consciously – influence their decisions. This is not an attempt to create some kind of grand conspiracy theory. However, I would suggest that you are as careful in reading numerical data as in reading literature and documents, to make sure you understand the arguments being put forward and can represent them correctly. I would also recommend a critical approach to numbers, as to text, to try to understand, as far as possible, the personal and political agendas that may have influenced their presentation.

Data analysis, too, should be done ethically. For a start, you need to use all the data you have collected. If you collect data that you don't use, you have misled your research participants and wasted their time. (This is a good reason for keeping your research project to a manageable size.) Then you need to make sure that you are representing your participants fully and accurately. Your findings should be firmly and clearly rooted in your data.

Writing your research also has ethical aspects. Consider the needs of your readers and write your report to meet those needs. Make sure the structure is user friendly, the narrative flows, and the prose is clear. Keep jargon and professional terminology to a minimum and, where these are absolutely necessary, give definitions. Be clear about how your conclusions spring from your findings and your findings spring from your data. As far as possible, ensure that your conclusions are dictated by the findings and the data you have collected, rather than by your own biases and preferences. And try to write the report in such a way that anyone reading it will be able to judge this for themselves.

If you are conducting workplace research such as a service evaluation, you will need to make recommendations for putting the research into practice (Robson, 2011: 506). This can be something of an ethical balancing act. On the one side, you have the need to accurately represent your findings, and on the other side, you have limited resources. You may also be under pressure from managers or commissioners, like this interviewee:

> They want me to find things other than what they've already found but there's nothing there. It's blindingly obvious where the problems are but they seem to want more and more detail. There's no point, it won't tell them anything different in the long run. Our biggest problem, I could have told them when they first did the survey, is that we haven't got enough staff to deal with the customers coming through the door, the footfall, it's just not possible. All the findings are people complaining about wait times. One day we had over 400 people through the door and four members of staff, so what do people expect? I'm trying to turn it round to be positive, four members of staff,

each saw 100 people that day, excellent bloomin' productivity. They're trying to get me to find something different, but in the long run it's all going to come out the same.

This kind of pressure is in itself unethical, and it's a researcher's job to resist it and protect the views of research participants. This is not always easy. Some years ago, I did a service audit that involved gathering views from all the staff of a public service. The research commissioner told me not to include a question about salaries, as it was a contentious issue and the management didn't want it to be highlighted through the research. I agreed to this, thinking that as I was doing semi-structured interviews, it would come up anyway if there were strong feelings about the subject. However, I was surprised when every single person I interviewed said they were aggrieved by their low salary. Given this, I felt a duty to report it in the findings, so I did – and the commissioner was furious.

Dissemination, also, has its ethical aspects. It is difficult to summarise a research project on one side of A4, or a poster or leaflet, while maintaining a true representation of all the literature, documents, and data that have contributed to the research. There is also the question of whom you disseminate the findings to. Of course your manager, supervisor, commissioner, or examiner will have to see your work. But what about the research participants? Do they have a right to see, and maybe even comment on, the results of your research? One interviewee felt very strongly about this:

> I think feeding back to the people you have involved in the research is something that should happen as standard every single time, and I think it should be built into a research plan. I don't think sending them a copy of whatever report you produce is good enough. I think it has to be something that definitely reflects what they've told you.

Dissemination methods are covered in more detail in Chapter Ten.

Looking after yourself

Something that is often forgotten is the ethical imperative for researchers to look after themselves. Doing research can be very stressful at times, particularly on top of a main job.

> It's the sort of thing that could bring on a panic attack if you think about it too hard.

> The pressure and stress on family life can be quite demanding, you've got to factor all that in. I have known marriages breaking up, I've got academic friends who've done so much work in academia that they've ended up divorced, you've got to be pretty careful.

> Doing a PhD, three or four years of no relaxing weekends or holidays where you can switch off, I think it affects your mental health and your relationships with friends and

family. Even those who do it in a shorter amount of time, you have these real spikes of depression. It's always there, so even if you do decide you're having a weekend off, it's still there.

It's essential that you plan ways to keep yourself physically, mentally, and emotionally safe. It is not ethical to wear yourself out doing research, and this book will advise you on healthy working practices, such as good time management, that can help to reduce your stress levels.

Different people have different ways of reducing stress. Interestingly, some of the interviewees for this book advocated linking research as closely as possible with your main job to reduce stress, but this could evidently be stressful too. Others recommended keeping a clear separation between research and other work.

If you can choose something that supports what you're doing in your day-to-day work, that's even better. It helped me to deal with things at work.

It never stops, it morphs, it's just all the time, because my main job is this as well, and that has its advantages in terms of access to resources and all kinds of things, but psychologically I find it a challenge, it feels like I'm just working working working working.

You need be able to compartmentalise work: do the practice work, leave it alone, walk away from it, concentrate on the academic work. That's very very important. What I've found is that cross-over can have a significant impact. There's no point doing research while you're worrying about a particular case, or being with a challenging client and worrying about your questionnaires.

If you're doing workplace research, you may be able to enlist the help of colleagues, or work to recruit volunteers with suitable skills.

One of the things that I want to do is get a student in who I can then delegate some of the work to, and I've been having a look at how I can go about doing that. Students do come with work attached but I think it would be worth it.

However, if you're doing academic research, it's all down to you.

Primary data collection is the phase that can be most obviously stressful for a researcher, particularly if you are working with a vulnerable group, as this interviewee did:

I think my main worry was that I knew I was going to hear some very harrowing stories, and how could I prepare myself for that? There was nothing in the literature anywhere that discussed that. The only thing I found was on change management and how people deal with stress. That's one element of it but it didn't really answer my question. I took advice that a friend gave me about it's OK to be upset but don't be

> hysterical, and it's OK, you're not being cold, you're just deferring the emotion. But there was nothing written anywhere about that. In my uni class I actually brought this up, I was there with a couple of people who were social workers, they don't get any training on how to deal with things like that.

This interviewee prepared by thinking through the problems that were likely to occur. Searching the literature, asking friends' advice, and bringing up the subject in class for discussion yielded nuggets of information and advice that the interviewee was able to use to prepare mentally and practically for the work ahead. This is excellent research practice.

Most UK central government departments, from the Health & Safety Executive to the Ministry of Defence, now have research ethics committees, and so do many universities. There is a national Association of Research Ethics Committees (AREC), whose website states: 'Research Ethics Committees review proposals for research on human participants so as to protect them from unduly risky or unethical research, while also encouraging research of high quality.' There is no mention of protecting researchers from unethical research, although AREC's aims and objects do include recognition that 'those engaged in the conduct or supervision of research' may have 'educational and training needs'. However, this seems to be more about promoting quality in research than in caring for the researchers.

This seems odd, as researchers are also human beings, and so may be vulnerable to the effects of stress and injustice. As there is little external recognition of the need to consider the safety and well-being of researchers, we have to take care of our own welfare. This is not always easy in the heat of a research project, when you are trying to juggle competing agendas and manage everything else in life too. Keeping to your ethical principles can be a hugely stressful experience in itself, as this interviewee found:

> Our tutor decided, earlyish on, that she wanted us all to send abstracts off to a national research conference. That led directly into some of the biggest difficulties, ethically. For me, it was a ... nightmare, because we weren't doing a proper research project, we were doing a practice one, that was how it was presented to us, but that changed because of our tutor's ambitions, so then you've got this conflict. Then it gets very difficult to manage, because you're doing this because you want to get qualified, and your tutor holds a lot of power within that. My own ethical position meant that at the end I didn't know whether I would fail because I'd stuck to my guns. That was a real personal journey for me.

The need to resist the power of others can also arise in workplace research, as this interviewee's experience shows:

> We did have a moment before the stuff was collated where we were in the middle of a meeting. I hadn't done the coding yet but I had the coding categories. The other

researcher and my boss sat down and started coming up with recommendations, and I was like, "Hang on a minute, should we not be making recommendations after we've done all the collation and stuff?" Some of what they were saying did turn out to be relevant, but I felt very uncomfortable about that. I don't think there was any malice involved, it was enthusiasm, but we had to stop it.

This quote helpfully demonstrates that ethical problems can arise from people's acting with the best of motives.

A number of interviewees found that a particularly stressful part of their research project was the process of obtaining ethical approval from research ethics committees. Not everyone has to do this, but it is becoming more widespread. The procedures of research ethics committees differ, but the application process is often long and complex. This does make you think through your research thoroughly at an early stage, which is a good thing, as that will save you time later on, but it can also be quite onerous.

We needed help to get through the local research ethics committee. Because we were working with NHS patients we needed their approval. It's designed for the boys, so if you're outside of that circle it's harder to get into. If you're part of the research community ... the language they use is in-house language and it's alienating, it's very long winded.

After application, there may be a wait of two or three months before a response is given by the committee. Even then, it may not be approval: the application may have to be rewritten and resubmitted, with another lengthy wait for a response, or at worst it may simply be refused. Although this might be for a good reason, it's frustrating and upsetting for the researcher. Luckily, there are ways to mitigate this, as this interviewee found:

It's such a steep learning curve, a lot of it, like ethics. Last week I went to an ethics committee for the research we're doing. That was really useful. It's the one I'll have to go to with my PhD and I've been now, I've seen what it's like. All the time it's been that on-going appreciation of, whilst it's something you have to navigate through, it is important if your research is going to have value.

Find someone else who has made a successful application to your research ethics committee, and ask for their help.

One interviewee's view was that the practices of some research ethics committees may themselves be unethical, such as in removing choice from potential participants:

> What I wanted to do was research asking people what they think about things. These people are quite capable of giving consent, so why does an ethics committee have to second-guess what people are going to say? This patronising attitude to asking people's opinions, it's still there. I haven't managed to make any inroads into ethics committees but other people have and they say people aren't allowed to have an informed choice. The second-guessing is there all the time.

It is worth considering that there are some circumstances in which even embarking on research could be regarded as unethical.

> There are so many consultations going on now that it's reached the ridiculous stage. One of the patients I spoke to had someone from a large professional consultancy firm come and ask questions about a month ago. Four years ago someone else from that company came and asked exactly the same questions and nothing changed since then so she said "I'm not prepared to talk to you". I had to work really hard to get her to take part in my research. I gave her examples of past pieces of work and what had happened as a result of that, and she very reluctantly took part. It definitely had an impact, if you're doing a piece of research you have to bear that in mind.

It can be very stressful to try to manage ethical difficulties where you have little or no control. Preparation is the key to foreseeing as many of these as possible and therefore minimising their impact. Many of the interviewees for this book emphasised the need to be well organised and manage your time so that you can deal with ethical difficulties as they arise.

Peer support can also be useful in reducing stress. I was part of a loose group of 'PhD buddies' who saw each other through the long and difficult process, and were always available between get-togethers for support by phone, e-mail, or face to face. I found that invaluable. Social networking sites such as Facebook and Twitter are also very useful for this kind of peer support. Some people are happiest in groups, whether online or in real life, while others prefer chatting or meeting one to one.

> We got together with people doing MPhils and PhDs once a month to talk about how it was going. That didn't work particularly well for me because I got anxious, I thought everyone else was doing better, but it did help for others in the group.

Work out what kind of support will be most effective in reducing your stress levels, and make sure it's in place.

The role of theory

Theory is a way of making sense of some aspect, or aspects, of the world around us. For the purposes of research, theory can usefully be divided into two types (Silverman and Marvasti, 2008: 52):

1. Formal theory, based primarily on thought, such as Marxism, constructivism, or attachment theory.
2. Informal theory, based primarily on experience, such as a police constable's theory of how best to manage an unruly crowd.

Research can be seen as a way to link formal and informal theories with a view to increasing knowledge and improving practice.

Formal theory plays a more explicit role in academic than in workplace research. If you are doing academic research, you will need to engage with formal theory, particularly when you are defining your research question and discussing your findings. If you are doing workplace research, you probably won't have to engage with formal theory, but it is likely to improve your research if you do. This is because each research method is rooted in a theoretical perspective – a particular way of making sense of some aspect of the world – and the better you understand the rationale behind that way of making sense, the more effectively you will be able to use the method (Rose, 2012: 45) and disseminate the findings.

> **Research sits in a void if it's not theoretically connected.**

Some of the formal theory literature is quite impenetrable. Here's an example: 'Unlike psychoanalysis, psychoanalytic competence (which confines every desire and statement to a genetic axis or overcoding structure, and makes infinite, monotonous tracings of the stages on that axis or the constituents of that structure), schizoanalysis rejects any idea of pretraced destiny, whatever name is given to it – divine, anagogic, historical, economic, structural, hereditary, or syntagmatic ...'. This is quite an extreme example, being taken out of context from a well-respected book by two French poststructuralists.[2] I do not include it here to criticise the

---

[2] G. Deleuze and F. Guattari (1987) *A thousand plateaus: Capitalism and schizophrenia,* translated from the original French by B. Massumi, p 13. Minneapolis: University of Minnesota Press.

book or its authors, who have made a unique and valuable contribution to social theory. However, many people do find their work, and that of other theorists, quite difficult to read.

> Academic language, oh, ow, it made my eyes bleed, and that was really time-consuming. I still can't … remember what 'hermeneutic' means.

> Sometimes, I'm sure some people would shoot me for saying this, when I've started to unpack some of it, some of it isn't complex in itself but it's the language that's used to make it complex. Like phenomenological analysis. You're analysing a phenomenon as experienced by someone else, that is fairly straightforward, but the language has made it complex.

Luckily there is a fair amount of formal theory that is written in more accessible language. However, the language of research practice can also be quite opaque.

> Some of the people I teach are expected to do small-scale research studies. Ninety per cent of them are practitioners within the service. They find the language quite difficult, it's a language they're not used to. Qualitative and quantitative research is not something that trips off the tongue.

> The language of research can put people off. I'm in practice and it's too academic for me.

In this book, I have tried to be clear about the meanings of the research terms I use, and to use those terms consistently. But other writers will use some of the same terms with slightly different meanings, such as 'document analysis', where I have used 'document review'. And other writers will use different terms to mean the same thing, such as 'subject' to mean a person who takes part in research, where I have used 'participant'. Also, I have not tried to include every possible research term in this book, just those that are necessary for understanding the points I want to make. As you read other people's work on research methods you will inevitably come across new research terms.

If you're struggling with the language of research, read *Understanding the Research Process* by Paul Oliver (2010), a short, accessible book that will help you to become familiar with research vocabulary as well as teaching you a lot about how research works.

It has to be said that the language of public services can also be difficult and off-putting. There are some good glossaries and jargon-busters online if you are struggling with this.

Write definitions of new words on Post-It notes and stick them where you will see them frequently, for example on the inside of your front door, next to the kettle, or on the bathroom mirror.

If you're doing academic study, depending on your research topic and question, you may have to get to grips with some unfamiliar and challenging concepts. After all, you're doing it to learn. If you find complex social theory exciting and appealing, you'll find plenty to amuse you. If, on the other hand, you prefer simpler explanations, there is so much literature available that you should be able to find readable commentaries on the theories you need to understand.

You don't have to read the unreadable.

As a researcher, it is as important to learn to identify and skip documents that won't help you, as to learn to identify and read those that will (Langridge and Hagger-Johnson, 2009: 19). Information about how to do this is in Chapter Five.

Informal theory is often undervalued, perhaps because it is formed from lived experience by lower-status public sector practitioners rather than being written down in long words by higher-status academics. But it can be every bit as valid, as a way of understanding the world, as formal theory (Glasby, 2011: 89), as these interviewees discovered:

> When I first came to academia, I shied away from my practice experience because I thought it's not academic, but now I realise that was stupid. I teach some subjects that are a real quagmire, and I can tell them what it means in practice, like when I worked with this person and the challenges we faced. Part of the reason you're here isn't just your academic skills, it's because you've been in practice. It's all part of the thing we're all banging on about all the time, about theory into practice.

> Research is almost a hidden extra but it's such an important part of the work that we do. From my perspective as a nurse, in nursing we don't do enough research. As nurses, we're hands-on, we're coal-face with patients, relatives, care providers, we see the impact of that care, and yet we don't utilise that information. Also there's a belief that research is done by academics, university people. We need to be bringing that more to the workplace, that's where I see bridging the gap between the theory and practice.

Formalising your own informal theories by writing them down can be a useful process that can help you define your research questions and hypotheses. Qualitative data collection often involves collecting the informal theories of practitioners, service users, and other stakeholders. Informal theories are like close-ups, while formal theories can take a wider view in a broader context. The most insightful research often, explicitly, uses both.

Theory, research, practice

Again, these are not separate entities – at least, they shouldn't be. In an ideal world, there would be a cyclical relationship between them as shown in Figure 2.1.

In the real world, there are a number of barriers to this relationship, such as organisational and sector cultures, lack of time, and lack of understanding. Then there is the human instinct to sort ourselves into groups on the basis of identity. Some researchers and academics see practitioners as so immersed in their day-to-day work that they can't stand back and take a wider view, while some practitioners see researchers and academics as out of touch with the real

Figure 2.1: Research, theory, and practice: a cyclical relationship

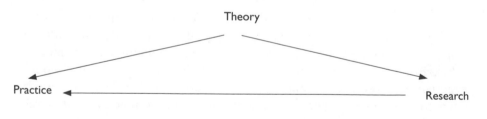

world. Also, poor research practice by some academics and some practitioners causes disillusionment among service users, which really doesn't help. Another barrier is the lack of resources and/or willingness to disseminate the findings of research. (This will be discussed in more detail in Chapter Ten.)

These barriers can be particularly frustrating for practitioners, who can see how theory and research could be used in practice to benefit their service users. One of the best ways to break down these barriers is to do research well and make good use of its findings. This book will show you how.

THREE

Research topics, proposals, and plans

No Plunging
Straight In

Research

Introduction

It can be tempting to rush through the early stages of the research process and plunge straight into data collection. This is a bad idea. The more careful thought and exploration you put in at the start, the more time you will save yourself later on. This chapter will guide you through the process of choosing and refining a research topic and writing a research proposal or plan. These are the first building blocks for the construction of your research, and it is always easier to build on solid than on flimsy foundations.

Choosing a research topic

Choosing a research topic can be a challenge, particularly if the choice is very wide, such as for a Master's dissertation or a PhD thesis. The best approach is to focus on whatever interests you most (Robson, 2011: 48).

If you're going to do a postgrad and you have the opportunity to design your own question, make sure it's something that *really* interests you, because you won't like it halfway through anyway.

Research can be a hard and lonely journey, and a passion for your topic will help you to keep going through the difficult times.

 *Choose the research topic that you find most interesting.*

Some people have topics chosen for them, whether they are doing workplace or academic research. This may feel like a blessing in the short term, but people who are not enthusiastic about their research topic may have difficulties later on.

I was talking to a colleague, someone else has chosen her topic for her, she's not committed to it. We've got some great topics she was really interested in doing but they were saying no. She's got something she's not that interested in, you can see her commitment wavering, she's already off her timeline.

One of the other problems that can occur is that services will decide what the research or the evaluation topic needs to be, and the person who's undertaking the thesis may well not actually be that interested in that area, but because it's a topic that's defined by the service they've got to do it, and that gets very taxing in terms of their personal motivation to continue.

People in positions of power, such as funders, supervisors, and managers, may attempt to influence – or even decide – your choice of research topic. If you are lucky, their interests and yours will coincide, but this seems to be quite rare. Where possible, I would advise you to resist such influence and focus on your own interests.

If you have to do a piece of research on a topic you don't find particularly interesting, the best way to get through it is to identify likely positive outcomes. For example: you will learn from the process; the qualification would look good on your CV; it should earn you brownie points with your manager. Stay focused on those outcomes as you carry out the research.

Write the positive outcomes that are likely to come from your research on Post-It notes, and stick them in places where you will see them every day.

In some cases, doing a research project on someone else's topic may give you leverage to ask for extra support, whether in terms of study time, help with administration, or other resources to make your life easier. This can also apply if you choose your own topic and it's closely related to your work. This will be discussed more fully in Chapter Four.

If you are intending to do academic research, you may be able to draw on existing workplace data, which can save a lot of time and effort. But it is still essential to make sure the topic interests you.

> One of the areas of advice I give is if possible do what I did. I was involved with some of the research officially within the police at the time; I got permission to use that as a base for the PhD. If people haven't decided on a specific subject, I say, "Look at what the force is doing. If there are any areas that fit, see if you can get permission to latch on and use some of that data." It can give a tremendous boost at the beginning. But it depends what people are interested in. You shouldn't just do it because you like the idea of having a PhD.

Refining your topic

Whether you choose for yourself or the choice is decided for you, your topic is likely to start by being huge and vague. Two examples are:

- How does education help people to succeed?
- What does our organisation do effectively, and where could it be improved?

These are important questions, but they are much too big to research as they stand. So you need to narrow your focus.

Photography offers a useful parallel. If you take a camera and point it at a landscape without focusing on something specific, the result will be unsatisfying: half sky, half land, altogether nothing much. However, if you focus on a gnarly tree in the foreground, and include enough scenery to give it context, you could have an interesting and appealing picture. In a landscape, there are many different things you could choose to focus on: cattle on a hillside, dew–pearled cobwebs, a hovering hawk. The same applies to research.

Whether you are doing academic or workplace research, the tools you use to refine your topic into useful questions are the same: reading, writing, and thinking. The way to formulate research questions is to read, and think, and write, and think some more. Reading other people's work in your topic area will help you to clarify your own thoughts, provide useful definitions to consider, and offer ideas for how to conduct your own research. Thinking about what you've read will help you to develop your ideas. Writing down your thoughts will help you to clarify those ideas. Thinking about them again will help you to develop them further.

The huge, vague topics mentioned earlier could be refined in many different ways, but in all cases you need to move from concepts (which are not measurable) to variables (which are) (Kumar, 2005: 56). 'Success' and 'effectiveness' are both concepts that are not, of themselves, measurable, but that can be measured by identified variables such as individual income or service take-up rates. Let's consider the topic of how education helps people succeed. To refine this, you would need to consider questions like: Are you interested in pre-school, child, teenage, college/university, or adult education? Do you want to take into account factors such as gender, ethnicity, or socio-economic status? How do you define 'success'? It might take a lot of reading and thinking and writing before you came up with your research question: What is the relationship between A level results and income for Asian men 10 years after taking their A levels?

You could go through a similar process with the topic of what an organisation does effectively and where it could be improved. Researching the effectiveness of a whole organisation, even a small one, is an enormous task, so to begin with you would need to define 'effectiveness'. Then you would need to consider questions like: Using your definition of 'effectiveness', which parts of the organisation do you think are effective now? Which do you think could be more effective? Can you evaluate one effective and one less effective part of the organisation, for the purposes of comparison, with the aim of learning lessons that could be applied more widely across the organisation? Write down your questions, write down your answers, and develop your thoughts.

I think the most important thing is to know what question you're going to ask.

Taking the time to define your research question or questions is the only way to give a clear focus to your research project (Jesson, Matheson and Lacey, 2011: 18). It may seem time consuming and onerous, particularly when other things are clamouring for your attention, but having clearly defined research questions to refer back to will save you much time and effort later in the process.

From question to data

In the same way that your research question is derived from your topic, your methods of collecting data should be derived from your research question. Again, you can work out how to do this by reading, thinking, and writing. You may already have read an existing study and want to use the same method yourself, which is fine, as long as you say where you got the idea. Alternatively, Chapters Six and Seven of this book introduce a variety of data-collection methods, and the research-methods literature explains these and other methods in more detail. (Some relevant books and papers are listed in the bibliography at the end of this book.) The important thing is to make sure that the methods you use are those most likely to help you find accurate and useful answers to your research question.

So, for example, let's say a local authority has had a lot of complaints about long waits at bus stops. It wants you to do some research to find out whether the bus company it's subsidising with taxpayers' money is providing the correct level of service. At first you think about talking to people as they get off the bus, to ask how long they had to wait for the bus to arrive at the start of their journey. However, common sense tells you that people's perception of time varies, depending on all sorts of factors, so the data you produce from such questioning probably wouldn't be very accurate. It might still be useful to collect that data, because complaints are likely to be based on people's perceptions, but you will need additional data for comparison. You realise that you could find out about the intended and actual frequency of bus services, which would be useful. Reading some other research into bus passenger experiences leads to the idea that you could spend some time at bus stops, observing how long people wait and how frequently buses come along. You decide that the combination of those three methods – asking people about their perceptions, checking the frequency of bus services, and observing people and buses at bus stops – should give you enough information to answer your research question.

Of course there are many other decisions to make. How will you ask people about their perceptions? Will you conduct a brief interview on the street or hand them a questionnaire? How will you find out about the intended and actual frequency of bus services? Is this information available on the World Wide Web, or do you need to contact the bus company, or go and look at timetables at the bus stops? How will you manage the direct observation? Which bus stops will you go to, on what days and at what times, and for how long? How will you record the data you collect?

For some people this is a very enjoyable part of the process, while others find it more difficult.

> I find formulating the questions to be the most difficult part. I know what I want to find out, I have no problem identifying where I want to be and what the outcomes of that information are, but I actually think choosing the right questions is a skill and I'm not quite sure, always. I still haven't mastered that, although I'm learning from what I see people change my questions into.

> I like writing questions and thinking about what to ask people, wording things so that they understand. I like writing questionnaires and discussion guides and thinking what we need and how to get what I want from the research process.

The information in Chapter Seven will help you to start thinking about these subjects, and research-methods books such as those listed in the bibliography at the end of this book will give you more detailed information.

How much data?

When doing research for the first time, it is common for people to think that the more data they collect, the better their research will be. This is not necessarily true (Davies, 2007: 53), as this interviewee found out when she was planning her Master's dissertation:

> The initial design was overly ambitious, completely over the top. My initial thing was about interviewing policy makers, national and local; a questionnaire to peers in the region; two focus groups; and using secondary data as well. And I then reflected with a friend who said, "This is ridiculous, that's more than I'm doing for my PhD."

Consider this. Ipsos MORI, which conducts opinion surveys, regularly carries out research on the whole of the adult UK population – around 42 million people – using a representative sample of only around 1,000 people.[1] However, almost everyone has an opinion, while not everyone is a victim of crime. The British Crime Survey aims to reach almost 50,000 people each year, from a total population of around 45 million aged 16 and over.[2] This is one of the largest social research surveys in the UK, but even so, at 0.001% of the population, it is a much smaller sample than most people would guess to be adequate.

The surveys conducted by Ipsos MORI and the Home Office (which carries out the British Crime Survey) are based on decades of experience. The difficult question for most practitioners is: how much data will be enough? It's often less than you think.

> I found out later that for my dissertation I only needed to speak to 20 people for it to be a valid qualitative study, and I spoke to 129. That's the difference between doing it for work and doing it for uni. You're not told at any point how many people you should do.

Ideally, you need to collect enough evidence to be able to answer your research question in full. In practice this isn't always possible, so sometimes you have to settle for a partial answer. However, this is rarely due to lack of data. It's more

---

[1] www.ipsos-mori.com/newsevents/ca/346/Three-Frequently-Asked-Questions.aspx.
[2] www.homeoffice.gov.uk/publications/science-research-statistics/research-statistics/crime-research/user-guide-crime-statistics/user-guide-crime-statistics?view=Binary. Note: the 'British Crime Survey' covers only England and Wales these days, as Scotland and Northern Ireland now each do their own survey.

often due to unforeseen circumstances, such as the research uncovering new factors that need to be taken into account but can't be addressed within the current research, due to limitations of budget and time-scale. That's not a problem as such, and it certainly doesn't mean the research has been badly done. It just needs to be clearly explained so that the next steps can be taken in a follow-up piece of research, whether that is done by you or by someone else.

Qualitative or quantitative methods?

As we saw in Chapter Two, the distinction between qualitative and quantitative research is not as clear as it seems. At its simplest level, there are always numerical aspects of qualitative research – the number of people interviewed, the age of respondents, the size of the geographical area covered – while quantitative research is reported in words that may have different meanings for their readers than they do for their writers (this is discussed in more detail in Chapter Five). Also, there is a growing movement towards 'mixed-method' research, which draws on the best that each approach has to offer, as appropriate to the research question(s) under consideration. Value-based research, while primarily a qualitative approach, also often includes some quantitative data collection and analysis.

There are many ways to describe quantitative and qualitative research, but essentially, quantitative research is based on numbers, while qualitative research is based on data in the form of words, pictures, audio, video, and so on.

Quantitative research terms include:

- independent variable – a measurable characteristic that changes in the course of the research;
- dependent variable – a measurable characteristic that stays constant in the course of the research;
- nominal data – data in categories with labels, such as categories of ethnicity;
- ordinal data – data in ranks without a defined numerical distance between them, such as the first, second, and third places in a competition;
- interval data – data in ranks with a defined numerical distance between them, such as age in years;
- questionnaire – a data-collection instrument that doesn't require the presence of the researcher;
- statistics – analytic calculations for describing data and using samples to make inferences about populations.

Qualitative research terms include:

- interview – a data-collection method that usually involves one researcher and one or two participants;
- focus group – a data-collection method that usually involves one or two researchers and several participants;

- observation – a data-collection method that usually involves one researcher and many participants;
- ethnography – a data-collection method that usually involves one researcher and many participants over a sustained period of time;
- action research or participatory action research – a data-collection method that involves participants in helping to construct the research alongside the researcher (see Chapter Two for more on this);
- content analysis – a technique for analysing the content of data;
- thematic analysis – a technique for identifying and analysing the themes in data.

You can use quantitative or qualitative methods, or both, to test a hypothesis. A hypothesis is a hunch, guess, or suspicion about something unknown. For example, you might hypothesise that your service would function better if managers had a fuller understanding of service users' priorities. You could test this by evaluating the service, training managers in service-user awareness, then evaluating the service again after a period of time to find out whether or not it had improved. You don't have to have a hypothesis to do research (Kumar, 2005: 73), but in practice many researchers do have one or more hypotheses, whether or not they define them as such. Hypotheses can help you to keep a clear focus on the core of your enquiry, but on the other hand they may prevent you from seeing other factors that might be of interest (Bryman and Cramer, 2009: 5).

Some people find quantitative research more appealing; others prefer qualitative research. It is rare to find a researcher who is equally comfortable in both modalities. Whichever is your preference, I would urge you not to ignore the other approach. It is important to let your research question(s) dictate your methods, rather than the other way around.

Sampling techniques

In most research projects it is impossible to involve everyone who might be relevant to the research question or questions. There are exceptions to this. For example, in workplace research, it would be necessary to involve everyone in a company or department if you were conducting a skills audit or training-needs analysis. Also, if you were doing research in a prison, it might be possible to include all the prisoners. In an evaluation of a small specialist service, you might be able to include all the staff and service users.

In most kinds of research you need to sample the population – that is, involve some of the people (the sample) from all the people you could involve (the population). Effective sampling makes it possible to draw conclusions about the population. On the other hand, sampling leaves room for error, because you have to use the findings from the sample to make calculations or inferences about the whole population, which may not be correct. It is important to be aware of this while you're deciding on your sampling strategy.

The guidance on sampling is more precise for quantitative research than for qualitative research (Punch, 2000: 55). However, in any research project, whether quantitative or qualitative, sampling may be constrained by time or budget limits. Also, no matter how well you plan your sampling technique, your plans may be overturned if potential participants don't turn up or refuse to participate, or if actual participants drop out part of the way through your data collection or decide to withdraw their data at a later stage. It is worth thinking this through as thoroughly as possible in your planning process to prevent problems later.

Samples do not only consist of people (Robson, 2011: 276). For example, in the transport survey described earlier, the researcher would also be thinking about suitable samples of place (how many bus stops, and which ones?) and time (do people experience longer waits at certain times, say at weekends, or when people are commuting to work?).

It might be undesirable to make firm decisions about your sampling strategy at the outset. You may wish to build in room for manoeuvre in case of unexpected findings early in the process. For example, the researcher for the transport survey may use local knowledge to hypothesise that people would experience the longest waits on Sunday evenings, and so decide to visit bus stops then. During the first session of data collection, three separate passengers mention that buses are often late on weekday mornings. The researcher is glad of the flexibility to add in some observations at those times.

If you are using qualitative methods such as interviews or focus groups, you may wish to continue until you are no longer hearing much new information. This is known as reaching 'saturation', a term drawn from grounded theory (Robson, 2011: 148), and is often held to be good practice. The difficulty is that you won't know at the outset whether you will reach saturation in 10 interviews or 100, so you may have to set an upper limit that is suitable for your time-scale and budget.

Your sampling strategy should be shaped by your research questions and how you are planning to approach those questions. Constraints of time and money will also play a part. For example, it might be fascinating and useful to compare whatever you're studying with a similar situation on another continent, but few practitioners can afford to do international research.

Probability samples

In probability samples, every member of the population has the same chance of being selected as part of the sample. This means you need two things: a 'sampling frame', that is, a list of all the members of the population with their contact details, and a way of generating random numbers. Tables of random numbers are available on the Web.

With probability sampling, the larger the sample, the more robust your findings will be. But as you can't go on and on collecting data, you will need to decide how large is large enough. In statistical terminology, you need a sample with the 'power' (that is, size) to allow you to make inferences about the population.

There are a number of online web pages that offer calculators of statistical power to determine the answer to this question.

The most straightforward type of probability sample is **simple random sampling**, where you use random numbers with your sampling frame to randomly select the required number of research participants.

If you don't have access to random numbers, or if you want a quicker way to sample, you can use **stratified sampling**. Here you do need one number generated at random to select the first research participant, but then you choose the other participants from the sampling frame at regular intervals, for example every third or every tenth person.

You can also do **stratified random sampling**. This is useful if you want to make sure, for example, that you include equal numbers of men and women, or equal numbers of people from different age groups. For this to be possible, the relevant information needs to be included in your sampling frame. Then you can divide the sampling frame into two or more parts, for example one for men and one for women, or one for each of your defined age groups. After that you pick the same number of participants at random from each subset of the sampling frame.

One benefit of probability samples is that you can use inferential statistical techniques to calculate how likely it is that your findings could have occurred by chance. This helps to reduce the impact of any sampling errors, and makes your findings more generalisable (Bryman and Cramer, 2009: 6). If you're not comfortable with numbers, don't be put off, because there are a range of computer applications that can do the calculations for you. There is more information about this in Chapter Eight.

Non-probability sampling

It may not be possible to create or gain access to a sampling frame. For example, if you're interested in the effect of custodial sentences on prisoners' families, or the impact of a health service on its users' carers, you probably won't be able to find or build a list of those families or carers. In research like this you have to use one or more types of non-probability sampling. Also, qualitative researchers, who aren't interested in using inferential statistics, are likely to choose non-probability sampling techniques.

With non-probability sampling, a larger sample doesn't necessarily mean more robust findings. In fact, some reputable research uses a sample of one, such as for a case study. In these research projects, the participant is studied in great detail, and the richness of the investigation is held to compensate for the lack of sample size. (There is more information about case studies in Chapter Seven.) However, in most research projects using non-probability sampling, you will have to make a judgement about how many participants to seek.

Convenience sampling effectively means choosing the first participants you can find who are willing to help. This is useful for some tasks, such as piloting questionnaires or interview questions, or in conjunction with other sampling techniques. However, I wouldn't recommend its use alone, as it is too vulnerable to researcher and other biases.

Quota sampling is akin to stratified sampling in that the population is divided into groups. The aim then is to find participants within those groups in proportion to the total number of people in each group. So if you wanted to research a community care service, with 40 users, an estimated 100 carers, and 16 care workers, you might decide to talk to 10 users, 10 carers, and 4 care workers. The perceptive reader will have noticed that this focuses on the numbers, and there is still a decision to be made about how to select the individual participants. Convenience sampling is often used for this, although other non-probability sampling techniques may be used.

Purposive sampling is where the researcher uses their own judgement about which participants will have most to contribute to the research. Again, this is best used alongside other types of sampling, to reduce bias.

Snowball sampling is where you use one participant to lead you to others. This is particularly helpful when you're trying to research groups that are difficult to contact, such as gang members or freegans.

There are other types of sampling (see, for example, Robson, 2011: 271–6), but these are the main ones used in practice-based research.

What is evidence?

In some quarters there is a lot of argument about what constitutes evidence. Anecdote is often considered to be the lowest of the low when it comes to evidence. However, if you collect a large number of anecdotes, perhaps through a series of research interviews, they may then become data that, once analysed and reported, yields useful evidence. Furthermore, you can use a single story from one interview as a quote to illustrate a point in your research report or thesis, and that is seen as perfectly proper. Yet the quote is indistinguishable from an anecdote.

So why doesn't an anecdote constitute evidence? Especially when it often does in everyday life? People listen to the anecdotes of trusted friends or family members, about which plumber to use or which restaurant to avoid, and use those anecdotes as evidence on which to base their own decisions. But I'm sure almost everyone has followed someone else's anecdotal recommendation and had a completely different experience from the one they were led to expect. This is why, in research terms, anecdote does not equal evidence: a single view is not likely to be representative of a wider population.

Researchers, whether qualitative, quantitative or mixed method, are seeking evidence that is representative of a wider population. Anecdotes may contribute to this – even in quantitative research, anecdotes told to the researcher may influence the planning or conducting of the research. We love anecdotes because they are stories, and a single story is much more likely to change our view of the world than even the most robust statistical finding (Kahneman, 2011: 174). Nevertheless, anecdotes alone, even lots of anecdotes, are unlikely to constitute strong enough data for a competent research project. Even if your research project was designed to study anecdote, you would need to use the literature, documents, and probably some secondary data, as well as collecting anecdotes of your own.

So, anecdotes collected for a research project may become data, as may diary entries, meeting minutes, photographs, collages, video recordings, and any number of other constructions and artefacts. And this data becomes evidence through the process of analysing it and reporting findings. However, you still need to consider what kind of evidence you are producing.

Some research commentators talk about a 'hierarchy of evidence', with randomised double-blind controlled trials seen as the gold standard and personal experience having the lowest value. This seems to me far too simplistic. For sure, if I'm going to take a new drug, I'll be reassured to know it's been through a randomised double-blind controlled trial or six. However, if I'm considering trying a new brand of wine, I'm happy to base my decision on a friend's personal experience.

For me, as a researcher, the important thing is to aim to produce the type of evidence that fits your research question. If you're interested in the impact of a new piece of legislation on certain organisations, a randomised double-blind controlled trial will get you nowhere, but a well-conducted piece of mixed-method research might well produce evidence to show how many organisations are affected and in what ways. The advice in this book will help you to conduct good-quality research that will produce robust evidence.

Do I need to write a research proposal?

A research proposal is a short document explaining what you intend to research and why, and how you intend to carry out the research. A research proposal is essential for most academic research, research funding applications, and commissioned workplace research. Even if a research proposal is not essential for the research you are doing, it is good practice to write one. The process of writing the proposal will help you to clarify your thoughts and decisions. Also, the proposal can be used to help you plan your research process, and for reference during that process to make sure your work stays on track. And, as one interviewee pointed out, it can give credibility to your research in your workplace.

> Every researcher should put together a formal proposal. I think if you make it a formal thing, people are more likely to pay attention and make the time for it, rather than something ad hoc. It's about formalising it and showing the importance of it. I think once you've done that, got something in writing and a formal procedure that you're going to follow, people see it as part of your job rather than an additional thing you have to squeeze in.

As we saw earlier in respect of data, one major mistake that new researchers make is to think that more equals better. People who are not experienced in research may also think they need to read as much literature or as many documents as possible. This is not true.

> All too often students new to research equate the breadth of their research with its value. Initial enthusiasm, combined with this common misconception, often results in broad, generalized and ambitious proposals. It is the progressive narrowing of the topic, through the literature review, that makes most research a practical consideration. (Hart, 1998: 13)

The people assessing your proposal will be more impressed with a proposal that is SMART – simple, measurable, achievable, realistic, and targeted – than with one that promises a great deal but is, by definition, highly unlikely to deliver. It is important to estimate how much time your research will take, taking into account the time you need for other aspects of your life (Jesson, Matheson and Lacey, 2011: 4), and there is more advice on how to manage your time in Chapter Four of this book.

Your research proposal should include information about:

1. Your topic area.
2. Your research question or questions.
3. The background information you are drawing on.
4. Why your research is important/worth doing.
5. Whether or not you are involving service users, and why.
6. Ethical considerations.
7. A timetable for your work.
8. Data collection:
     - what you intend to collect;
     - how you will collect it;
     - how much you plan to collect;
     - why you think this will enable you to answer your research question(s).
9. How you will prepare and analyse your data.
10. How you intend to disseminate your findings.
11. Who could benefit from your conclusions and how they might benefit.
12. References.

For your proposal to be truly convincing, it should be readable and understandable by someone who has no prior knowledge of your plans. It was allegedly Albert Einstein who said, 'If you can't explain it simply, you don't understand it well enough.'

Test your research proposal on a family member or friend, to make sure it is completely clear, before submitting it to a tutor, commissioner, or funder.

And it's not just the explanation that needs to be simple, it is the research itself (Silverman and Marvasti, 2008: 434). Complicated research does not equal better research, and writing a research proposal or plan is a good way to assess whether or not your plans are sufficiently straightforward.

The process of writing a research proposal or plan may seem like a tedious chore, especially if you're longing to get on with collecting your data. However, time spent thinking your research through well enough to write a convincing proposal or plan will undoubtedly save you from time-consuming problems later on, so it is definitely worth doing.

Research funders

Funding for social research may be obtained from local and national government departments, charitable trusts and research bodies, and research councils or their equivalent that are usually mostly or entirely government funded. These include:

- Economic and Social Research Council (UK)
- Arts and Humanities Research Council (UK)
- Joint Information Systems Committee (UK)
- National Endowment for the Humanities (US)
- National Science Foundation (US)
- Social Sciences and Humanities Research Council (Canada)
- Australian Research Council
- Research Australia
- Health Research Council (New Zealand)
- New Zealand Council for Educational Research.

It is difficult to get funding from any of these bodies unless you are a professional academic or a PhD student with academic aspirations. Even then, it's not easy. Each department, trust, body, or council will have its own application system, most of which are quite onerous. Also, some of these processes will have deadlines that don't suit your project. However, I don't mean to put you off, because if you think you have a chance of securing funding, it's well worth having a go. This is especially true when you can include an element of funding to free up your time, for example to pay for someone to do your main job for a while so that you can concentrate on your research.

If you decide to apply for funding, you need to write a killer proposal, using all the advice outlined in this chapter and the rest of the book, and make sure you work through the application process with meticulous accuracy and thoroughness.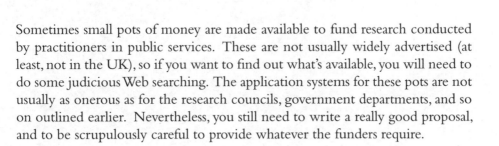

Sometimes small pots of money are made available to fund research conducted by practitioners in public services. These are not usually widely advertised (at least, not in the UK), so if you want to find out what's available, you will need to do some judicious Web searching. The application systems for these pots are not usually as onerous as for the research councils, government departments, and so on outlined earlier. Nevertheless, you still need to write a really good proposal, and to be scrupulously careful to provide whatever the funders require.

FOUR

Managing the research process

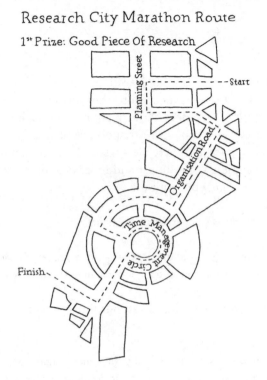

Research City Marathon Route

1ˢᵗ Prize: Good Piece Of Research

Introduction

Research isn't a sprint, it's a marathon. Successful completion of a marathon takes planning, organisation and time management. This chapter will help you to learn techniques for these essential parts of the research process. It contains a great deal of advice from practitioners who are experienced in conducting research, in the hope that their hindsight can be your foresight.

Research by Richard Wiseman from the University of Hertfordshire in 2009 (reported in the *Guardian* newspaper on 28 December 2009) showed that people were more likely to stick to their New Year's resolutions if they followed six easy steps:

1. Made a plan for their project.
2. Broke down their overall goal into smaller goals, for each week or fortnight, that were SMART (specific, measurable, achievable, realistic, and time-based).
3. Told their friends and family about their goals.

4. Rewarded themselves whenever they achieved one of the smaller goals.
5. Kept a diary of their progress.
6. Regularly focused on the benefits of success.

These steps are also ideal for helping researchers to complete their projects successfully.

Planning

The people I interviewed for this book were unanimous about the need to plan research carefully. You may feel inclined to skip this section. Perhaps you don't think there's any point in reading about planning, either because you're not a natural planner, or because you're already good at planning. However, I would advise you to read on, because there are specific ways of planning research that will help you to complete your project and meet deadlines more easily. I think these interviewees would agree with me.

> The first major hurdle is going to be the planning.

> I used to have to plan my year at the beginning of the year, my family life, my work, my academic studies, planning is essential, good planning and time management.

The process of planning isn't always easy, but putting work in at this stage will save time later.

> The preparation work is the most challenging, most important and most difficult. Once you get the research process going, it develops momentum and is quite fun and rewarding.

And not everyone finds preparation and planning to be the most difficult part. In fact for some, it's the easiest.

> I love sitting down and doing concepts, and making action plans of where this could lead and where I need to go to find it out. I love fleshing out beginnings of projects, I really enjoy that part ... if it's going to be a project that's collaborative you really have to start from that blank page. I like looking for resources, sources of information, people I might have to talk to.

> Once you've narrowed down your question, I enjoy designing research to fit the question because it's a bit of a puzzle, isn't it, and you know there's not a right or wrong answer, you've just got to justify. And there may be limitations of time or money, so they've got to be built in.

First, you need an outline plan for your whole research project. If you've written a research proposal, as suggested in Chapter Three, this can form the basis of your plan. If not, you'll need to start from scratch. Either way, you should be able to break down your overall plan into a few chunks such as: background research, writing your proposal (or plan), collecting data, analysing data, writing up your research, dissemination. Then you can break down each chunk into monthly goals, bearing in mind that you are likely to be working on two or more chunks at the same time in most months. The next step is to break down your monthly goals into weekly to-do lists. Then each day you can refer to your list to make sure you're on track.

It's best to make weekly to-do lists just a week or two ahead of the present day, rather than for the whole project at once. Life is full of surprises, as is research, so sometimes plans have to be changed. It is essential to build in time to deal with unexpected occurrences at all levels, from running out of milk to serious illness. It is equally essential not to use unexpected occurrences as an excuse for procrastination.

Visual learners may prefer charts to lists. Perhaps the best-known type of project management chart is the Gantt chart. Figure 4.1 shows a Gantt chart for the outline plan of a simple research project.

You can see from the chart that this researcher plans to read throughout the project, do the research proposal at the start, then data collection that overlaps with data analysis. Two chunks of formal writing are planned, the first in December – perhaps for an interim report, if one is required, or just to get ahead – and the second in February, when most of the other work has been done. Dissemination is also planned in two chunks, one in January – perhaps to report interim findings at a meeting or an academic conference – and one in March when the rest of the research work is finished.

Figure 4.1: Gantt chart for a research project

Task	Sep	Oct	Nov	Dec	Jan	Feb	Mar
Reading	xxx	xxx	xxx	xxx	xxx	xxx	
Research proposal		xxx					
Collecting data			xxx	xxx			
Analysing data				xxx	xxx		
Writing	xxx	xxx	xxx	xxx	xxx	xxx	
Writing report/thesis				xxx		xxx	
Dissemination					xxx		xxx

A real-life example

As with all the other skills you'll be using during your research, you will get better at planning as you go along. My own PhD plans demonstrate this. At the start I didn't have much idea how to tackle the project: studying the emotion work of Sure Start partnership managers. In my first supervision meeting, I asked my supervisors to construct a brief timeline with milestones for completing the research and thesis within three years. The notes from my first PhD supervision meeting, in July 2003, say:

- First draft of methodology chapter by September 2003.
- Sept–Dec 2003: pilot method [of data collection].
- Jan 2004–July 2005: iterative process of data collection/analysis and chapter drafting.
- From July 2005: third drafts of chapters.
- Last two months for polishing.

This formed the basis of more detailed project plans that I revised and updated as I went along. So, my 'to do' list for February to September 2004 read as follows:

1. Read up on data coding.
2. Write piece on data coding, explaining method and rationale (before May/June supervision).
3. Go back to first participants and ask them for a 'three months on' response.
4. Do two more data-collection sessions.
5. Download and analyse Sure Start governance/partnership guidance.
6. Sift professional journals for Sure Start managers' stories.
7. Write piece on document analysis, explaining method and rationale.
8. Do participant observation meetings.
9. Write background info piece with lots about what I've done and why.
10. Write up programme managers' day.
11. Do map of the whole thing.
12. Read supervisor's papers.
13. Plan next stage: more data collection (?); first drafts of data collection and analysis chapters; second drafts of methodology, partnership and emotion chapters.

Then, each month I would refer to this plan and decide which parts to do in that month. Those went on my overall work plan for the month, which included paid and domestic work. I broke that down into weekly to-do lists and referred to those daily – sometimes several times a day – to make sure I was on track.

By July 2005, I was able to formulate a timetable for finishing the project over the next 12 months. I had one chapter almost finished, two at second-draft stage and another at first-draft stage. Plus I hadn't finished my data analysis, so I still had plenty of work to do. I wrote out a timetable for this work. At this stage I was taking a much more professional approach, and used the timetable I'd written to produce the discussion paper in Box 4.1 for my supervisors.

Box 4.1: PhD – Work plan July 2005 to July 2006

This work plan is based on two main assumptions: first, that each chapter will need to go through exactly three drafts; second, that there will be nine chapters. There are also some minor assumptions, for example that some drafts will be quicker than others (based on experience to date). Many of these assumptions may prove incorrect, so it is intended to be an illustrative guide rather than a prescription. Reading continues to provide a backdrop for my work.

Still to do at 1 July 2005

Chapter 1 – Introduction – draft 1, draft 2, draft 3, polish
Chapter 2 – Partnership – draft 2, draft 3, polish
Chapter 3 – Emotion – draft 3, polish
Chapter 4 – Methodology – polish
Chapter 5 – Thematic Analysis (TA) – draft 2, draft 3, polish
Chapter 6 – Narrative Analysis (NA) – analyse, draft 1, draft 2, draft 3, polish
Chapter 7 – Discussion – draft 1, draft 2, draft 3, polish
Chapter 8 – Reflexivity – draft 1, draft 2, draft 3, polish
Chapter 9 – Conclusion – draft 1, draft 2, draft 3, polish
Final stage – knitting everything together, checking refs and cross-refs, appendices, prelims etc.

Workplan month by month

July 2005: narrative analysis, start NA chapter 6 draft 1
August: finish chapter 6 draft 1, start partnership chapter 2 draft 2
September: finish partnership chapter 2 draft 2, start TA chapter 5 draft 2
October: Finish TA chapter 5 draft 2, do NA chapter 6 draft 2
November: Partnership chapter 2 draft 3, emotion chapter 3 draft 3
December: TA chapter 5 draft 3, NA chapter 6 draft 3
January 2006: Discussion chapter 7 draft 1
February: Reflexivity chapter 8 draft 1
March: Discussion chapter 7 draft 2, reflexivity chapter 8 draft 2
April: Discussion chapter 7 draft 3, reflexivity chapter 8 draft 3
May: Introduction chapter 1 draft 1, conclusion chapter 9 draft 1, polishing/knitting together, appendices
June: Introduction chapter 1 draft 2, conclusion chapter 9 draft 2, polishing/knitting together, appendices
July: Introduction chapter 1 draft 3, conclusion chapter 9 draft 3, polishing/knitting together, prelims

Questions for supervision:
1. Does this look like a plausible workplan for the next year?
2. From my perspective, I think it's feasible; from yours, do you think it's realistic?
3. Any other comments?

My supervisors were happy with the plan. My thesis was ready for submission in May 2006, two months ahead of schedule, which shows that this approach to planning works. (If you think it also shows that I can be a bit smug, you could be right.)

Organisation

Once you've got the planning sorted, you need to be organised in how you use that planning.

> Be extremely organised with your time and block off time in your diary each day or week to do research.

> I used to highlight things and have charts and graphs all over the place telling me what was coming up and what I needed to do by then. I have it all in my head these days but it's important to plot and plan things.

> Good administrative set-up right at the start is not time wasted. I wish I'd known that. It's about trying to manage the process, and feeds into how you manage when you've got work and family and domestic and all that other stuff going on. You need a level of organisation that can help to manage the research.

Doing research as part of a non-research main job can be particularly challenging. Research adds pressure to already pressured jobs, and is often a low priority compared to other aspects of people's work. People interviewed for this book spoke of how they experienced this.

> Evaluation, the stuff that's statutorily required, it's easier I think to structure in time to do it. It's the more non-statutory stuff that is going to be very difficult to figure in. Getting a skills audit done is going to be difficult, it all keeps being crowded out by other needs. Getting some research done around marketing and publicity is going to be very difficult. But those are things that have to happen.

> The way things work out in academia now is that because you have teaching, if you want to be research active you basically have to use whatever time you can. During term times you can have such a high teaching load that you would effectively have to stop researching if you were to work to rule.

> Quite often it's easy for that kind of thing to fall to the back of your priority list. It's not meeting the bottom line at the end of the day. Everything is always deadline driven. You have to continuously remind other people that evaluation is also important.

Planning, organisation, and time management are the three keys to successfully fitting research obligations in with the rest of your work. Even then, as the latest quotes show, you can end up putting in extra hours. Yet professional practice and service delivery can benefit enormously from research and, as we saw in Chapter One, this is being recognised more widely.

Time management

Time management is more of an art than a science, but there are some basic principles that can help you to manage your time more effectively. First of all, make sure that everyone close to you knows that you have research to do and that it's a priority for you.

> If you want to do research you've got to be up front about that with yourself and other people and you have to prioritise it and make it happen, because nobody else will.

If people know you're doing something that matters to you, they're more likely to accept that you need to spend time on it.

> Because it was for my dissertation, and had an end point, it wasn't going to go on for ever, my mum said, "Don't worry, we'll see you once you've reached the other end." Most people were like that.

> You need your family behind you, or your support networks behind you, they need to be aware of the commitment involved.

> There is something about it won't go on for ever, and I think, certainly with the social life, if friends and family know what's going on, then hopefully they can understand that you're just not so available and they'll still be there at the end and won't have buggered off entirely!

Second, and counter-intuitively, it is not always the case that more time equals more productivity. In fact, people are often more productive when they work in short bursts in between other activities.

> When you've got family, it's pulling aside a sensible chunk of time. If you had a whole day and went and sat in the library, you'd probably file your nails, you wouldn't use the time properly.

> Because I'm reporting to the chief exec, I'm trying to make time because it is fairly important, so I take time out of my normal job. It's the only way to do it.

> I've tried to set aside certain times when I focus on *my* work – usually part of Saturday and Sunday – or later in the evenings after dinner.

> I'm an anal calendar lady! I allocate time. It sounds so … [giggling] I allocate slots
> of time, now I use an Outlook calendar, I'm not technically savvy but I think it's the
> absolute best thing since sliced bread.

> I'm not one for sitting in libraries, I like to read while I'm waiting for the bath to fill
> up or something like that.

It is a common misconception that you need a whole free day, or even a whole week, to be able to work on your research. Small chunks of time, well used, can be very productive. A colleague told me recently that twice a day, while she cleans her teeth with her electric toothbrush in one hand, she holds her Kindle in the other hand and reads for two minutes until the toothbrush's timer sounds. It takes only five minutes to read one page of a book, enter data from a questionnaire into a spreadsheet, or think about a problem you are facing. In quarter of an hour you can make notes from a chapter you have read, search the World Wide Web for journal articles on a particular subject, or make a few phone calls to set up interviews. In half an hour you can transcribe part of an interview, read a journal article, or write 250 words of your research report or thesis. Small chunks of time are very valuable for researchers; the art lies in learning to use them well.

> I do think if you don't do something fairly regularly, it becomes like an enormous
> mountain and you just don't want to do it even though you do.

It's also useful to identify thinking time, perhaps when you're doing repetitive tasks that don't need much thought, standing in a queue, or walking to the bus stop.

> When I did my PhD, because I was doing something that wasn't directly work related,
> and because I was a police constable at the time, I had lots of time where I was
> walking the beat or other duties that weren't taxing where I could think about things.

A third useful principle is to remember that you can say 'no'. If you are in the habit of saying 'yes' to every invitation and request for help, or even to most of them, try being more selective. One way to do this is, instead of giving an immediate response to an invitation or request, to take time to think about whether you really want to accept. Another option is to ration yourself. For example, in the last three months of writing this book, I restricted myself to two social activities per week. In the final month, I reduced this to one social activity per week. I explained my plans to my family and friends, and they were very understanding.

One very helpful piece of advice is to look at your 'to do' list, and do the job you least want to do first of all.[1] There are two reasons for this. First, if you leave

---

[1] Personal communication, Julie Miller, regularly over the last four decades. Thanks, Mother.

that job till last, it may well not get done at all, because motivating yourself to do an unpleasant job is harder when your energy is low. Second, if you do it first, the other tasks feel easier to tackle.

Another useful piece of advice is to identify your time eaters. Everyone has these, and they're all different. Using social media, pottering in the garden, playing computer games, talking on the phone, watching TV – normal, everyday activities, in which you can lose anything from a few minutes to several hours. When you have identified your time eaters, work out a way to allow yourself enough time to do the things you love without either feeling deprived or encroaching on the work you need to do to achieve the goals you have set yourself. Social media is one of my great time eaters, because I love to communicate, so I restrict the amount of time I allow myself on social media sites, and where possible hide or ignore the associated time eaters, like online games.

Time management isn't easy, as this interviewee discovered:

> That's something that you do need to work in, a bit of time management and a bit of time out, I wasn't particularly good at that. I am a bit of a Last Minute Lulu. I think timelines and working to deadlines, there needs to be training and support around that, I didn't get that right.

Many people think every waking hour is filled, but there is almost always scope for better time management. If you're unsure how you could manage your time better, I suggest you do a time audit. Write out a blank schedule on a sheet of paper, or use a spreadsheet, with days of the week across the top and half-hour slots down the side. Then fill in your actual activities. Be honest! The first few entries might look as shown in Figure 4.2.

Figure 4.2: Weekly time schedule

		Mon	Tue	Wed	Thur	Fri	Sat	Sun
6.30 am	Tea; shower							
7	Breakfast							
7.30	Walk dog							
8	Read magazine							
8.30	Housework							
9	Data entry							

Completing the audit over an entire week enables you to see exactly how you're using your time. This then makes it possible for you to decide where adjustments could be made. For example, on looking at her audit, this person realises that she gets up at 6.30 am but doesn't start work on her research project until 9 am. This leads her to wonder whether she really needs two and a half hours for her morning tasks. After some reflection, she decides that she does need to dawdle through the first half hour, to ease herself into the day. She also needs to walk the dog for half an hour, as this is useful exercise for her as well as for her dog. However, she thinks she could compress the other one-and-a-half hours into 45 minutes, by leaving out the magazine reading, taking 20 minutes over breakfast rather than half an hour, and doing 25 rather than 30 minutes of housework. Now she can start work on her research project at 8.15 am, having freed up another 45 minutes in her day.

Where possible, play to your strengths. So if you're a morning person, don't try to do creative research work late in the evening, and vice versa.

Support from employers

Some employers of people interviewed for this research were supportive in some ways, and a few were very supportive, although none was entirely supportive without requiring anything in return. Some employers paid for academic courses, some provided a small amount of support, such as study leave or administrative support, and some provided no support at all.

> I was working for a local authority and they paid for me to do it at uni. I had time, I think it was one day a week in term time, to come to uni, they were full days' teaching. Then I had some days of study leave as well, not loads, but it was good, it was there.

> Work agreed to pay for it ... I had to do all the rest myself ... My manager agreed that I could leave early once a month to go and attend what was referred to as a learning circle, so you could talk about your research and hear other people's research, so I did get time for tutorials.

> It benefited the organisation. When I was promoted they put me into special departments at headquarters to use the knowledge. The organisation never paid for any of it but they certainly got a return from it at the end of the day.

Most people conducting workplace research, or work-related academic research, said they had to fit it in as and when they could, among all their other tasks.

> I am expected to do research as part of both jobs. The time is part of my working hours, I must factor it into my working day.

We had to squeeze it in where we could. We were all aware that was not the best way of doing it, but it was a case of needs must.

'Normal' work has to take priority, as it's my job – and sometimes this is really frustrating, especially when you feel you're at a crucial point with something and have to put it to one side.

Surprisingly, this was even the case for academics.

Officially – and this is important – officially, in my faculty we get a number of days out of our full year's work that can go towards scholarly activity. So at the most basic you should be able to block out days to either write bids, but also then if they're successful to carry out the research. So the university, I think, would say it's contributing those days. But in practice it's very hard to take those days. I've just booked five of them out in my electronic diary, so that anybody in my team can see when I am on a research day, and people don't respect them, they ask you to come in for a meeting so it is a bit frustrating.

My post is 70% teaching and admin and 30% research. It works as long as I can keep the teaching within the 70%, that's really the trick! And that's the hard bit, so it's recognising that the 70% for the teaching takes up entire chunks of time when there isn't any research time, but then scheduling in research time to make sure you've got adequate time to do things you need to do.

Interviewees who did receive support from their employer, however little, evidently found it helpful.

I think what helped was my manager valued my studies. We discussed it and I felt that he valued academic research and doing it, and his supervision in that area was really good. He valued what I was doing, in supervision he'd say, "I found this article from the *British Journal of Social Work*," and that was really helpful.

And some employers were notably more supportive, particularly those that could see their organisation stood to benefit from the research.

My employers were very supportive. Even though it was extensively my own time, they allowed me to talk to the trainees across several districts and use the work support networks, and allowed me to write that research up. The only precursor was that once I'd finished the paper I sent a copy to them.

They contributed admin support, they contributed help and advice ... Work were brilliant, actually. Because they were going to get the benefit of it.

But this can also come with a cost, as the employer then has an investment in, and so may claim partial ownership of, your research.

> I think there was an element towards the end of apprehension because they weren't sure what they were going to get because they hadn't seen any of the writing. From my point of view that was additional stress. I ended up writing two different sections, one for my dissertation and one for my employer. That probably wasn't the best use of my time but I was worried about it so they got the big results before they got the dissertation.

There can be other difficulties, too.

> It's compulsory, it's part of my contract of employment, which gives it a slightly different tone. I do it within the university. It's been more challenging in terms of having the time to do it. After I started it I had to intermit, to take time out from doing it. It clashed with a lot of my teaching, and when I raised it, and said, "How can I manage it?" – hoping they would review my teaching – they said I would have to intermit, which was quite frustrating. I felt blocked, they were telling me I had to do it, but I've had to manage and navigate my workload to do it rather than it being supported for me to do it.

Most interviewees ended up doing at least some of their research work in their own time, even if it was workplace research.

> This report's basically been pretty much handed over to me. There are pages and pages of stats and things. I'm trying to make something out of it. I get it done by bringing it home, to be honest.

> There were a lot of late evenings and a lot of take-aways in the office.

If you do academic study as part of your continuing professional development, even with some study leave from your employer, it will eat up a lot of your 'leisure' and other time.

> One of the things I found to do with research is that any academic course is very difficult to fit in and you have to learn to make use of time. You have to be very focused and dedicated.

> As a researcher, sometimes the line between personal and professional becomes very blurred, it's because you get involved in projects and have commitments and deadlines and things that you drive yourself that bit harder.

People spoke about how they managed this.

My studies took place in the evenings once the children went to bed and at some weekends when I was against deadlines.

I didn't get out much!

I sleep less. True fact. It was sleep less or give up on family time. No contest really.

Also, it can be hard to switch off.

It's always there, so even if you do decide you're having a weekend off, it's still there. I can remember having weekends off and I couldn't concentrate on what people were saying to me because I should have been working on that chapter or that bit of data analysis.

It's like a little rucksack you take with you everywhere. You wake up and think about it, you go to bed and think about it, you don't get any peace, it's constantly there.

Even with effective time management, it can be a heavy load.

I worked stupid hours. I worked pretty much seven days a week. I got very knackered and pushed myself a lot. I couldn't really see any other way of doing it, though, there was no other way. It was a life-style, maintaining that family–work–study balance, but I wanted to study. I really needed to study to keep my brain going, I needed to be around for my family, and I needed to work because I couldn't afford anything. I didn't want to give any of those things up. It was 'work hard now it'll pay off later' type of thing.

And effective time management is essential.

The thing I've tended to do always in my research time is to consider there need to be specific hours that are given to it. I did the same with the PhD. My approach to the PhD time was if I had two days' teaching work or other research work, that I still had to do 40 hours that week on the PhD. During my time as a research fellow, they gave me one day a week, point two, so I gave it one day as well, point four, half the weekend. It's recognising that whatever you choose to do is fine but you've got to have the hours to do it.

I also try to link, kill two birds with one stone, so the research we're doing is around a particular aspect of adult social care but I also teach in that area so by looking into it for the research, that can feed into my teaching. I do that where I can.

Negotiate for support from your employer, wherever possible, while retaining as much of your autonomy as you can.

Creative time management

Conducting research requires flexibility of thought. This applies to the research work itself, and to managing the research process. You need to be able to take an open-minded and creative approach, both to conducting your research and to managing your research. Inflexible thought will hamper your progress at every stage.

The kinds of inflexible thoughts that create problems for time management include:

'I can't start working on my research until all the housework is done.'
'There's no time for my research in the working day, because I am either in meetings or people are in my office asking me about stuff.'
'My children's needs must come first.'

Words and phrases like 'have to', 'must', 'can't', 'no time', 'always', and 'never' often signal inflexible thoughts.

Use these words and phrases to identify your own inflexible thoughts. Then create a more flexible version that will help you with your research.

Of course housework is necessary, but it is rarely 'all done'; there is almost always something else that can be tidied or cleaned or de-cluttered, so the key here is to do only what is necessary and leave the rest for another time. For workplace research, putting a 'do not disturb' sign on the office door for an hour or two or, for those in shared offices, booking a meeting room to work alone for a while can work wonders.

It might be about taking yourself out of the environment, so you can focus, because when you're there, particularly if you're in the social sector, people are so needy and greedy, you might need to make yourself unavailable at particular times. Be clear about that. If you can't respect the value of what it is that you're doing, then nobody else is going to.

Children's needs are indeed paramount, but don't have to be met by just one person, even if s/he is a single parent; relatives, friends, and other parents can help to share the load. These interviewees offer real-life examples:

> Sometimes you just have to live in a bit of domestic chaos. It's disruption to the routine, and I do resent that a bit. I don't want to have to be stumbling over piles of laundry and books, but I also recognise that there's a deadline. The laundry is never going to end but at least the research project will.

> If I have half an hour at work before a meeting, I'll do half an hour of searching for the text that I need. I can build it into my day.

> My experience as a single parent, that really is … difficult. My boyfriend was brilliant. Once a week he would take my daughter from school, feed her, be with her for the evening, and I would have that evening to work like a bastard.

The point here is that you almost always have a choice. You don't *have* to watch the next episode of your favourite TV programme; you are choosing to do so. It is not *essential* that you complete the crossword and sudoku puzzles in the daily newspaper; it may be an enjoyable part of your usual routine, but it's still a choice you make, every time. Nobody is *making* you go out with your friends every week: for sure, they like your company, and you like theirs; they may encourage you to join them, but in the end it is your decision.

Of course, for people with heavy workloads, this can apply in reverse. It may feel as if you *must* spend evening after evening at your desk – but it's still a choice.

> I think in terms of having a life, it won't happen unless you make it happen. You've got to say, "Right, enough is enough." A concrete example: a friend, we sometimes go out for curry, he was saying, "Can you do this week?" And I was saying, "I can't, I've got this and this and this to do," and then I thought, "What's important here?" I said yes to the curry. You've got to make a conscious decision.

The key factor in managing decisions like these is self-discipline. Self-discipline is a term that makes many people recoil, because to them it means all the hard tasks and none of the enjoyable activities. The stereotype of a self-disciplined person is someone who rises at dawn, exercises vigorously for an hour, takes a quick shower, eats muesli, works hard all day, and so on. I don't agree with this stereotype, and, more importantly, neither does Professor Windy Dryden, who published an excellent and accessible book, *Self-Discipline*, in 2009.

Dryden is a very experienced academic, practitioner, writer and trainer from the UK. He sees self-discipline as belonging to three aspects of the personality:

the short-term self, the long-term self, and the executive self. The short-term self knows what it wants, and it wants it now: playing computer games, eating cake, phoning a friend. The long-term self looks after the longer-term goals: health, career, relationships, and so on. The stereotype of the really self-disciplined person, mentioned in the previous paragraph, is a person whose long-term self is acting at the expense of their short-term self. Conversely, for someone's short-term self to act at the expense of their long-term self, they would need to be very wealthy so that they could gratify every whim – and they would be unlikely to be happy.

The third aspect of the personality that Dryden identifies, the executive self, works to balance the needs of the short-term and long-term selves. Self-discipline is most effective if long-term goals are attended to first, with time and space built in for the short-term self to play.

If you would like to improve your own self-discipline, read Professor Dryden's book and put his ideas into practice.

Self-discipline is an essential skill for researchers, whether their research is workplace or academic or both. Another essential skill is negotiating.

> There were two of us. We convinced the person in HR[2] to give us our CPD[3] hours for actual study time. So we'd have a Friday working from home on CPD leave, where other people were going on courses. We did some negotiating like that, it helped at the crucial moments where you've got something to submit.

> I bribed my son to do the techie work for me. He made all the tables and charts for my Master's. He must have been about 12. And he's so savvy, and I think it helped him feel involved.

> I have had to have quite strong words with the assistant director, go through his timetable and get him to see he is not giving us the time he is committed to giving us. I've got a commitment from him that he will book in the time he is going to spend each week. That will help.

The classic stereotype of a good negotiator is someone who is hard-nosed and out for everything they can get. Negotiating skills were developed by business people

---

[2] Human Resources.
[3] Continuing professional development.

who were competitive, aggressive, and comfortable with using techniques such as deception and manipulation to get what they wanted. This does not sit easily alongside research ethics. Luckily, negotiating skills have developed further, such as through the work of Professor Stuart Diamond, a very experienced academic, practitioner, writer, and trainer from the US, who published a useful book on negotiating, *Getting More*, in 2010.

Diamond deals with real-world negotiation. He covers negotiation with colleagues, friends, family members, spouses or partners, people in positions of authority, and toddlers. He sees a range of factors as essential, including emotional sensitivity, understanding the wishes and needs of the person you are negotiating with, communicating honestly, and recognising that every situation is different. He also points out that negotiating can be achieved by exchanging things that don't have equal value in the market. So, for example, while I was working on this book, a former client of mine wanted my help with some new research he was commissioning. It wasn't within my area of expertise, so he hadn't asked me to bid for the research myself. He runs a local charity and didn't have any money in his budget to pay consultancy fees, so he called to ask me to help him at one meeting, for free, as a favour. I hesitated, using the technique of not giving an immediate response while I worked out whether I wanted to say 'yes'. He knew I was writing to a deadline and my time was limited, so he said, "We could make it a lunchtime meeting and I would give you lunch." That clinched the deal. In terms of the market, the cost of a sandwich lunch is a fraction of the cost of my time spent attending a meeting. But in my own terms, it made me feel valued; saved me from having to prepare my own lunch that day; and provided some tangible recompense for my time and effort. While the lunch my client offered was not of equal market value to the time and skills he needed, it was enough to persuade me to help.

Diamond's negotiators are self-aware, aware of others, honest, assertive, and creative. Researchers also need these skills to manage the research process. Here's a great example of this in practice, from an interviewee who completed a part-time Master's degree while supporting herself financially and helping with the childcare of her brother, who is over 20 years younger than her.

> Explain to your tutors from the off, not apologising for it, but explain that you have a lot of responsibilities and you're juggling very many balls and you strive to keep on top of it but there is always a risk that something may take precedence, like family. I was pushed to say that I had to take study over work, and my tutor got very annoyed if I said, "I might have to work that day." She was quite passionate about, "You must be involved in everything," but be honest about the facts. Not like in a way that you're being a martyr, but just say, "This is what I have going on in my life, research is important to me but these things might come into play." I ended up bringing my brother to a field trip, I didn't want to miss the field trip so I took him on the trip, and it actually showed people that, yes, there's a real child involved. In a way it made it a bit better when people actually saw that I had a child to look after as well.

If you would like to improve your own negotiating skills, read Professor Diamond's book and put his ideas into practice.

Reward yourself

Rewarding yourself for completing tasks will help your motivation. You can give yourself small rewards several times a day. Everyone has different ideas about what constitutes a reward. That doesn't matter; what matters is that you can identify rewards that work for you: 10 minutes on a social media site, a drink and a snack, or a walk around the block. On a daily level, I might promise myself that when I have reached my daily word count, I can call a friend for a chat; or when I have finished today's data entry task, I can have a break and do the crossword over a cup of tea.

Completing bigger tasks deserves bigger rewards. So after the first draft of this book has gone to the publisher, I plan to spend a week catching up with friends. After the final draft is done, I will take a holiday with my partner. Again, you need to identify rewards that work for you, whatever those might be: tickets to a show or a sporting event, time with family or friends, a new book or a new item of clothing.

Also, if you fail to complete a task as planned, don't beat yourself up. Life gets in the way, and people make mistakes. The last thing you need is to spiral into a vortex of feeling like a failure, deciding there's no point in trying, and giving up on your research. Regroup, replan, and keep going.

Look after yourself

It is essential that you take care of yourself because nobody else is going to do that for you. Other people may help: someone might make you a meal, or listen to your woes. But it is your responsibility to keep track of, and maintain, your physical and mental health. For optimum research/life management you need to:

- eat a healthy, balanced diet, with a few treats;
- take regular exercise;
- make sure you get enough sleep;
- have regular breaks in your daily, weekly, monthly, and annual routines;
- find time each day and week to do some things purely for enjoyment;
- network with other researchers for peer support;
- ask for help when you need help;
- learn from your mistakes, but don't dwell on them;
- celebrate your achievements.

Highlighting the need to eat and sleep may seem obvious, trivial, or irrelevant. Some people claim to do their best work in caffeine-fuelled all-nighters. They are likely to be deluding themselves. Research has demonstrated that food is necessary for the exercise of will-power, and sleep for good decision making (Baumeister and Tierney, 2012: 49, 59–60). Will-power and good decision making are key ingredients of successful research.

Keeping a research diary or journal can help you to manage your research and your life. Some people advocate the use of research journals for reflective learning, or learning from the process. A journal can certainly be useful for this, but it also has other potential benefits: as a way to express uncomfortable feelings or concerns; as a place for anything from the unspeakable, to thoughts you really don't want to forget; or simply as somewhere to offload.

> I did keep a journal, and the journal was really useful, and that was from the research qualification because you had to do it for that. Initially I thought, "This is a pain," but actually having the journal was really useful. The journal I used more about my experiences of the subject I was studying, the wake up screaming at 4 o'clock in the morning type stuff, and to reflect on things I'd had to do in my work life that I hadn't felt comfortable about.

> At the moment I'm doing a diary of each time I have a project about who's come, how they're interacting with each other, how I've felt about it. That was encouraged by the last person in my job and my line manager, that's been quite useful doing a learning journal.

Some professions, such as nursing, regularly make use of learning journals (Alaszewski, 2006: 10–11), so you may be comfortable with this technique. Even if you have no experience of diary writing and feel appalled at the very idea, I would encourage you to give it a try. There is no right way to keep a research diary (Silverman and Marvasti, 2008: 304) – which, comfortingly, means there isn't a wrong way to do it either. I am an ad hoc journal writer at best, but I do find it useful to write down odd thoughts and feelings and bits and bobs as I work through the research process. In the day-to-day business of research work, such a huge amount of information passes through your thoughts and senses that it's easy to forget even very relevant pieces of information or ideas (Jesson, Matheson and Lacey, 2011: 58). It is surprising how often my ad hoc records of oddities prove useful when I'm writing my research reports.

You also need to take care of yourself within the process of conducting research. Potentially, research can endanger you physically, emotionally, and politically, and it is your responsibility to keep yourself safe.

Most of the physical dangers of research consist of spending too long sitting at a desk staring at a screen. However, the data-collection phase may at times lead to physical danger for researchers. Some researchers will be sharply aware of this possibility, such as Simon Winlow in his investigations of cultures of violence and organised crime (Westmarland, 2011: 133–7). For others, it may come as a surprise.

Here's an example from my own experience. Soon after I became an independent researcher, I was asked to evaluate a partnership-based mental health service. To do this, I needed to interview users of the service, some of whom were in secure psychiatric wards. I'd had previous experience of locked wards so the prospect didn't faze me. Arrangements were made for the ward staff to identify willing and able interviewees. When I arrived at one hospital, the nurse in charge pointed to a man sitting in a side room with a glass panel in the door, and said, "There's your first interviewee. He said he's happy to do it, but he's a bit unpredictable with strangers, especially women." My jaw must have dropped, because the nurse grinned and added, "Don't worry, we'll keep an eye on you."

My pulse was racing but I tried to appear calm as I went into the side room to begin the interview. Luckily, the interviewee was even tempered and helpful, but the interview felt very long and I was relieved to reach the end. I still don't know what 'a bit unpredictable' meant, but I certainly didn't feel safe, and the regular appearance of a concerned face in the glass door panel did more to prolong my feeling of alarm than to reassure me about my safety.

People generally are 'a bit unpredictable'. Some people don't like researchers, or intellectuals, or clever Dicks. Someone may be sexist, or racist, or uncomfortable around people who dress in certain ways. A participant may have been angered by something unconnected with your research, and choose to take it out on you. Or someone may just be in a bad mood. Whatever the reason, you can't assume that everyone will be well mannered and helpful, and that you will always be safe.

So take appropriate precautions. If you are going out alone into an unfamiliar environment, you should make sure someone knows where you are going and when you expect to be back, so they can take action if you don't return on time. Don't research topics that could take you into dangerous encounters unless you are confident that you can manage such situations. Be aware of the possibility of danger, and be prepared to abandon a piece of data collection if necessary.

Finding yourself in physical danger takes an emotional toll, but researchers can also be in emotional danger without the physical aspect. Interviewees for this book talked of distressing experiences in researching subjects such as chronic illness or bereavement. As with physical danger, when it is obvious that a topic may lead to emotional danger, steps can be taken to manage this, although there seems to be little advice available on how to do so. One interviewee really grappled with this situation.

> If anything, in actually doing the research, that was the bit that worried me, there were some people I knew were having end-of-life care, and I knew some bits were going to be harrowing. It's not just about how I deal with it, but how to deal with someone who is getting upset. Maybe because of the research I was doing, I knew about that but I didn't read it anywhere. I prepared an exit strategy, I had ready prepared statements I could use that were comforting but would call an end to the

research interview and enable me to calm them down, make sure they were safe and happy and OK and remove myself from the situation. I had to use them once when a woman got very distressed, and they worked, but I have to tell you, thank God I had them, because if I hadn't had that at my fingertips I don't know what I would have done. I'm pretty intuitive, and I probably would have handled it OK, but you can't guarantee, and knowing what I'd planned to do meant the planning kicked in. It was stuff that I would do intuitively, but having the steps written down and in the back of my head helped me manage that situation. I like people, that's why I do social research, but having ideas about how to deal with it meant that I wasn't flustered and panicked, because what she needed was somebody calm. And bless her, she rang me the next day to thank me, and to apologise for being upset. I think I'd have been more upset if she hadn't been. It's not just how you're going to handle your own emotions, but how you're going to handle someone else's.

And sometimes you can't see it coming. For example, I have conducted research in the areas of mental ill-health and drug misuse, both areas where I have enough experience to be reasonably inured to the misery involved. However, in both areas, I encountered parents who had been forcibly separated from their children because of their situation, and their grief was intense. I found this very upsetting because I couldn't do anything but listen and sympathise, and that wasn't enough; it felt like trying to treat an amputation with a sticking plaster.

Again, with emotional danger, you need to take appropriate precautions. If you have a distressing encounter, take some time for yourself as soon as you can after the event. Find someone supportive to talk it over with, ideally someone who will help you sort through your feelings and find a sensible perspective. Write about it in your journal – or, if you don't keep a journal, write about it anyway: the act of writing will help you to process the experience, and the write-up may prove useful as data. (This might seem a horribly callous thing to say, but everything is potential grist to the researcher's mill.)

Political danger is another difficulty you may come across in your research work. What I mean by 'political danger' is that everyone has their own agenda and some people may try to hi-jack part or all of your research for their own ends. You may experience this from managers, commissioners, supervisors, tutors, participants, colleagues, and others, at any stage of the process, from plans to dissemination and beyond. Yet this kind of hi-jacking isn't always malicious, or even intentional. The interviewee quoted in Chapter Two, who had to stand firm against another researcher and her boss when they were getting over-enthusiastic and trying to make recommendations before the data had been analysed, reflected on this:

> The danger from my point of view was, some people come up with an idea they don't want to let go of, and the idea works from one angle and won't work from another, and I was worried that we could go far too far down that road. Then the research might say something else but the idea wouldn't be let go of. So I nipped that in the

bud, and said, "Hang on, all this information's in my head but the coding may turn up something I haven't seen, and that's the point of coding."

At times, however, hi-jacking can be absolutely intentional. For example, I was once asked to evaluate a residential service. The commissioner was completely open about the fact that he wanted to close the service down, and he asked me to find evidence that would support his plans. I was equally open with him, saying that I was not prepared to work to his agenda, but I was prepared to conduct a professional independent evaluation and present my findings. He accepted this and gave me a contract for the work. My findings did not support his plans to close the service, as its users, its staff, and staff of partner agencies who referred users to the service, were all unanimous in their opinion of its high value, and this was supported by monitoring and other data. So the commissioner couldn't use my evaluation report as evidence to support his plans, but he was very nice about it, paid my invoice, and, sadly, found another way to close down the service.

In both of these examples, the researcher's job was to remain fully aware of what they were doing, why they were doing it, and how they were doing it, and to hold those boundaries in place when others tried to bend them. This is the best way to maintain your political safety as a researcher. It won't protect you against every political danger, because research is in itself a political act, and you can find yourself treading on unexpected toes. But boundary management is your greatest safeguard, as well as being a sound ethical way to conduct research.

What works, and what doesn't work

Table 4.1 summarises what works, and what doesn't work, in managing the research process on top of your main job.

But, as I said in Chapter One, I can only write the guidebook. Now you know where the safe places are, and which paths might lead to danger. What route will you take?

Table 4.1: What works, and what doesn't work

What works	What doesn't work
Being clear and realistic about your workload from the start.	Putting off thinking about the work you need to do – and then putting it off some more.
Establishing a routine for studying so that you work at the same times each day or week.	Waiting until you're in the right mood to start studying.
Finding or creating a quiet, uncluttered space in which to study so that you are free of distractions.	Trying to study with the TV or talk radio playing, social media flashing up messages on your computer screen, children running in and out.
Turning off your phone and letting your voice-mail take messages.	Trying to concentrate while your phone is beeping and ringing.
Working in blocks of 30–90 minutes, with short exercise/snack breaks in between of 5–10 minutes.	Working for long periods without breaks – you can't maintain concentration.
Using time when your mind is under-occupied – for example, while exercising, waiting for a bus, walking to the shops – to think about your research.	Putting your research out of your mind except when you're at your desk.
Taking proper breaks: at least one day off a week and one holiday a year.	Studying for days, weeks, months on end without a break.
Setting milestones and rewarding yourself for each one you reach.	Beating yourself up for failing to meet deadlines.
Sharing experiences and support with other people doing similar work.	Trying to do the work and cope with the pressure all on your own.
Eating nutritious food.	Living on junk food and coffee or cola.
Taking regular exercise.	Sitting hunched over your desk all day.

FIVE

Background research

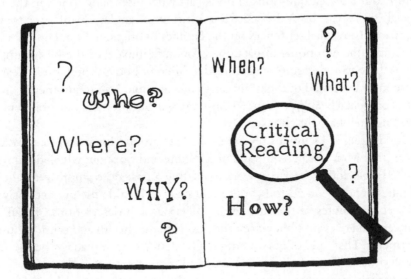

Introduction

Whatever kind of research or evaluation you're doing, some background research is always helpful. This can range from just a few project documents and perhaps one or two pieces of national policy, for a small evaluation, to several hundred items of published and 'grey' literature for a full-scale literature review.

> When you're dealing with material that you can engage with and understand, the bit where it's exciting, firing off all sorts, the thrill of it, it's the bit that's pleasurable.

The main point of background research is to provide the context for your own research. As a result, much of the work on this is best done at an early stage – although it may also be necessary to include any legislation, policy, and/or key articles or books that are published as you do your research. Also, you may decide to do more background research at a later stage, such as if your data analysis reveals something unexpected and you want to put that finding into context for your readers.

Document review or literature review?

If you're doing research for postgraduate academic study, you will be required to do a formal literature review. This is covered later in the chapter. If you're doing research in and for your workplace, you will need to do a document review.[1] So what is the difference?

In conducting a literature review for academic research, you start from the literature and work towards your research topic, using the literature to help you develop your research questions. This is partly because many topics in the field of social studies can be addressed from a variety of angles. So if your topic is the impact of custodial sentences on the families of offenders, you could look at, for example, the emotional impact, the economic impact, or the health impact. Each of these would require you to read a different body of literature. Let's say you are most interested in the health angle. That could lead to another decision: physical or mental health, or both? Again, there will be different bodies of literature, depending on what you choose.

In conducting a document review as the background for workplace research, you start from your research question or questions and work out which documents you need to include. So if you were evaluating a project to improve the health of families of people in custody, you might need to include the project's original funding bid, minutes of steering group meetings, job descriptions of staff and volunteers, and relevant policy from the government's health and criminal justice departments. That kind of document review is quite easy to manage, but in other research projects it can be a much larger and more complex undertaking.

For example, let's say you work in a service that is set up to give debt and benefit advice. You notice that more of your service users have mental health problems – perhaps because of the closure of a neighbouring service, or the reduction of social stigma around mental health (which means more people are open about their condition), or a wider change in policy, or for some other reason. Your manager develops an informal theory that your service is not entirely meeting the needs of people with mental health problems, and asks you to do a piece of research to find some evidence one way or the other. The research questions are: Are we meeting all the needs of our service users who have mental health problems? If not, what do we need to change to ensure that we do meet all their needs? Your manager wants you to collect primary data from interviews with service users, and also to carry out a document review to research best practice in service provision for people with mental health problems. This will involve you spending time on the World Wide Web tracking down documents from sources including:

- specialist mental health organisations, such as Mind and SANE in the UK;
- other service providers in a variety of fields who have produced guidance about working with people who have mental health problems;

---

[1] Documents can be used for background research, as discussed here, and/or as data, which is discussed in Chapter Seven.

- research organisations and think-tanks, like the Joseph Rowntree Foundation, Demos and the King's Fund in the UK, that have published relevant research;
- national government departments.

That sounds very complicated, but actually all you have to do is put your search terms into a web-based search engine, and it will find documents for you.

What your search terms will be is another question. Whether you see your background research as a literature review or a document review or something between the two, your work will be richer if you don't limit your reading to your own subject or discipline. Of course you have to limit your reading in some ways, or you'd never do anything but read. Nevertheless, a bit of lateral thinking can greatly enhance your research. So, for example, in the project mentioned in the previous paragraph, as well as looking for information about best practice in service provision for people with mental health problems, you might also look at best practice in occupational health for the purposes of comparison. If you were researching the impact of custodial sentences on the families of offenders, you might do some reading around other ways in which a family member can be temporarily separated from the family home, such as through being in the forces or being kidnapped, to see whether these experiences have parallels or contrasts that might throw light on the experiences of offenders' families.

Rather than reading only from your own subject or discipline, think laterally about which bodies of literature might help to throw light on your research question(s).

Whether you are conducting a document review or a literature review, you may wish to draw on 'grey' literature and ephemera. 'Grey' literature refers to research reports and other documents that are not formally published, but may be available in hard copy and/or electronic formats from individuals, organisations, or governments. Examples include research that has not been peer reviewed, policy documents, and technical reports. Ephemera are also written in hard copy and electronic formats, and are not intended to be kept or stored. These include e-zines, leaflets, and social media updates, such as tweets.

While I am suggesting you read as widely as you can, there is a danger for avid readers. When you are searching through documents or literature, it's easy to get side-tracked and go off on an interesting tangent.

> If you're reading a lot, you can go through bibliographies and keep on going and going and going. You can find yourself getting distracted by insignificant things that are interesting but have no relevance to you or anyone else.

While this may be enjoyable, if it is not potentially or actually relevant to your research questions, it is a poor use of your research time. Of course, if you have all the time in the world, go right ahead. But most of us need to exercise some self-discipline in this situation.

> Go back to what your research objectives were. If what you're doing isn't helping you get there, then stop.

In this chapter, I have drawn a distinction between a document review and a literature review, because the former is usually referred to in workplace research and the latter in academic research. But this is not a hard-and-fast distinction, and there are many areas of overlap between the two. Depending on the approach taken and the literature available, one person's document review may look much more like someone else's literature review, or vice versa. As I have already said, they are both forms of background research that can provide the wider context for your work, which is useful for you and for the readers and users of your research. They also both offer:

- a chance to clarify parts of your thinking about aspects of your research questions;
- an opportunity to hone your research questions against the work of others;
- support for the importance, necessity, or relevance of your research;
- a way to find and develop your own standpoint.

And they both require:

- careful and critical reading;
- considerable thought;
- the making of connections between theories, ideas, and perspectives;
- the development of a new view of the subject.

The requirement to develop your own standpoint, and a new view of the subject, can be quite daunting. It is more onerous for academic researchers, who *must* produce original work, than for workplace researchers, who *should* produce original work. But any research that ignores this requirement is likely to be poor research. The good news is, it's not as hard as you might think, and the way to do it is simply to keep reading, thinking, and writing. Your standpoint already exists; the reading and thinking you do will help you identify and express it through your writing. Your new view of the subject, which you will convey in the completed research, does not exist at the start. In fact, it may not exist until close to the end. Nevertheless, it is essential, because whether you are doing a document review or a literature review, the final result should not simply be a list of 'person 1 says this, person 2 says that'. Of course you need to include some explanation of the thoughts, ideas, and concepts put forward by the key writers in your field. But where your view will come in is in the synthesising of those thoughts, ideas, and concepts, from your own standpoint, such that it is unique (Silverman and Marvasti, 2008: 98).

The words 'unique' and 'original' are quite scary for some people. It can help to step back and take a wider perspective. A commonly used phrase is 'the whole body of human knowledge', so let's compare that to a human body. Nobody knows how many cells a human body contains, but estimates suggest there may be approximately 10 trillion, or 10 to the power of 14, or 100,000,000,000,000 – which is a very big number. Every time you touch another person's skin, several of your cells rub off on them, and several of their cells rub off on you. Similarly, as you read and learn, several cells of knowledge will rub off on you – but your research only needs to add one tiny cell to the whole body of human knowledge.

Record keeping

Whether you're doing a document review or an academic literature review, you need to keep an accurate record of what you read, where you found it, and how it might fit in to your research (Hart, 2001: 23). This is because, at a later stage, you will need to explain what documents and/or literature you have drawn on in your research, and how you assessed and analysed them. The best way to keep these records is to make a grid for yourself and fill it in as you go along.

> We had a learning circle and one of the other people was talking about how he organised his reading and his notes, and I suddenly thought, "I could have been doing that, it sounds like a really good idea." And it was dead simple, it was a grid: author, title, publisher, date, very brief précis of what it was about and whether you liked it or not, another section that had quotes related to what you were interested in. I added another column later on that said, "This would work in chapter so-and-so." I'd got about six different reading lists at the time and could I find anything? Could I hell. It was about how I organised it, and that was the turning-point.

This interviewee kindly gave me permission to use an example of her grid in this book, which you will find in Appendix 2.

You can make a grid on the computer in a spreadsheet or a text document, or on paper if you prefer. There is no set format for a grid, the important thing is to work out what you need to include for your own research project. Figure 5.1 shows another example.

Figure 5.1: Example of record keeping for a document or literature review

Reference	Where found	Where stored	Key message	Fits where?
Bunting, M. (2004) *Willing Slaves: How the Overwork Culture is Ruling Our Lives*. London: HarperCollins.	Library	Notes in folder	Work is too stressful	Links emotion and work – discussion section

There is a third example on page 30 of Jesson, Matheson and Lacey (2011).

If you use spreadsheet software, you can use a similar grid system in much more detail. For example, you might have columns headed:

1. Number
2. Date
3. Author
4. Title
5. Publisher
6. Edition number
7. Where found
8. Where stored
9. Quote/page
10. Main subject(s)
11. Key message
12. Why is this important?
13. Who agrees with this?
14. Who disagrees with this?
15. Where might it fit into my research?

The sorting function of spreadsheets is a very useful tool in helping you to manage and process your reading material, especially if you've read a lot of literature. For example, you could sort on 'main subject' to see whether you've read enough across each of the different subject areas; you could sort on 'edition number' to check whether there are any books that might have a more up-to-date edition than the one you've read; and you could sort on 'author' to help you construct your bibliography.

This may seem complicated and time-consuming, but it will save time later on (Jesson, Matheson and Lacey, 2011: 28), as this interviewee acknowledged:

> The literature search, if you are very clear at the beginning about the different elements of this – set that up right at the beginning and keep it up to date, that means you don't actually have to go back and try and dig that information out later. It's about trying to reduce the amount of work. Good administrative set-up right at the start is not time wasted. I wish I'd known that.

You are, of course, free to copy any of the grids in this book for your own use if you wish. However, I would urge you to spend a little time thinking through what you need to record for your own purposes. It is likely that an adaptation of one of these grids will work better for you than simply copying one as it stands.

Some people don't like grids and spreadsheets, and are much happier with hard copies. If you are one of these people, you can:

- use different coloured boxes and files to store information on different subjects;
- highlight photocopies or print-outs in different colours for specific reasons, for example green for 'theme', yellow for 'important', blue for 'possible quote' and red for 'key message';
- categorise your documents with different-coloured stars for different levels of relevance, for example gold for very relevant, silver for quite relevant, and blue for some relevant sections (which you could then mark with Post-It notes);
- use different coloured Post-It notes to mark different types of passage.

Again, you will need to devise your own system that suits your approach, resources, and topic.

Post-It notes are ideal for marking passages in books that need to be returned to the library.

There are also computer software packages that can help you manage your references. Dedicated applications such as EndNote and Reference Manager will help you to keep track of your references and compile the reference list for your report, dissertation, or thesis. Online research services, such as Zotero and Menderley, also include this function (see later in this chapter for more information about these).

Critical and strategic reading

If you're doing research, the odds are that you can read English fluently and have been reading for a long time. However, reading for research is different from other kinds of reading, and I think it's worth taking a moment to define and consider that difference.

There is a common perception that the process of reading involves ideas from the writer's brain, communicated via the writer's hands into words on a page, which are then transmitted through the reader's eyes into the reader's brain. With some types of writing, this is more or less true, but with research, the process is much more like the illustration in Box 5.1.

Box 5.1: The writing and reading process

Writer has idea.
↓

Writer filters their idea through their past experience and present emotions.
↓

Writer chooses language, grammar, structure and so on to express their idea.
↓

Editor intervenes to alter language, grammar, structure and so on (and sometimes even content, for example if word count needs to be reduced).
↓

Final version is published.
↓

Reader reads writer's idea.
↓

Reader filters writer's idea through their own past experience and present emotions.
↓

Reader considers writer's idea.
↓

Reader reaches some level of understanding of writer's idea.

One way to summarise this might be: I write in my terms, you read in yours. There are two main reasons for this.

The first is emotion. There are times when I've been reading for research and I've come across a chapter or article that has made me so cross that I can't bear to finish reading it, let alone give dispassionate consideration to the point it makes. There are other times when I read something that excites me, I think it's marvellous and the writer becomes my new hero.

The second is the richness of the English language. Writers frequently have to choose from a wide range of synonymous words, each with a slightly different meaning and resonance. Readers bring their own understanding to the chosen words. For example, one person's 'careful' might be another's 'cautious' or 'wary' or 'vigilant'. Choices writers make about grammar, syntax, structure, and so on also interact with readers' understandings in unpredictable ways.

So the emotions of writers and readers, the choices made by writers and editors, and the understanding of readers can all lead to misunderstanding when reading for research, even when written work is comparatively clear and coherent. And some of it isn't. Some documents and academic texts are abstruse and difficult, whether because they are poorly written, or poorly edited, or the authors are grappling with complex concepts, or some combination of those factors. But the good news is, there's so much literature available that you don't have to read the unreadable. If you're finding a piece of writing too difficult to read, stop trying, and find another relevant document instead.

If you're reading a complicated piece of writing, and you're struggling to understand, try reading it out loud.

So what is the best way to manage this potential for misunderstanding? I would recommend careful, critical reading. You need to read carefully enough to understand what the writer is saying. However, just because somebody has written something down in words and numbers does not mean it is true or useful or correct. Therefore you also need to read critically. This concept comes from critical theory, a formal theory that encourages scepticism and critical reading and thinking across a range of disciplines. Critical reading does not simply mean finding things to criticise, it means analysing the positive and negative aspects of the text (Jesson, Matheson and Lacey, 2011: 16) and making a careful assessment of the document's value, both to your own research and more widely. In practice, 'critical reading' means assessing what you are reading against a range of parameters including the document's age, relevance to your work, wider relevance, the skills of the author(s), any perceptible political stance, the quality of the explanations and reasoning, and so on. Critical reading requires critical thinking, which in this context has been described as the process of identifying another author's position, line of reasoning, and conclusions (Cottrell, 2005, in Jesson, Matheson and Lacey, 2011: 48). One way of learning to think critically is always to ask yourself these questions: Could there have been another explanation? Could a different conclusion have been reached?

You should also 'determine … the authenticity and usefulness of particular documents, taking into account the original purpose of each document, the context in which it was produced, and the intended audience' (Bowen, 2009: 38). When research is being reported, it is important to assess the quality of the report and sometimes of the research. If it is a second-hand report, like the last citation in the previous paragraph, the reporter should cite their source in full (in this case Jesson, Matheson and Lacey, 2011: 48), which should in turn cite the original source in full (that is, Cottrell, 2005, with the relevant page number if given), so that, if you wish, you can make a full assessment of Cottrell's work. It is important to include page numbers to make this process easier. (There is more information about citation in Chapter Nine.)

If you are reading a researcher's own report of their work, you should be able to understand what they have done, why they have done it, how they did it, and why they drew the conclusions they reached. This doesn't mean you have to agree with their conclusions, just that you need to be able to understand where those conclusions have come from. If you have read their report carefully, and you do not understand it fully, there may be a fault in their reporting and/or in their research. Your skills in critical reading and critical thinking will help you to work out where the fault lies.

It is easy to read carefully from the start. Reading and thinking critically is more difficult at the beginning, although it becomes easier with practice. As you begin to read for your research, be as critical as you can, but don't worry if you feel as if you're reading in a vacuum with no context within which to make sense of your learning. As you continue, you will start to make connections between theories, concepts, findings, and ideas, and this will help you to develop your critical faculties.

For a master class in critical reading, read *Bad Science* by Ben Goldacre (2008).

You can read strategically to save time. So, if you find an article with a promising title, read the abstract first. Does it still seem relevant? If not, discard it. If it does, then read the introduction and the conclusion and, if it still seems relevant, begin to read the rest.

> I've become very good at scanning texts quickly. This gets easier the more experienced you become. You get to learn which articles are worth spending more time on, which you don't need at all, and which have got good or useful references for you to backtrack on and dig a bit deeper.

The same applies with book chapters: read the first paragraph or two of each chapter, and skim the headings, to see what's relevant. With whole books, read the contents list, and perhaps part of the preface or introduction, to decide which chapters you need to read. Then you can read more thoroughly where necessary.

If you want to get a quick overview of a book's approach to its subject, read the first and last paragraphs of each chapter.

Don't ignore basic works of reference such as dictionaries and encyclopaedias. These can both be found online, as well as in print. In general, in this book, I have tried to avoid giving website addresses because of the speed with which they can change, and have focused instead on suggesting search terms. Here, though, I feel on safe ground, because www.dictionary.com has been around since 1995 and www.wikipedia.com since 2001. Both are free to use (although

Wikipedia appreciates donations from its users) and both are invaluable resources for researchers.

Dictionary.com draws on 15 different high-quality dictionaries to provide a range of definitions for each word. It is very useful to look through when you need to define a term you are using, or when you're unsure about the meaning of a word, or when you need to choose a word to help you make a point (its sister site, www.thesaurus.com, can also be helpful here). The site is run by a private corporation and funded by advertising.

Wikipedia is a collaborative encyclopaedia, run as a non-profit organisation, that currently has around 90,000 active volunteer contributors. At the time of writing, it has around 20 million articles, of which about 3.75 million are in English, and covers most subjects. Wikipedia is regarded by some as insufficiently authoritative because the articles are written and edited by volunteers, and some content is highly disputed between different contributors. It is certainly not good practice to use Wikipedia itself as a reference, for these reasons and because its content may change. Wikipedia is most useful as a starting-point for investigation.

Interestingly, in 2005, research showed that the level of errors in Wikipedia was similar to the level of errors in printed encyclopaedias.[2] This is an important point. It's easy to forget to read critically when you're looking at a dictionary or an encyclopaedia, whether online or in print. However, encyclopaedias and dictionaries are produced by humans, so there is scope for human error, bias, and even misinformation. Also, the publishers of dictionaries have a history of including one or more fake definitions to help identify plagiarism.[3] So it is essential to read critically at all times, even when you're looking up a subject in an encylopaedia or a word in a dictionary.

Finding academic journal articles

Journal articles, particularly those that have been peer reviewed, are an important source of information for researchers (Hart, 2001: 93). Tens of thousands of articles are published each year, but they can be surprisingly difficult to find, particularly if you don't belong to a university.

> If you're not part of academia, where do you even look? I'm thinking specifically now around the academic research project we had to do, oh my God, where do you look?

> If you're in practice, bang goes your Athens password, how do you access some of this stuff?

---

[2] J. Giles (2005) 'Internet encyclopaedias go head to head', *Nature*, vol 438, no 7070, pp 900–1.

[3] Mark Miller, former lexicographical proof-reader, personal communication 2011.

Access to many academic journals is restricted to individual or organisational subscribers. Most of these journals are accessed electronically through the Athens service, which can be joined only by institutions (which pay the subscription costs) and which issue passwords to individual members of those institutions (for whom access is free). This was originally just for students and staff in academic institutions, but has slowly widened to include, at the time of writing, staff in health services in many countries, including the UK, Australia, Canada, New Zealand, and the US, and staff in some public sector organisations in the UK, Canada, Australia, and the US. Nevertheless, access is still barred to most third sector, education, and criminal justice professionals, and to independent researchers.

There is a growing movement to provide open access to academic journal articles. Researchers from Finland and Iceland found that, in 2008, approximately 20% of all academic literature was openly accessible (Björk et al, 2010). More specifically, Björk et al found that 5.6% of social science articles were available free from the point of publication, while 17.9% were available after a delay. This figure is likely to have increased. In 2011, multi-lingual researchers from Finland and Germany found that the publication of open access journals had increased rapidly between 2000 and 2009 (Laakso et al, 2011), so was likely to continue to increase. Richard Poynder, a British technology journalist who has a particular interest in the open access movement, estimated in 2011 that 30% of all academic literature published in that year was freely available, one third of it immediately and two-thirds after a delay.[4] As this book goes to press, there is a mounting worldwide campaign to increase access to academic journals, including a boycott of journals that restrict access. This is being supported by prestigious research institutions such as Harvard University in the US and the Wellcome Trust in the UK. It looks likely that, in the future, more and more research papers that have been publicly funded will be openly accessible.

Existing 'open access' journal articles are not easy to find, because access is provided in several different ways and there is (at the time of writing) no single searchable database. The main ways in which access is provided are:

- in open access journals, that is, those that are entirely free to everyone;
- in subscription journals that make their electronic versions free after a delay;
- as individual open articles in otherwise fee-paying subscription journals;
- in subject-based online repositories;
- in institution-based online repositories;
- on the authors' websites;
- on the websites of the authors' employers;
- on research funders' websites.

---

[4] http://poynder.blogspot.com/2011/06/open-access-by-numbers.html, accessed 5 December 2011.

So how do you find these resources? Some of the largest open access journals are published by the Public Library of Science (PLoS) in the US, BioMed Central in the UK and Hindawi Publishing in Egypt. However, these are heavily weighted towards medicine and laboratory science, with just a handful of social science journals published by Hindawi. The Directory of Open Access Journals (DOAJ) includes listings of peer-reviewed or editorially quality-controlled journals that are openly accessible. Most of these are in English and cover other areas: at the time of writing this included 627 for education, 19 for criminology, 22 for social work, and 24 for government. However, its search function is a little idiosyncratic; I found that the search terms 'crime' and 'criminal justice' both yielded journals that were not covered by 'criminology' (although each yielded fewer journals overall).

When using DOAJ, try as many search terms as you can.

Two more useful websites, which list a range of free resources by subject including open access journals, are http://library.open.ac.uk/find/free/ from the UK, and http://infomine.ucr.edu/ from the US (use the advanced search function to select free resources).

You may be able to find other useful websites by using search engines to look for 'open access journals'.

Finding open access articles from subscription journals is harder, as there is no equivalent of the DOAJ for these publications. The best way is to use Google Scholar to search for the articles you would like to read, then check whether they are freely available anywhere on the Web. This will also help you to find them on the websites of the authors, their employers, or their funders, if they are held in those places. Another option is to track down journals covering the subjects that interest you, and then check the website of each journal to see which articles are available for free.

Subject-based online repositories can also be difficult to find. At the time of writing, the main English language ones are:

- for health – OpenMED at the National Informatics Centre in India (OpenMED@NIC), PubMed Central (PMC) in the US;
- for education – Higher Education Empirical Research (HEER) in the UK, Open Educational Resources (OER) in the UK;
- for government – Policy Archive in the US;
- for general social science (including criminology, third sector, and so on) – Social Science Research Network (SSRN) in the US.

If you would like to delve further, there is an online Ranking Web of World Repositories, listing 1,222 repositories in December 2011 (with the SSRN at number 1). You may also be able to find other subject-based online repositories by using search engines.

For institution-based online repositories, a useful place to start is the Registry of Open Access Repositories (ROAR), based in the UK. ROAR holds information about institution-based repositories of journals and other academic literature, including Master's dissertations and PhD theses. New repositories are being created and registered with ROAR all the time. At the time of writing, there were 400 from the US, 219 from the UK, 70 from Canada, 66 from Australia, and 16 from New Zealand. The site isn't very user friendly – for example, you can search by type of software, but not by academic discipline or subject – so I would suggest that you start by searching the repositories from your home country until you find one or more that look as if they could help to meet your needs.

It can also be useful to look at online research services that enable people to share information about the literature they are using, and therefore help others to find literature that is new to them. The leaders, at the time of writing, are Zotero and Mendeley. Both are free to use. They have a variety of pros and cons. For example, at the time of writing, Zotero allows you to add other types of information such as audio files, video files, images, and web page screenshots, but Mendeley offers more free storage space. I am not going to compare the two in detail, as they are evolving rapidly and information I give here will no doubt be out of date by the time you read this. If you are reasonably computer literate, it would be worth investigating these resources, and if you like social networking you will probably adore them.

However you find your literature, do remember that you need to read it critically and assess its weight through features such as the presence or absence of peer review (although some commentators are also critical of the benefits of peer review) or the clarity of methods used.

How to conduct a document review

If you're doing a document review for a piece of workplace research, you are likely to have quite a clear idea of the kind of information you want to find. As most, if not all, of the documents you will review are available in electronic form, you can search them using key terms to find the parts you need to read. This is particularly helpful with long policy documents or reports where only a page or two may be directly relevant. So, for the example used earlier in this chapter, our initial key terms might be 'mental health', 'best practice', and 'service user'. Searching a document electronically with these terms doesn't take long. Then you can copy and paste any relevant sections that you find into a new document, perhaps giving it a number from your spreadsheet if you're storing information electronically, or printing it out and colour coding it if you prefer to work that way.

As you search the first few documents, you might notice writers using other, similar key terms that you want to add to your list. For example, 'mental illness' and 'service delivery' might be relevant. The more key terms you have, the longer searching takes, but you can also be more confident that you're finding everything of relevance to your research.

Remember that for any research project, 'documents' may cover a huge variety of material, including letters, diaries, publicity materials such as brochures and leaflets, web pages, newspaper or magazine articles, and extracts from social media sites.

Some documents will be relevant in their entirety. When you have identified all of these, and have taken extracts from all the documents you can find that are partially relevant, you are ready to start your analysis. This involves careful reading, note making, and thought. It's similar to the analysis of textual data, which is covered in Chapter Eight of this book, although it does not involve detailed coding of the data. You will be looking for content and themes to help you develop your ideas, and quotations to use in your report, and you will need to make notes as you go along. The process of note making is the same for document and literature reviews, and is covered later in this chapter.

If you have made a thorough search and you can find few or no relevant documents, this is a finding in itself, so explain your search methods and techniques to show what you were looking for and how.

Document review is primarily a qualitative technique, but in some cases it may be helpful to include a quantitative element. For example, if you have a series of meeting minutes, you might want to count the number of times each person attended a meeting, or the number of times each topic was raised. If you are looking at a set of diaries, it might be useful to count the number of entries made in each diary or within a specific period of time. This kind of quantitative information can add a useful dimension to some document reviews by helping you to think in a different way about what the documents can tell you.

How to conduct a literature review

An academic literature review is not like a review of a book or a concert, written by a critic whose role is to inform a potential audience and entertain readers. Your role as a researcher is to show that you have read, considered, understood, and made connections with the academic literature in your field. When academics want to talk about this, they often say someone has 'engaged with the literature'. You literally need to 're-view' the literature (Jesson, Matheson and Lacey, 2011: 10): to look at it again, with fresh eyes, and bring your unique perspective to the process to create an original review.

Students often ask how many references they need to include, but it's not a numbers game (Jesson, Matheson and Lacey, 2011: 31). 'More' does not equal 'better'. You need to identify and engage with key texts – which in some cases will have been written several decades ago – and with recent developments in the literature, including academic journal articles (where the latest thinking is often found) that have been published within the last year or two. Then you need some texts in between to show how thinking developed.

If you are researching a very broad and long-standing topic, such as motivation, the literature can stretch back over a century or more, so you will need to be selective. In this case, you should define your selection criteria (Jesson, Matheson and Lacey, 2011: 30) and explain them to your reader. For example, you might use your research question to help you decide that you want to restrict your initial reading to texts covering both motivation and contact with the criminal justice system. Or you might use other criteria, such as time (for example, including only texts from the last five years, unless they are key texts) or research method (for example, including only texts based on interview data, if you are planning a series of interviews yourself). You are the only person who can decide what your selection criteria should be, and these examples should help you to do that piece of thinking.

On the other hand, if you are researching a narrower or newer topic, such as a recently identified illness or disability, there will be less literature to draw on. This will probably mean that you need to think more laterally and read further beyond the boundaries of your topic. Either way, once again you are the only person who can decide whether a particular text is relevant for your document review or literature review (Jesson, Matheson and Lacy, 2011: 23).

Using libraries

> The other thing around accessing information, as an absolute non-academic, is thinking, "Oh yes, the British Library, that's where all the books go, isn't it?" and not knowing how to access that resource, and in the end we never did because we couldn't work it out, sad to say.

University and other librarians are experts in finding information. It is well worth making contact with them, because they will be happy to help you, and their expertise can save you a great deal of time and effort.

Many universities have research libraries, and if you have access to one of those, that will make your life easier – but if not, don't despair; there is lots of help available for you from other libraries and librarians. Don't think your local lending library is too small to be of use. I live in a town with a population of around 15,000, and our library produced several useful books for me as I was writing this book. The librarians there, like librarians everywhere, are always ready to help me if I get stuck, and to advise me on ways to find information.

National library websites hold a great deal of useful information, and are putting more online all the time. They all have 'ask a librarian' features – although not all are called that; for example, on the British Library website you need to search for the relevant 'reference team'. All offer specific help for researchers, and have a variety of ways for you to get in touch, with e-mail being the most common, then post, phone, online chat, and so on. They also have digital collections from which you can request copies of documents to be sent to you online, although there is usually a charge for this, to cover copyright and other fees. And each site has special features, with new features being developed all the time. An example is the Social Welfare Portal at http://socialwelfare.bl.uk. This is a single point of access to the British Library's huge print and digital collections of research and information on all aspects of social welfare, which went live in mid-2012. It is free to use and provides access to a lot of free information, although there is still a charge for academic journal articles.

 Invest a little time in checking out the resources for researchers on your national library's website.

Generally speaking, national libraries will not want to hear from you until you have exhausted the available local and regional resources. Most national libraries will not lend books or other documents to individuals; your local library usually has to request anything you need, on your behalf, for you to read, which as a rule has to be done on library premises. Do bear in mind that these inter-library loans can take some time to arrange, and work out what you're likely to need early in your research process, or you run the risk of missing out or missing deadlines.

The British Library was set up to keep a copy of every publication from the UK and Ireland (although this is dependent on publishing organisations lodging copies of the documents they produce, which doesn't always happen – but the collection is fairly comprehensive). The national research library in America is the Library of Congress, which claims to be the largest library in the world. In Canada, the national library is Libraries and Archives Canada (LAC), which focuses on collecting Canadian publications, and materials published elsewhere that are about, or relevant to, Canada. The National Library of Australia and the National Library of New Zealand take a similar approach to the LAC. Other countries have national libraries with websites that you can access if you speak the language. All national libraries will accept requests for information, from people in other countries, about the collections they hold.

Don't be afraid to contact librarians and ask questions, whether at local, regional, or national level. Librarians are experts in finding and using information, and it's part of their job to help researchers (Robson, 2011: 52), so do make use of them. If they don't hold the information you need in their own library, they will know where to direct you.

Making notes

Whether you are reading for a document review or a literature review, you will need to make notes. This is not just a recording task; writing your own notes will help you to work out what you think (Becker, 2007: xi). Reading, note making, and writing is an iterative process that is both underpinned by, and supports, the development of your thinking (Jesson, Matheson and Lacey, 2011: 58–9).

If you have good keyboard skills or your computer supports voice recognition, I would suggest making notes electronically. You are likely to end up with copious notes, and electronic storage makes them easy to search. This is a bonus when you're in the middle of writing your research report or thesis and something triggers a memory of a really useful paragraph you saw somewhere that would be relevant to the section you're writing now. As long as you can remember a key word or phrase, you can find the paragraph you want in seconds, even if you have hundreds of pages of notes – as long as they're stored electronically. Doing the same search manually, however good your colour-coding system may be, would take much longer.

Alternatively, if you are a visual learner, you may prefer to make your notes in visual form, perhaps as mind maps or flow charts (Jesson, Matheson and Lacey, 2011: 61). Some computer applications enable this kind of visual modelling, such as FreeMind and NVivo 9, or you can use large sheets of paper and add Post-It notes, stickers, and so on, to help you visualise and record your reading and ideas.

In reading for research, there may be times when you lose track of what you're supposed to be doing and why. If this happens, go back to your research questions to help you refocus.

As you make notes, it is useful to categorise your sources. This can be done using tags in Zotero or Menderley, with attributes in NVivo, similarly in other computer software applications, or by hand on your electronic or hard-copy notes. You can define the categories as you please, depending on your subject, but I would like to suggest a couple of categories that might be useful: the author's location and the document's time. The author's location is not restricted to geography; it may be equally or more important to log their political or theoretical location, their location in terms of experience, and so on. Both location and time are useful for grouping literature and documents. It is always interesting to see what a range of authors from a similar location have to say on a subject. Equally, it is useful to arrange your notes on a particular subject in time sequence, from earliest to most recent, to show how thinking in that field has developed. Either of these approaches will help you to look at your literature more analytically. I hope these examples will help you to identify other categories that may be useful in your own project.

Keep meticulous records of document names and page numbers with your notes – it will save you time in the long run.

The iterative process of reading, writing, and thinking will also help you to identify your own location. Some aspects of your location may be immediately obvious to you: your gender, perhaps, or your social class, or your political views. Other aspects may become apparent only as you test yourself against the work of others. You will need to be able to identify your own location in your review, to position your own line of reasoning within the wider body of literature you are reviewing, so it will be useful to bear this in mind.

You will need to write more notes about the findings from your source categorisations, and at some point you will have to start writing up your literature review or document review. Advice on writing for research can be found in Chapter Nine of this book, but for now, please just bear in mind that you are aiming for a synthesis that is *as rigorous and as transparent as possible* (Bowen, 2009: 38).

Knowing when to stop

> Some areas of research, there are vast amounts of information, where do you stop? How do you know when it's enough?

Although you are likely to do the bulk of your reading at the start of your research, you will probably continue reading all the way through your project and you are unlikely to finish until close to the end of your write-up. This can make it particularly difficult to know when to stop. However, you should eventually reach a place where you find that the same points are being made, the same key texts being cited, and you feel as if you know what's going on (Jesson, Matheson and Lacey, 2011: 30). This is a sign that you are approaching the end of your reading.

In reading for a research proposal, you can stop when you are confident that you have identified the key texts for your subject, and are clear about how the thinking in the field has developed between the date of the first key text and the present time. For a literature or document review, where possible you need to find and read all the relevant literature and documents. Usually there are too many for you to read them all, in which case you need to read enough to develop your own view of the subject (that is, your location) and know where it sits within the existing views.

It is useful to remember that there is no such thing as the perfect document or literature review (Hart, 1998: 25). Any piece of writing can always be revised, polished, improved, but doing this endlessly will not help you or your research. The important thing is to produce a piece of writing that is good enough and fit for purpose. For this to be the case, your review will need a structure in which information given to the reader flows logically from one point to the next. Within that, it will need:

- a short introduction outlining what the review will cover;
- discussion of all key texts or documents;
- citation of some other relevant, but perhaps more peripheral, texts or documents (see Chapter Nine for methods of citation);
- a report of the ways in which thinking around the topic has developed over the time between the earliest texts or documents and the present day;
- location of your own position in the context of your review;
- details of your own line of reasoning, linked with the evidence from which this grew;
- explanation of how this fills a gap in knowledge or understanding;
- a short conclusion summarising the key points of the review.

There is one most important 'do' and there is one most important 'don't'. Do write as clearly, consistently, and coherently as you can (Hart, 1998: 10). And don't simply describe the literature or documents that you read, but extract the arguments from the texts and reflect on those arguments to create your own interpretation and analysis (Jesson, Matheson and Lacey, 2011: 66).

It is very hard to read your own work critically, so seek and use feedback from others – colleagues, tutors, supervisors, peers – to help you assess the quality of your work. And when it is good enough, that's when you can stop.

SIX

Secondary data

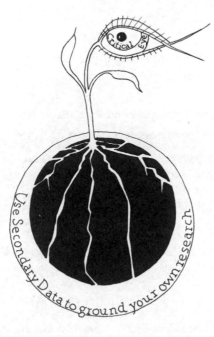

Introduction

Secondary data is data that has been collected by someone else for a purpose other than your research project and has been made available for reuse. Most of this is in digital form, and each individual collection of digital research data is known as a 'dataset'; these can include numbers, texts, images, blog posts, and so on. Due to great efforts to open up data to the public, there is now a huge amount of secondary data freely available on the World Wide Web, and more is being added all the time. Secondary data is also held in libraries, museums, and archives. Examples of quantitative secondary data are government statistics and census data. Examples of qualitative secondary data are criminological data, health data, web archive data, and oral history data.

Freely available secondary data is a tremendous resource for any research project. However, only two of the people I interviewed for this book mentioned secondary data, and then only in passing. This makes me wonder whether there is sufficient awareness of the potential value of secondary data among practitioners. So there will be no quotes in this chapter, and only one tip.

Use secondary data wherever possible, especially data that is freely available online, as it will save you a great deal of time.

Although there are several advantages to using secondary data, there are also some disadvantages. Both are summarised in Table 6.1.

Table 6.1: Pros and cons of using secondary data

Pros	Cons
Quick, easy, free access to datasets with far more data than you could ever collect yourself.	So much data available that it can be hard to find what you need.
Opportunities to identify gaps in data that your own project might help to fill.	Secondary data will have been collected and presented by people with different priorities from yours.
The ability to compare your primary data with local, regional, and national equivalents.	Data from different sources may use different categories, for example different age bands or different socio-economic classifications, which can make comparison difficult or meaningless.
The option of a historical, longitudinal, or cross-cultural perspective.	Data from different sources may be collected differently, for example in some countries it is a legal requirement to participate in national surveys while in others it is not, which can make comparison difficult or meaningless.
Often collected and presented by professional research teams with high-level expertise.	Not infallible – even professional and expert teams can, and do, make mistakes in data entry and analysis.
Re-using existing data is good ethical practice, to minimise the burden on research participants.	It can be more difficult to understand data you have not collected yourself, especially when it's in large, complicated datasets.
Data collection can be much quicker than with primary data.	Secondary data may be old and out of date, and so less relevant.
Less time spent on data collection means more time for data analysis.	Some people find secondary data so fascinating that it becomes a time eater.
Scope for enormous creativity.	It can be hard to find out why and how secondary data was collected and analysed, which can leave you unsure of its quality.

Despite the disadvantages, I would recommend the use of secondary data where possible, particularly at the start of a project. It's an excellent way of exploring a research question and finding background information to give context, evidence, and justification for your own work. But, as with everything else in research, it is important to look at secondary data with a critical eye.

Where possible, you need to ask questions to assess the integrity of the data as well as interrogating the data itself. Useful questions include:

- Why was this data collected?
- Who collected the data?
- How did they collect the data?
- When was the data collected?
- What kind of sampling was used?
- What variables were included?
- How were those variables categorised?
- How was the data prepared for analysis?
- How was the data analysed?

Some datasets will include answers to these questions, perhaps on a 'frequently asked questions' or FAQ page, and sometimes with other useful information such as response rates for questionnaires. Other datasets will not offer this kind of information, although in some cases answers may be found or deduced through careful exploration of the website concerned or wider searches of the Web. Overall, the less you can discover about the background to a dataset, the more careful you need to be about trusting its findings.

You also need to use your critical eye on the data itself. Useful questions here include:

- How has the data been presented?
- Has any of the data collected been left out of the presentation? If so, are the reasons for any exclusions made clear?
- Is there any evidence of bias in the way the data has been presented?
- Is the data raw (that is, every piece of data collected is presented separately) or aggregated? If the latter, which analytic methods have been chosen? Do you think those methods are appropriate, given the nature of the data? Why?

If you can conclude from the evidence available that the researchers asked sensible questions, and used robust methodology to collect, analyse, and present the data, you can place a high degree of trust in their findings. If your conclusion is any less confident, then the level of trust you place in the findings should decrease accordingly.

Some types of official data are notorious for problems with their accuracy and thoroughness. The main example is crime statistics (Bryman, 2011: 321–3), due to under-reporting of crime and to the number of judgements that go into each statistic that does become part of a dataset (Westmarland, 2011: 64–5). Westmarland points out that before any event can officially be called a crime, discretionary decisions are taken by at least three people: the person who decides whether or not to make an arrest, the person who decides whether and how to record that arrest, and the person who decides whether and how to prosecute the arrested person. Therefore, as she says, it is essential to question the integrity of crime data (Westmarland, 2011: 81).

It is unlikely that you can do an entire research project based on secondary data (Robson, 2011: 359), although it may be possible if you have access to secondary data that is both relevant and recent. However, secondary data can offer a great deal of reward for a surprisingly small investment of time, especially if you know where to start. The rest of this chapter contains information about the main sources of openly accessible secondary data worldwide.

Online secondary data sources

Online social science data archives are held by many countries around the world. I will give you their names and locations, rather than their websites, so you can find them even if the URL has changed.

In the US, there are several:

- Columbia University Electronic Data Services, New York
- Princeton University Data Library, New Jersey
- The Roper Center, Connecticut
- Harvard Data Center, Massachusetts
- Geospatial and Statistical (Geostat) Data Center, Virginia
- The Inter-University Consortium for Political and Social Science Research (ICPSR) based in Ann Arbor, Michigan
- DPLS Data and Program Library Service, Wisconsin
- Social Science Data Archives, University of California, Irvine, California
- San Diego Social Science Data Center, California.

There are also several in Canada, such as:

- British Columbia Inter-university Research Data Centre
- University of Alberta Research Data Centre
- South Western Ontario Research Data Centre
- Carleton, Ottawa, Outaouais Local Research Data Centre.

These and many others are part of the country's Research Data Centres Network, which has a useful website.

Europe has social science data sources in a range of countries, with acronyms/ names as follows:

- Austria – WISDOM
- Czech Republic – SDA
- Denmark – DDA
- Estonia – ESDDA
- Finland – FSD
- France – Réseau Quetelet
- Greece – GSDB-EKKE
- Germany – GESIS
- Hungary – TARKI
- Ireland – ISSDA
- Italy – ADPSS Sociodata
- Luxembourg – CEPS
- Netherlands – DANS
- Norway – NSD
- Romania – RODA
- Slovenia – ADP
- Spain – ARCES/CIS
- Sweden – SND
- Switzerland – FORS
- UK – UKDA, Mimas, and EDINA (Scotland).

Australia has the Social Science Data Archives, based in Canberra.

The New Zealand Social Science Data Service is based in Auckland.

The South African Data Archive is based in Pretoria.

At the time of writing, there are also online data archives based in Jerusalem and Montevideo, and by the time you read this, there will probably be others; you should be able to find out by searching the Web.

Secondary qualitative data

Most of the data in the archives already mentioned is quantitative, but there is also a growing interest in online data archives for qualitative social science. Again, their names and locations should enable you to find them on the Web. The first online qualitative data archive, Qualidata, was established in the UK in 1994, and at the time of writing it holds over 350 qualitative datasets. Other archives that hold qualitative data, sometimes alongside quantitative data, include:

- The Henry A. Murray Research Archive in the US
- ADA Qualitative in Australia
- NIQA in Northern Ireland
- The Irish Qualitative Data Archive in Eire
- DARIS in Switzerland
- ADJ in Poland
- FSD in Finland.

Some of these hold only a small number of qualitative datasets.

Other countries working towards collections of qualitative data, at the time of writing, include Austria, the Czech Republic, Denmark, France, Germany, Lithuania, and Slovenia.

There are some specific ethical concerns about re-using qualitative data. When quantitative data is collected at national or local governmental level, it is usually understood that the aggregated findings will be made public and called 'data'. In most quantitative datasets, the data has been prepared and analysed into categories, so there is no chance of anyone using it to identify individuals. Qualitative data, however, is a different matter. Participants in qualitative research often speak openly, trusting the researcher to omit any identifying details from their analysis and reporting. Also, it is rare for qualitative researchers to seek consent from their participants to the use of the data they provide for anything beyond the project in hand. Where consent has not been obtained, and/or details that could identify an individual have not been removed, it would be highly unethical to share qualitative data.

Some online commentators have expressed concerns that the reuse of qualitative data could be hampered by the reuser's lack of knowledge of the context and drivers for the original research. Other people see this as a positive advantage. Either way, the UK's Economic and Social Data Service, which hosts Qualidata, has identified six ways of re-using qualitative data:[1]

1. Description – of the original participants at the time of the project;
2. Comparison – over time, between social groups, between geographic locations, and so on;
3. Re-analysis – to see what the data will yield to a new researcher, at a later time, who may be using different analytic methods or asking different research questions;
4. Research design – studying existing data enables assessment of the research design used in the light of the quality of the data it yielded, and the ability to draw conclusions to inform future research designs;
5. Methodological advancement – study of methods used and the resulting data can enable existing methods to be improved and new methods to be devised;
6. Teaching and learning – genuine data is an excellent aid to the study of research methods and individual social science disciplines.

Open data

The open data movement is lobbying for more data to be freely available to the public. This has led to many governments making national non-personal data freely available via the Web. The UK open-data website contains data on health, social care, crime, and education, as well as on transport, housing, and so on. There are also regional open-data websites such as the London Datastore and DataGM, which covers Greater Manchester. Other countries work in a similar way. The open-data websites of the main English-speaking countries are listed here, with the number of datasets recorded on their home pages on 25 November 2011.

• US: http://data.gov – 390,144 datasets (including geospatial datasets);
• Canada: http://data.gc.ca – 261,134 datasets (including geospatial datasets);

---

[1] www.esds.ac.uk/qualidata/support/reuse.asp, accessed viewed 26 November 2011.

- UK: http://data.gov.uk – 7,700 datasets;
- New Zealand: http://data.govt.nz – 1,684 datasets;
- Australia: http://data.gov.au – 819 datasets.

The UK, New Zealand, and Australian databases may also include geospatial datasets, but they don't explicitly state this on their home pages. The home page for the Canadian database spells out that its 261,134 datasets include 260,296 geospatial and 838 general datasets. Conversely, the home page for the US database doesn't make this distinction, so you can't tell how many of its datasets are geospatial and how many are general (although you might be able to find out if you investigate the website beyond the home page). These very simple differences may give you an initial idea of the difficulties you could face if you chose to try to compare secondary data from different countries.

At the time of writing, in late 2011, Holland, Norway, Kenya, and Italy also had open-data websites. No doubt many more countries will soon have such websites; you should be able to find out by searching the Web. One good place to start might be the Open Government Partnership (OGP), set up by eight founding governments in September 2011. The OGP has four 'key areas' that governments must commit to in order to join, one of which includes 'access to government data' for all.

There is a movement to make datasets as easy to find, identify, and cite as books or journal articles (see Chapter Nine for more on citation). This is being spearheaded by an international group called Datacite, which supports a system for identifying datasets reliably on the Web even if they move from one web page to another. This system is called the digital object identifier or DOI. The DOI for a dataset would be permanent – a bit like an article's title, or a book's ISBN number – so it could lead people to the dataset itself, not just to the place on the Web where that dataset is (or was) located. This would also mean that the researcher or researchers who collected the data could be credited every time it was reused. (Journal articles are also now being given DOIs – you will find some in the bibliography of this book.)

Application programming interfaces[2]

Application programming interfaces, or APIs, are being used to release some open data. An API is a piece of source code that provides a mechanism by which external applications can communicate with it and access or exchange data. Sites such as Google and Facebook use APIs to keep their stream of data and content coming at you through applications, so they can be very powerful tools. Many companies and organisations are making data available like this for free, but you

---

[2] I am indebted to John Kaye, Lead Curator of e-social science at the British Library, for the first draft of this section.

need to know how to use APIs to access their content. If you're interested, The Programmable Web at www.programmableweb.com is a good place to start. This user-friendly site provides lists of APIs and information on ways to interact with and use them, including the 'data mashup' or mixture of data from two or more APIs that can offer different perspectives on that data. This sounds complicated, but the mashup tools are often surprisingly simple, requiring no great level of technical skill to use.

There are countless APIs providing data globally, and more are being created all the time. A few of the APIs that could be useful to researchers are:

- Transport APIs – for example Transport for London uses an API to release live data on tube, road, and bicycle-hire status, and has even released sample Oyster Card travel data via its API.
- If you are interested in researching social networks, Twitter data is available through an API.
- The UK National Archives has released its Legislation API, which gives access to the statute book in html.
- The World Bank API allows you to access 114 indicators from key data sources and 12,000 development photos.
- Bloomberg has released an Open Market Data API for financial market data.
- Ordnance Survey has released geographic data via API, as have projects such as Google Maps and Open Street Map.
- The British Library and DataCite have released their catalogue and metadata via Open APIs, as has the National Library of Australia.

Some computer programming skills are usually required to connect to an API and make it work, but as web development is becoming more accessible these skills are coming within the reach of researchers. There is more information about these skills on The Programmable Web. There is a huge amount of free data available via APIs, and they offer an easy way of keeping data up to date – often in real time. So, for anyone who isn't too daunted by the technical aspects, this is a research method worth investigating.

Large-scale surveys

Most countries regularly carry out large-scale surveys of the population on subjects such as health, crime, education, and so on. The census is one of the best-known, and is carried out every five years in some countries, such as Australia, and every 10 years in others, such as the UK. However, there are many other surveys that may be of interest to social researchers. For example, in the UK, some of these include:

- **1946 Birth Cohort** – the study of all mothers who gave birth in a week in March in England, Wales and Scotland, whose children are still being followed up today. Also known as the National Survey of Health and Development.
- **1958 Birth Cohort** – the study of over 17,000 people born in a week in March in the UK, and followed up at irregular intervals since. Also known as the National Child Development Study.
- **1970 Birth Cohort** – the study of babies born in a week in April in the UK, and followed up at irregular intervals since.
- **Annual Population Survey** – a survey introduced in the mid-2000s, providing information on a range of topics, such as health and education, between the 10-yearly censuses.
- **British Crime Survey** – carried out biennially from 1982, then annually from 2001, focusing on people's experience of crime rather than reported crime, and one of the largest social surveys conducted in the UK.
- **British Social Attitudes** – annual since 1983, covering attitudes to a range of subjects including health and social care, education, and social inequality.
- **English Housing Survey** – in its current form since April 2008, when it was formed by a merger between the Survey of English Housing (annual from 1993) and the English House Condition Survey.
- **Family Resources Survey** – annual since 1992, covering family resources including welfare benefits, savings, and housing costs.
- **General Lifestyle Survey** (formerly the General Household Survey) – annual since 1971, covering a range of topics including health and education. A longitudinal design component was introduced in the mid-2000s, the survey closed in its current format in January 2012, and is now part of the Integrated Household Survey.
- **Health Survey for England** – annual since 1994.
- **Integrated Household Survey**, also known as Continuous Population Survey – a new approach that began in 2009 and will encompass the General Lifestyle Survey, the Expenditure and Food Survey, and three other large-scale surveys.
- **Labour Force Survey** – biennial from 1973, quarterly from 1992, covering employment and earnings.
- **Life Opportunities Survey** – a new longitudinal survey, started in June 2009, exploring disability in terms of social barriers.
- **Living Costs and Food Survey** (formerly the Expenditure and Food Survey, which included the National Food Survey set up in 1940) – annual since 1957, covering family incomes and domestic spending. Part of the Integrated Household Survey since 2008.
- **Millennium Cohort Study** – a longitudinal survey following the lives of around 19,000 babies born in the UK in 2000–01.
- **National Transport Survey** – carried out periodically from the mid-1960s to the mid-1980s, and continuously since mid-1988, to assess people's travelling choices.

- **Scottish Health Survey** – carried out in 1995, 1998, 2003, and continuously from 2008 to 2011.
- **Survey of Carers in Households** – a one-off study in 2009/10.
- **Time Use Survey** – a one-off study in 2000.
- **Understanding Society** (incorporating the British Household Panel Survey) – following 40,000 households in the UK since 2008.
- **Welsh Health Survey** – conducted periodically since the mid-1980s.

Much of this data collection is now being standardised across Europe through Eurostat, which is the Statistical Office of the European Communities, based in Luxembourg.

Surveys in America include:

- **Current Population Survey** – a monthly survey that has been conducted since 1940 and includes labour force and earnings data.
- **General Social Survey** – an annual survey conducted since 1972 that covers a wide range of topics and attitudes, and has had an international component since 1982 (there is more information on international surveys later in this chapter).
- **National Crime Victimization Survey** – a bi-annual survey, similar to the British Crime Survey, which has been conducted since 1972.
- **National Health Interview Survey** – annual since 1957.

Surveys in Canada include:

- **General Social Survey** – a five-yearly survey conducted since 1985 covering a range of topics including population, health, time use, victimisation (similar to the British Crime Survey), education, work, family, housing, ageing, and social engagement.

Surveys in Australia include:

- **Australian Health Survey** – five-yearly from 1977 to 2001, then three-yearly, with a new survey in 2011–13, claiming to be the most comprehensive ever undertaken in Australia.
- **Longitudinal Surveys of Australian Youth** – began in 1995, designed to track young people through the transitions in their lives.
- **Monthly Population Survey** – carried out since 1960, covering employment and sometimes supplementary topics such as education or crime and safety.
- **National Crime and Safety Survey** – conducted in 1975, 1983, 1993, 1998 and 2005, as a supplementary part of the Monthly Population Survey.

Surveys in New Zealand include:

- **Household Economic Survey** – conducted annually since 1973, full survey run every three years since 1998, with smaller versions each year in between; includes population and income/spending.
- **Household Labour Force Survey** – conducted quarterly since October 1985.
- **New Zealand Crime and Safety Survey** – every three years since 2003 (formerly National Survey of Crime Victims, conducted in 1996 and 2001).
- **New Zealand General Social Survey** – biennial survey of individual well-being since 2008.
- **New Zealand Health Survey** – every five years since 1992, continuous since 2011.

International surveys

There are a number of international groups that collect and disseminate potentially useful data. For example, the Organisation for Economic Co-operation and Development (OECD) is an international alliance of, at the time of writing, 30 member countries representing two-thirds of the world's goods and services. The OECD collects and disseminates data on education, social expenditure, and the labour force, among other things. At the time of writing, the International Social Survey Programme (ISSP) has 48 member countries and works on cross-national collaboration in general social surveys. Even more impressively, the United Nations website provides access to a free database that includes data from many countries on population, education, health, labour force, crime, social, and economic issues.

Working with secondary data

Many other websites hold, or act as portals for, secondary data. These include census websites, local government websites at city, county, and regional/state levels, health service websites and even national newspaper websites. Faced with this immense wealth of data, it can be hard to find data that is directly relevant to your own research questions; it is a bit like looking for the proverbial needle in a haystack. The best way to look for useful data is to take a step-by-step approach.

1. Identify a website that seems likely to hold data that is relevant to your research.
2. Read the website's FAQs – if only the headlines – to ensure you know enough about how the site works for your purposes.
3. Search the site, using appropriate search terms.
4. Save any data you find that looks useful (if you can't download the data, then save the URL by using a 'bookmark' or 'favourite' in your web browser, or copying and pasting the URL into a document, with a note of where it leads).
5. When you have finished searching, assess your saved data more thoroughly to establish how useful it can be for your research.

You can repeat this process until you have enough secondary data for your needs.
    You will then be able to analyse the data using the same analytic techniques you would use for primary data. These methods are covered in Chapter Eight.

SEVEN

Primary data collection

Introduction

The collection of data is often the first thing people think of in connection with research. A common misconception is that more data always leads to better research. As we saw in Chapter Three, this is not the case. Too much data, particularly qualitative data or data in a variety of formats, can become unwieldy and difficult to analyse. However, insufficient data will definitely lead to poorer-quality research.

When you're planning your data collection, try to work out the smallest amount of data you can collect that is likely to provide an adequate answer to your research questions.

You don't have to collect data using one method alone. In fact, using more than one method can be helpful, and this is known as 'triangulation'. The term has its origins in physical sciences, such as land surveying and water navigation, where two known points are used to find the location of a third. In social research, collecting data using two or more different methods can help you to look at your research topic in different ways. Triangulation doesn't apply only to primary data collection. Depending on your research question, you may be able to: use more than one theory to underpin your work; collect more than one kind of document or literature; analyse your data in different ways; and so on. I am not suggesting that you should try to do all of this, or even any of it if it is not relevant to your research. However, it is important for you to know that it is an option, and to do the necessary thinking to decide whether or not you want to take it up.

Almost half of the interviewees for this book said data collection was their favourite part of the research process – not necessarily the easiest part (although it was for some), but definitely the most enjoyable.

Collecting quantitative data

Some research questions lend themselves to the collection of quantitative data. In particular, questions of 'how many' or 'how much' require numerical answers. Much quantitative data can be collected from existing sources such as organisational monitoring information, or national statistics such as those discussed in Chapter Six. For now, we're looking at quantitative data that you need to collect yourself.

Your research may be entirely quantitative, entirely qualitative, or a mixture of the two. Mixed-method research is becoming more and more common. Even research that is essentially quantitative, such as drug trials, is now likely to include a qualitative element, such as patients' self-reports of possible side-effects. And even research that is mostly qualitative, such as an investigation of users' and carers' views of a service for people with learning disabilities, will include a quantitative element, such as the numbers of people who use the service.

So it may be that you need to collect only a little quantitative data, and all you have to do is ask for it. But if you are conducting, say, a needs assessment, or an evaluation in which you want to compare baseline data with outcome measures, you will have to collect a sizeable amount of quantitative data.

There are three main methods of collecting quantitative data: counting, measuring, and using questionnaires.

Counting

Collection of primary data by counting is not used often in social research, but it does have a role to play. For example, in the transport survey discussed in Chapter Three of this book, the researcher might count the number of buses that arrive in a given time period.

Counting itself is often used in social research, but mostly in the context of secondary data (as we saw in Chapter Six). Nevertheless, when you are planning your research project, it is worth giving a little thought to whether there is anything you can usefully count, and, if so, what that is and how it can best be counted.

Measuring

Some practitioners, such as health professionals, will be familiar with scales used to measure particular variables in people's lives, such as depression or quality of life. People who work in human resources will know of personality-profiling tools that aim to measure someone's personality type. This kind of measuring device is also widely used in research (Pallant, 2010: 5).

If you are interested in a specific variable of individual people, such as motivation, intelligence, or spiritual beliefs, you will find it useful to know that many devices exist to measure this kind of variable. Such a device may be called a scale, tool, inventory, or instrument. They consist of a series of questions that are designed to measure the variable. Some of these measuring devices include several hundred questions, while others are of a more manageable size. If you want to use one of the more complex measuring devices, you are likely to need training first, while the simpler ones can be used straight away.

Most measuring devices will have been tested to ensure that they work and that they are reliable, generalisable, and valid. In this context, 'reliable' means that a device will yield consistent results even if it is used by different researchers, in different environments, at different times, or with different groups of participants. 'Generalisable' means that findings from the use of a device can be generalised from your sample to the population.

There are several types of validity. For example, face validity (also known as content validity) refers to whether the device actually measures what it is supposed to measure. Internal validity assesses whether every item in the device is clearly related to the overall aim of the device. External validity checks that the overall aim of the device is closely related to other indicators of the variable.

Use a measuring device that has been thoroughly tested for reliability, generalisability, and validity.

Even though there are hundreds, perhaps thousands, of these devices, finding a suitable measuring device for your own research can be a challenge (Pallant, 2010: 5). You may find one that appeals to you through the literature. If not, the World Wide Web is a rich source of measuring devices, many of which are free to use for non-commercial purposes. It is worth using a measuring device that has been thoroughly tested, because then you will have a range of studies with which to compare your own research.

 Search the Web using the name of the variable you are interested in, plus 'measurement', plus 'scale', 'tool', 'inventory', and 'instrument' in turn. So, if you are researching anxiety, you would search on: anxiety measurement scale, anxiety measurement tool, anxiety measurement inventory, and anxiety measurement instrument.

A device may be completed by the research participant or by the researcher. The researcher can complete a device face-to-face with the participant, over the telephone, or using an online communication system such as a chat room, video conferencing, or software that lets you make calls over the Internet, for example Skype (see later in this chapter for more on data collection online). Some devices enable a researcher to complete them using observation alone, but this method has more limited application.

It is possible to develop and test your own measuring device, but this is a complex and time-consuming process. It is not advisable to attempt this unless you are doing it in the course of your work, with sufficient resources and support from your management, or perhaps for a PhD thesis.

Questionnaires

Questionnaires are primarily instruments for collecting quantitative data. They can also be used to collect qualitative data in the form of open questions with text answers. These enable the person answering the questionnaire to write down their response in their own words, rather than marking one or more options from a list or range. Here is an example:

Please could you tell us what we can do to improve our service?

....

However, open questions with text answers are not used frequently, for two main reasons. First, they put some people off answering, as they take a comparatively long time to answer and require more literacy and creativity than marking a predetermined option. Second, the data collected from these questions is more complicated to code and analyse than the numerical data yielded by questions with predefined answer options. If you are designing a questionnaire and you find that you want to include a lot of open questions, you should consider doing interviews instead.

Some people think closed questions just mean binary answers such as 'yes/no' or 'agree/disagree'. In fact there are several kinds of closed question. For example, you can ask people to choose one from a range of options, several from a range of options, rank their responses, or complete rating scales. Here are examples of each of those question types.

Choose one option

Which activity do you like best from the following list? Please tick one only.

☐ Reading
☐ Gardening
☐ Eating out
☐ Cooking
☐ Visiting museums or art galleries
☐ Going to a play, musical, gig, etc

☐ Listening to music at home
☐ Playing sport
☐ Watching TV
☐ Social networking (Facebook, Twitter, etc)
☐ None of the above

Choose more than one option

Which of these activities have you enjoyed in the past month? Please tick all that apply.

☐ Reading
☐ Gardening
☐ Eating out
☐ Cooking
☐ Visiting museums or art galleries
☐ Going to a play, musical, gig, etc

☐ Listening to music at home
☐ Playing sport
☐ Watching TV
☐ Social networking (Facebook, Twitter, etc)
☐ None of the above

Ranked responses

Please rank these activities in order of preference, starting with number 1 for the activity you like best.

☐ Reading
☐ Gardening
☐ Eating out
☐ Cooking
☐ Visiting museums or art galleries
☐ Going to a play, musical, gig, etc
☐ Listening to music at home
☐ Playing sport
☐ Watching TV

☐ Social networking (Facebook, Twitter, etc)
☐ None of the above

Rating scale (sometimes called Likert scale)

Please circle one number to indicate how satisfied you are with the service you received.

Very satisfied   1   2   3   4   5   6   7   Very dissatisfied

There are several arguments for and against using questionnaires, which are summarised in Table 7.1.

Table 7.1: Pros and cons of questionnaires

Pros	Cons
Questionnaires are quick and cheap to develop and administer.	Standards of design and development are often so low that the results are not worth having.
E-mail can be used to send questionnaires, with higher response rates than other methods, and to chase up unreturned questionnaires.	E-mail is no use for contacting people who don't have access to computers/Internet; and for those who do, questionnaires can be difficult to open and use if software is incompatible.
Participants can complete the questionnaire at their own convenience.	Response rates are often low, so results are unrepresentative.
Participants have time to think about their answers.	Questionnaires assume that people have answers available in an organised way.
It is easy to maintain participants' anonymity.	It is difficult to motivate potential participants.
There is no interaction between researchers and participants to affect participants' answers.	The way questions are worded can affect the answers given.
It is easy to get information from a lot of people in a short time.	Data may be incomplete and/or inaccurate, and misunderstandings cannot be corrected.
Each participant is asked exactly the same questions, and can be given exactly the same responses to choose from.	Participants have little or no input into the research agenda, and may feel frustrated if the questions or the permitted responses don't fit their view or experience of the subject.
Flexibility is available with open-ended or text response options.	People with low levels of literacy, or whose first language is not that of the questionnaire, are unlikely to be able to respond at all.
Questionnaire data can enable you to test a hypothesis.	There is no way to check the honesty or accuracy of the responses.
Data analysis is, in general, quicker and easier than analysis of other types of data.	There is no way of knowing what lies behind the responses given, or what participants might have contributed if they had been able to choose how they responded, so interpreting the analysed data can be problematic.
With a big enough response rate from a representative sample and careful statistical analysis, results can be robust.	Questionnaires are more liable to superficial questions than other methods, which can lead to irrelevant or unhelpful results (particularly if the questions are prepared by researchers who have little or no experience of the subject).

Anyone can put together a questionnaire that looks convincing, but a questionnaire that will yield useful results needs to be developed carefully (Gillham, 2000: 1). There are some established good practice points in designing questionnaires, and these are covered in the literature recommended in the bibliography at the end of this book.

Questionnaire tips

Ask closed questions wherever possible because this will make analysis easier (also response rates to closed questions are higher).

Use open questions only when: you don't know enough about the subject to write appropriate options for people to choose from; you are asking about particularly sensitive issues; or you want to give the participant the opportunity to contribute to the research agenda.

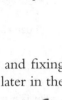

Pilot a draft version of the questionnaire with people from outside your target group, to check the questions and the layout for any problems. Then revise and refine the questionnaire on the basis of your participants' feedback.

Piloting your questionnaire may seem like extra work, but finding and fixing any problems at an early stage can save you a huge amount of time later in the research process.

If you are comfortable with technology, you can set up a questionnaire online.

There is free and user-friendly software to help you do this such as www. surveymonkey.com/ that will give you a unique survey link that you can use to reach people by e-mail, on web pages, in Facebook links, through a blog, via Twitter, and so on. This is more flexible and less prone to errors than sending out questionnaires by e-mail, and it also prevents mistakes at the data inputting stage. However, again, you won't be able to use it if your target group includes people who don't readily use computers and the Internet.

Collecting qualitative data

Qualitative data is any data that is not in the form of numbers. This data is often in the form of words, but also includes audio data, video data, photographs, artwork, and so on. There are a wide range of methods for collecting qualitative data. These include: interviews, focus groups, collecting documents, observation, and collecting visual data.

Interviews

If you enjoy talking to people and hearing their stories, you will probably enjoy doing some interviews for your research. Interviews were very popular with the interviewees for this book.

> I love the listening to people's stories, and I find it so rewarding and such a gift that people are willing to sit down and tell you about themselves. People you've never met, you ring them up, not dissimilar to this, but with addiction recovery they're telling you their major epiphanies and people are so generous, I get a lot from that, it feels like a privilege.

> I loved conducting the interviews during the research. It wasn't as easy as I thought it was going to be but the views and insights shared by the participants were truly fascinating – brought ideas that I would never have considered; and humbling to have practitioners share thoughts about practice that I would never have heard without the research. The skills that I developed to hear all perspectives, to fully listen and to think about what else is going on in the interaction, including myself, are something I use regularly now.

If you are planning to conduct interviews, I have a few recommendations. First, wherever possible, don't use the word 'interview' when communicating with potential interviewees. It is the technical term in research, but for many people, 'interview' has negative connotations of being tested against covert standards through job interviews, university interviews, disciplinary interviews, and so on. I tend to say things like, 'I'd like to hear what you think of X for my research,' or, 'Could we have a chat about X for my research?' rather than, 'Can I interview you for my research?'

Second, people must be able to give free and informed consent to taking part in a research interview (Davies, 2007: 101). 'Informed consent' is another technical term in research which means that someone must be able to understand why the research is being done, by whom, how any information they give you will be used, and so on. 'Free' means they must not be forced or coerced into taking part, as that would be highly unethical. It's fine to ask; even to be a little bit persuasive; but nothing more than that, and you must always take 'no' for an answer. People are not just repositories of data that researchers can download at will, they are human beings with complex lives to manage. Everyone has the right to say 'no' to voluntary work – and taking part in research, unpaid, is voluntary work. A reward such as a gift voucher for interviewees or focus group members is a nice gesture, if you have the budget, but should be given as a 'thank you' rather than used as a lure. Furthermore, you should make it clear to anyone you interview that they have the right to stop the interview at any point and to have their data withdrawn from your research, either then or later, if they wish. It is helpful to give a cut-off point after which this won't be possible because, as you get into the data analysis and writing, it becomes more and more difficult to extract the contribution of one individual's data from your interpretations.

Third, please make sure you look after your own safety – and, by implication, that of your interviewees – when conducting research interviews (Davies, 2007: 101). Try to choose a location where there are other people around, such as a room in a community centre, workplace, or college, or any public place where confidentiality would not be compromised. Don't invite people to your home, or go to theirs, unless you're absolutely sure it would be safe to do so.

Interviews are a great exercise in listening. This is a much undervalued skill in our society, where we teach children how to talk but we don't teach them how to listen. When you are doing a research interview, try to listen actively, that is, to hear and understand not only the person's words but their whole message. To do this, you need to:

- pay attention to the interviewee's body language and facial expression;
- make sure your own body language is conveying receptive attentiveness (open relaxed posture, appropriate facial expressions in response to their words);
- encourage the interviewee to keep talking: nodding your head and short utterances like 'yeah' and 'mm-hm' are helpful here;
- check you understand what they're saying, by asking questions about anything you're not sure you understand fully, and using gaps to summarise their comments;
- react and show emotion if they tell you something shocking or upsetting – don't be afraid to do this; the interviewee will be reassured by your humanity.

Most importantly, you need to concentrate on whatever the interviewee is telling you. As far as possible, don't let yourself get distracted by noise and movement around you, or by your own thoughts of appointments you need to make and what you should pick up at the supermarket on your way home. Focusing on someone else's opinions for a while is often a surprisingly therapeutic experience for the researcher as well as for the interviewee. You will find that interviewees tell you they value the experience.

There are several arguments for and against using interviews, which are summarised in Table 7.2.

Table 7.2: Pros and cons of interviews

Pros	Cons
Interviews yield rich data.	Interviews are time-consuming for researchers and participants.
Face-to-face interviews let the interviewer include observational elements, for example from the participant's appearance or body language, that are not available with other methods.	The researcher's interpretation of the data from a face-to-face interview may be affected by the quality of the rapport they developed with their participant.
Interviews can be conducted by telephone, which saves time and costs and increases anonymity.	Not everyone is comfortable using the telephone, and it can be harder to create a rapport over the phone than in person.
An interview equivalent can be conducted by e-mail, which avoids transcription and so saves time and money; this also helps in reaching some groups of people, for example those with severe hearing impairment.	Conducting an 'interview' by e-mail can make it more difficult to follow up interesting answers with supplementary questions.
Interviewers can follow up interesting answers with supplementary questions.	Interviewers' input can influence participants' answers.
Unstructured interviews can be particularly useful at the exploratory stage of a research project.	Unstructured interviews run the risks of missing important issues or degenerating into a general chat.
Semi-structured interviews allow participants to participate in setting the research agenda, which may be more politically acceptable, lead to more useful data, or both.	Semi-structured interviews make it harder to compare data from different individuals or groups.
Structured interviews enable clearer comparison of data from different individuals or groups.	Structured interviews require the question designer to be able to consider all the issues that are relevant to the participants.
Recording data enables exact reproduction of someone's words and pauses.	Transcribing interview data is time-consuming and expensive.

Interview tips

Send interview questions to participants in advance.

Giving participants a chance to see your questions before the interview is good, ethical research practice. It shows participants exactly what you're interested in, and reassures them that they will be able to contribute. Doing this also enables participants to prepare – not all will take the opportunity, but the interviews will often be quicker when they do.

You can interview people in pairs, thereby getting two views in the time it would otherwise take to get one.

For pair interviews, the participants would need to be from the same target group and happy to be interviewed together. People in pairs are less likely to indulge in small talk or start telling you their life story. However, there is a risk that one may inhibit the other to some extent.

If you can touch-type at a reasonable speed, you can record interview data straight into a laptop or desktop computer.

Data collected by touch-typing while an interviewee speaks won't be as exact as recorded and transcribed data, but it will be close, especially if you leave out people's speech tics (for example 'you know' and 'I mean'), fillers ('er', 'um'), and repetitions. Also, if you use acronyms and abbreviations, and don't worry about any spelling mistakes, you can tidy up your data straight after the interview. (And I do mean *straight* after - otherwise you'll forget what those abbreviations meant.)

There is more information about how to conduct interviews in the bibliography at the end of this book.

Focus groups – pros and cons

A focus group is in fact a type of interview, but conducted with a group rather than an individual or a pair of people (Robson, 2011: 294). However, while one person having a chat with one or two other people is a fairly normal social situation, one person facilitating a group discussion is much less usual. Therefore, running a focus group will, in general, demand more skills and energy from you, as a researcher, than conducting an interview.

Several interviewees expressed an awareness of and interest in focus groups, but few people actually used them for collecting data, and those who did found that the process was full of pitfalls.

I don't think I fully anticipated how long it would take to get people and to get everything organised. To work out where the focus groups were going to be, and when, and start recruiting people. I think you also need to look at what communities you're trying to engage – some will take longer than others. Two focus groups filled quite quickly, two others that were specifically for the BME (Black and minority ethnic) community, they took time. So it's not just about what you're doing, but how long it's going to take you, and don't underestimate that.

There are several arguments for and against using focus groups, which are summarised in Table 7.3.

Table 7.3: Pros and cons of focus groups

Pros	Cons
Focus groups can yield rich data.	To be conducted effectively, traditional focus groups need two moderators, one to facilitate and one to take notes.
Focus groups enable you to get the views of several people at once.	Focus groups can be time consuming to arrange.
Some people are more relaxed in groups than in one-to-one.	Not everyone is comfortable speaking in a group.
Focus group moderators can follow up interesting answers with supplementary questions.	Moderators' input can influence participants' answers.
Unstructured focus groups can be particularly useful at the exploratory stage of a research project.	Unstructured focus groups run the risks of missing important issues or degenerating into a general chat.
Semi-structured focus groups allow participants to participate in setting the research agenda, which may be more politically acceptable, lead to more useful data, or both.	Semi-structured focus groups make it harder to compare data from different groups.
Structured focus groups enable clearer comparison of data from different individuals or groups.	Structured focus groups require the question designer to be able to consider all the issues that are relevant to the participants.
A single moderator can use participatory action research techniques (see Chapter Two for more on this) to enable focus group participants to construct research data.	Research data constructed through participatory action research techniques is not as rich as recorded verbal data.
Recording focus group data enables a fairly exact reproduction of what was said.	Transcribing focus group data is time consuming and expensive. Also, it is sometimes difficult to identify the different speakers, and often impossible to understand what is said if more than one person is speaking at the same time.

Focus group tips

Instead of setting up a focus group especially for your research, think about whether there are existing groups you can use to make contact with potential participants.

For example, you can reach teenagers through youth clubs, students via student unions, parents of young children at toddler groups, drug users through support groups, and so on. Negotiating contact with an existing group will save you all the time it would take to set up a group of your own, find a venue, and so on. But do make sure that the group's gatekeeper understands what you need, and that you can have an appropriate amount of time with the group's members. It's frustrating to sit through someone else's meeting and then be allocated five minutes at the end just as everyone is putting on their coats to leave.

Send focus group questions to potential participants or gatekeepers in advance.

Giving people a chance to see your questions before the group meets is good, ethical research practice. It shows participants exactly what you're interested in and reassures them that they will be able to contribute. Doing this also enables people to prepare. Not all will take the opportunity, but if some do, the group is likely to run more smoothly.

If you can touch-type at a reasonable speed, you can record focus group data straight into a laptop computer.

Data collected by touch-typing won't be as exact as recorded and transcribed data, but it will be close, especially if you leave out people's speech tics (for example 'you know' and 'I mean'), fillers ('er', 'um'), and repetitions. Also, if you use acronyms and abbreviations, and don't worry about any spelling mistakes, you can tidy up your data straight after the focus group. (And I do mean *straight* after – otherwise you'll forget what those abbreviations meant.)

If you decide to use focus groups, you can find more information about how to do this in the bibliography at the end of this book.

Documents as data

In Chapter Five I wrote about how you can use documents to give background and context to your research. Using documents as data is subtly different. When you're using documents for background and context, you are primarily interested in the content of those documents. Of course you need to read critically, and take into account relevant aspects such as the author's location and perhaps the source of funding for the work you're reading. But when you're using documents as data, the identity of the document is also relevant.

A document is not just a container for content (Prior, 2011: 95). Documents are also tools for people to use as they act in the world. For example, one of the negotiating techniques suggested by Professor Stuart Diamond in *Getting More* (see Chapter Four) is to use organisational standards to help you get what you want. So if you receive poor service from a business, instead of ranting and raving, you may be able to find its customer service standards on the World Wide Web and then calmly quote them. Diamond suggests that this use of documents as tools can have astonishing results (2010: 83–112). And of course the organisation's customer service standards are in the form of a document.

Some documents have a wider impact on society. Government enactments and legal judgments fall into this category. Other documents hold people's instructions and wishes, whether a child's letter to Santa or an adult's last will and testament, and so are, in a sense, an extension of the writer. A document may be anywhere on the spectrum from intensely private, such as a diary that was only ever intended for the writer to read, to very public, such as a newspaper article published on the Web.

As we saw in Chapter Five, when you use documents for background, you need to read and think critically to help you select and evaluate documents. Using documents as data requires you to develop your skills in critical reading and thinking further, so that you can also categorise, compare and contrast documents, find patterns, identify interesting phenomena, and recognise items of significance (Cottrell, 2005: 17).

As with other methods of data collection, there are pros and cons to using documents. These are set out in Table 7.4.

There are no particular short cuts when it comes to using documents, apart from those already covered in Chapter Five.

Observation

This is data recorded by a researcher from their observations of an event or phenomenon. The observations may be conducted in real time, or the event may be filmed and the resulting video data converted into text. This process is similar to transcribing recorded audio data, but with extra complexity because of the need to record both visible and audible information. As a result, it is even more time consuming than transcribing recorded data, and should be used sparingly if at all. It can seem simple just to go and watch people at a business meeting, or a police station custody suite, or a children's playground. But as soon as you try it, you will realise that there is a lot going on (Robson, 2011:318). Comings and goings, interactions, facial expressions, body contact, speech – what can it all tell you? There is no way you can record everything, so you need to decide what you're interested in and create a recording system, such as a list or grid, to act as an aide-memoire and enable you to record observations of interest quickly and easily.

Table 7.4: Pros and cons of using documents as data

Pros	Cons
Huge quantities of documents are freely available in libraries and on the Web.	The sheer number of documents available can make it difficult to find and select those that will be most relevant for your research.
Documents at the private end of the spectrum can offer fascinating insights into people's lives and social topics.	Documents at the private end of the spectrum can be difficult to obtain, and to get consent to use in research.
Newspapers and magazines offer contemporaneous data.	Newspapers and magazines have an 'angle' that is designed to please their readers, because their main concern is sales (which also means they cost money).
Newspaper and magazine journalists can often interview people whom researchers would find difficult to access.	Newspaper and magazine journalists are unlikely to ask questions about everything that would interest a researcher.
Documents can contain information that is not accessible in any other way.	Some documents are written in languages and/or styles that make them difficult to understand.
Documents can contain a great deal of rich and detailed information.	Researchers have no control over the structure or content of documents that may not address research questions directly.
The use of documents as data can make research more accessible for people who find it difficult to interact with others.	Documents alone may not provide all the information needed to answer the research questions.

So, for example, if you were going to observe people with advanced dementia in a nursing home, you might choose to record:

- independent action: hand gestures, body movement, vocalisation, eating, drinking, sleep;
- dependent action: receiving food, drinks, personal care, medication;
- interaction: with other residents, with staff, with family/friends, with other visitors.

You could use these to create a grid, with each form of action listed in a column on the left, time periods of 10 minutes across the top, and cells large enough to enter a number of minutes (or simply a tick, if someone is doing an action for the whole 10-minute period), with a few words of explanation if necessary. You might also want to leave a few blank rows for recording observations that were not predetermined, such as the particular behaviour of one individual, or simply something you didn't think of in advance.

Observation may be unstructured, where you simply record whatever you notice; semi-structured, where you have a recording system that also allows you the freedom to record other items of interest; or structured, where you record only what you previously decided to record. There is a role for each type of observation, at different stages of research projects and in answering different research questions.

You may have heard of a specific type of observational data collection known as 'participant observation', which was briefly touched on in Chapter Two. This technique was developed by anthropologists and involves observing a defined group of people very closely over a considerable period of time. For example, a participant observer might go to live in a community far from their own home, or be taken on by an organisation as a full-time worker, or go to several religious services per day – often for many months or even years. While participant observation is fascinating to do, and yields rich findings when conducted by experienced researchers, it is difficult for novices and far too time consuming for busy practitioners.

As with the transport survey discussed earlier and in Chapter Three, observational data can yield quantitative as well as qualitative data. However, it is primarily a qualitative method.

There are several arguments for and against using observational data, which are summarised in Table 7.5.

Unstructured observation is quicker than semi-structured or structured observation, because you don't have to spend time thinking through what you want to record and preparing a grid. But this is a false economy of time if it doesn't yield the results you need.

Really, there are no effective short cuts when it comes to observational data, so I would recommend that you use it sparingly, and only when your research question(s) cannot be answered in any other way. If you do decide to use observational data, you can find out more about it through the references in the bibliography at the end of this book.

Visual data

Visual data includes photographs, drawings, collages, paintings, diagrams, and so on. Visual data may be collected from existing sources, such as magazines, the World Wide Web, or art exhibitions, or created specifically for your research, perhaps through techniques such as photo-elicitation or 'draw and write'.

Table 7.5: Pros and cons of observational data

Pros	Cons
Observational data can be rich and specific.	Observational data recorded by hand may be very subjective, as usually it is not possible to record everything that is said and done.
Two researchers, observing the same situation or group, can compare their data after the event to reduce subjectivity.	It is not always possible to use two researchers.
One researcher can check their data with some or all of the participants after an event to reduce subjectivity.	It can be difficult to check data with participants if they are not willing to help, or if different participants have different views of the event, or if a participant feels unfairly represented.
Observational data can be useful to confirm (or deny) findings from other methods, for example questionnaires or interviews.	The presence of the observer may affect the behaviour of the people being observed, and there is no way to know whether or not this is the case.
Observation is a direct technique that can be useful in situations where other techniques are difficult to use, for example prison visiting rooms, school gates, hospital reception areas.	Observation raises difficult ethical issues: how detached or involved should the researcher be? How can consent be obtained from participants?
Covert observation of people in public places – hospitals, cemeteries, courts, streets – avoids the need to negotiate access through a gatekeeper.	The covert observation of people for research purposes is ethically dubious.
Unstructured observation, where a researcher records whatever catches her eye, can be useful at the exploratory stage of a project.	Unstructured observation may produce data that is not easily comparable with data from other observations.
Semi-structured observation, where a researcher takes notes on a grid and records whatever else catches her eye, can help you to pick up aspects of a situation you might otherwise have missed.	If the situation being observed is very complex or busy, there may be no time for the researcher to do anything other than take notes on the grid.
Structured observation, using a grid alone, may be easier for the researcher to manage and produce data that is more comparable, reliable, and valid.	Data from structured observation may not represent the full complexity of the situation being observed.
If recording observational data by hand, thinking through what you want to record and preparing a grid can help you to clarify your research question and themes.	Recording observational data by hand can be slow and the researcher may miss things in the situation while they're writing.
Video can be used to record observational data at an event where a researcher also needs to participate.	A researcher won't be able to record observational data by hand at an event where they also need to participate.
Recording observational data using video enables a fairly exact reproduction of what was said and done.	Transcribing recorded observational data from video is very time consuming and expensive.

If you want to collect visual images from existing sources to use as data, there are a huge number of places you can look (Rose, 2012: 47). Examples include:

- image collections on the Internet, such as Google Images
- art galleries
- museums
- libraries
- books
- magazines

- catalogues
- web pages
- screenshots, for example of particular moments in video games
- posters
- leaflets
- street advertisements.

You can view some images in a range of ways (Rose, 2012: 48), and this is another form of triangulation. For example, you might see a painting in an art gallery, buy a postcard of it in the gallery shop, view an online reproduction on screen, and print out that reproduction to look at on paper. You might see an advertisement on a hoarding in the street, take a photo with your phone to help you remember, and later find the same advertisement in a magazine. Using different media to view the same image can help to enrich your experience of that image, as we perceive images differently in different contexts. Where there is a unique image that you want to use, such as a specific artwork, do try to see the original if you can.

Photo-elicitation may involve participants' existing photographs, or photos created specifically for the research, either by participants or by the researcher or both (Prosser and Schwartz, 1998: 123). The rather impenetrable academic term 'photo-elicitation' conceals an everyday activity for people in many parts of the world: one person showing another their photos and telling them about the context for each picture and the histories and relationships of people in the pictures. This everyday activity can be fun for participants and for researchers, and can yield rich data. For example, some years ago, I conducted a research project in which I asked parents and carers of pre-school children to take some photographs, as they went about their daily lives, of things that helped or hindered them in looking after their children. As this was in the days before camera phones, they were each given a disposable camera. The participants were encouraged to use some of the film in taking photos for the research and the rest in taking photos for themselves, and they were given a set of prints to keep as a thank you for helping with the research. One photo was of a little girl sleeping, and the notes I took as her carer told me about the picture are as follows:

> That was giving me a break, she went to sleep on the settee. She's just so active and into everything I seem to need that little break. I know I try to keep young but you do get tired, when you're, not getting on, but I mean I'm 67 now, so you do get tired. She's so active during the day. I have her from 9 till 3 so it's quite a full day really.

This shows how much information can be elicited from just a few comments on one photograph.

The 'draw and write' technique was devised in Nottingham, England, in the 1970s to enable children to express their views and opinions in their own terms (Wetton and McWhirter, 1998: 273). Again, it is based on an everyday activity, drawing, which most children enjoy. The children are given simple and age-appropriate questions and asked to draw their answer, and then add a few words of explanation or as a title (this can be done by an adult helper, under a child's instruction, if any child's writing skills are not yet up to the task). This also elicits surprisingly rich and fascinating data.

There are some specific ethical issues that you need to consider if you want to use visual data. First, images in the public domain may be under copyright. Photographers and artists earn their living from making and selling these images, and might take a dim view of a researcher's using one without permission. One way around this is for a researcher, or their participants, to create images specifically for the research, but that raises our next ethical problem: consent. If created images include any recognisable people, those people should be asked to give written agreement to their image being used for research (or, if they were unable to consent for themselves, for example because they were too young, then consent should be given by an appropriate person). Then images themselves may be ethically questionable, particularly if they are potentially shocking for readers, such as images depicting gruesome medical matters, violence, or pornography.

There are several arguments for and against using visual data, which are summarised in Table 7.6.

In some cases, the use of visual data can save you time at the data-collection stage, because participants will do most of the work. Sometimes this can happen without you even having to be present, for example by arranging for the art coordinator of a project for ex-offenders to help his service users to produce work around a particular theme for your research.

However, with visual data, you may need to spend more time on data interpretation and analysis than with other forms of data. This depends on the amount and complexity of the data, and the nature of the client group. For example, data can be collected using the 'draw and write' technique outlined earlier in this section. This can be speedy to collect if you can persuade schools to help you, and can be relatively quick to analyse – but the results yielded are likely to be quite brief. Conversely, collages created by non-English-speaking refugees from war-torn countries may yield rich data, but may also be very difficult for an English-speaking researcher from a peaceful country to interpret and analyse. So you will have to balance the type of data you need with the amount of time you have available for data analysis.

More information about the use of visual data can be found in the bibliography at the end of the book.

Table 7.6: Pros and cons of visual data

Pros	Cons
Visual data is useful in contexts where literacy levels, difficulty in speaking English, learning disability, or sensitivities mean that collecting spoken or written data is impossible or unhelpful.	Interpreting visual data can be challenging, particularly where there are language barriers.
Participants can create much of the data themselves, through photography, painting, collage, and so on.	You have to convert any visual data into text before it can be fully analysed.
Some visual techniques, such as the use of digital cameras and the draw-and-write technique, are suitable for use with young children.	Photography of people, for use in research, requires written consent, which may make this method impractical in practice.
Visual data can enable participants to convey experiences that are difficult or impossible for them to put into words.	Visual data needs to be carefully analysed and then checked against a range of other sources to ensure that it is not being interpreted to fit your theories.
Visual data collection can be useful when working with disparate groups, as the shared activity can help to bring people together.	Some people are not comfortable with visual techniques and may feel their skills in painting, photography, and so on are 'not good enough'.
Visual data can add an extra dimension to research reports, dissertations, theses, and so on.	Visual data alone is very unlikely to provide robust answers to complex research questions.

Case studies

A case study is not really a method in itself, it's a way of using a range of methods to look at a single case. That case may be a person, an organisation, a sporting event – any single thing. Case study research is different from most other kinds of research because you don't try to generalise from it; you are interested in a holistic, 360°, complete view of the case in all its uniqueness (Thomas, 2011: 3). To gain such a complete view, you would need to look at the case in several different ways, using a variety of methods with rigorous analysis to obtain new insights about the case under scrutiny (Thomas, 2011: 23).

A research case study is different from a journalistic case study, in which an individual example is used to illustrate more general points in a newspaper or magazine article. With a case study for research, you would need to make decisions about what kinds of data to collect, how much data to collect, how to analyse your data, how to manage ethical issues, and so on, just as you would for any other type of research. And as with any other type of research, the quality of a case study will depend on how well you have thought through your key decisions (Thomas, 2011: 71).

More information about conducting case studies can be found via the bibliography at the end of this book.

Collecting data online

The Internet and the World Wide Web have increased researchers' choices about how to collect quantitative and qualitative data. Every Internet user will be familiar with online and e-mailed surveys, but it may be less obvious that interviews and focus groups can be conducted online, and observational and visual data can be collected online.

Market researchers have led the way in collecting primary data online through dedicated 'access panels' of people who volunteer to be involved, usually in return for a small 'reward' every so often, such as a gift voucher or some air miles. If you want to find out more about access panels, or experience them as a participant, sites like Ipsos Access Panels, Toluna, and Brainjuicer are good places to start. Primary and secondary data can also be collected from existing sites such as social media sites (Twitter, Facebook, and so on), blogs, forums, or other interactive sites, such as newspaper comment boards (Poynter, 2010: 163–6).

There are specific and complicated ethical issues involved in online data collection. The boundaries of public and private space are not always clear; anonymity cannot be guaranteed; it is not always possible to identify and safeguard vulnerable participants (Markham, 2011: 122–3). The Association of Internet Researchers, an international body, produced a set of recommendations about ethical decision making and Internet research in 2002, which are still useful today (Hine, 2005: 5).

As well as the ethical dilemmas, there are other pros and cons of conducting research in virtual environments. These are summarised in Table 7.7.

As the Internet develops, so do the associated research methods. There is huge scope for creativity – market researchers are producing some very innovative practice here – but there are also many ways for problems to arise. If you think your research questions can best be answered through data collected online, you will need to think very carefully about how to collect that data.

More information about collecting data online can be found in the bibliography at the end of this book. However, as this is such a fast-moving field, I would also recommend searching for information on the Web.

For any method of data collection, always run a pilot.

For online data collection, as with all the other methods outlined in this chapter, I can't emphasise enough that you should always run a pilot (Robson, 2011: 405). This means testing the method you have adopted or devised with a small number of people from the target group, to find out how well it works. Then revise and refine your method on the basis of your participants' feedback and/or your own observations. This can seem like extra work, but it will save you time later in the process, and will also help to ensure that your research is as good as it can be.

Table 7.7: Pros and cons of online data collection

Pros	Cons
Online data collection enables you to reach more people.	You may not be able to verify that your participants are who they say they are.
Online data collection is often free of cost.	Online data collection requires a degree of technical know-how.
Observational research can be carried out in public and semi-public areas of the Web.	It may be difficult or impossible to obtain full informed consent from all potential participants in public or semi-public areas of the Web.
Interviews can be conducted online, via Facebook, Twitter, in chat rooms, and so on.	Participants recruited online often use pseudonyms that may conceal their gender, ethnicity, disability, and so on – and there is no way to assess the credibility of the data collected.
Interviews can be conducted by telephone worldwide using software that lets you make calls over the Internet, for example Skype.	Not all potential participants will be able and willing to use the Internet in the same way as you, which can be a barrier.
Chat rooms, video conferencing, and so on enable focus groups to be conducted online.	It can be difficult to persuade people to participate in online research.
Focus groups can be conducted online via chat rooms or conferencing software, which needs only one moderator, is useful where potential participants are not co-located, and provides instant textual data.	It can be difficult to moderate a group with no non-verbal cues. Also, there is no guarantee that the person responding is who you think they are. And this method will not reach people on the other side of the digital divide.
Good relationships can be created and developed online.	It is often hard to perceive emotion accurately in online communication.
With some online data-collection methods, data arrives ready prepared for coding and analysis.	You will need a system for storing data securely and backing it up frequently.

EIGHT

Data analysis

Introduction

When you have collected all your data, you need to analyse it, to find a way to understand what it can tell you. This is both one of the most challenging and one of the most rewarding parts of the research process.

One of the people I interviewed for this book said they found data analysis to be the easiest part of the research process. Another said quantitative data analysis was the easiest. On the other hand, four said that for them, data analysis was the hardest part of the research process. Also, two of the interviewees who teach novice researchers commented that new researchers often find data analysis to be one of the most difficult parts of the process.

Starting to work with your data can feel quite daunting.

> You've got it all, you've got this great mountain of *stuff* and then it's OK, what do I do with it now? This is all very interesting, but what do you do with it? I didn't have a computer program or anything like that, so it was your highlighter pen and your cut-and-paste to get things into categories. How was I deciding how to get things

into categories? Was it what people said? If they said 'integrated working', did they mean the same thing or something different?

Even if your own data is mostly quantitative or mostly qualitative, you need to understand the principles of data analysis for both types of research. This chapter will cover each approach separately before looking at how to cross-analyse and synthesise your data. I would urge you to read the sections on both quantitative and qualitative data, even if you feel a definite antipathy to one or the other. This is because you will need to understand both kinds of data analysis to be able to read critically reports of quantitative, qualitative, mixed-method, and value-based research.

Data preparation

Before you can analyse your data, you will need to prepare it for analysis. How you do this depends on the form of your data. For example, data from a pile of handwritten questionnaires with numeric answers, such as from rating scales, would need to be collated by hand or entered into a computer application such as Microsoft Excel, StatsDirect or SPSS. Audio data from interviews or focus groups would need to be transcribed, either by hand or using computer-assisted qualitative data analysis software such as NVivo. Pictorial data would need to be converted into text for thematic analysis, whether by hand or using computer software such as Microsoft Word, or the data could be scanned and loaded into a computer application that facilitates analysis of visual data, such as NVivo.

If you are analysing visual data by hand, where possible, you may make your life easier by creating electronic copies of images that you have only in hard copy, and then enlarging them before printing them out. This will give you more room to code and annotate each image. If your images are very rich in content, you may need two or more print-outs of each one. Another helpful tool for analysis by hand is the metadata record, similar to the literature grids discussed in Chapter Five. As with those grids, you would need to devise your own metadata record to meet your particular needs, but if, for example, you were using photographs as data, you might create a metadata record like the one shown in Figure 8.1.

Then you can use one metadata record for each photo, which will help you to compare and contrast the significant features of your data. You can see that I have left some blank rows at the end of the metadata record, which is good practice, as you may think of significant features as you work through your data preparation that you didn't consider at the start. I expect you realise that this system would also work with documents, interviews, and so on.

Figure 8.1: Sample of a metadata record sheet for visual data

Photograph number	
Date photo taken	
Location	
People in photo	
Buildings in photo	
Objects in photo	
Landscape in photo	
Other photo content	
Other features (blurred, horizon angled, etc)	
Purpose of photo	
Any other comments	

Create and use your record sheets electronically to save time at the analysis stage.

Data preparation can be surprisingly time-consuming.

> You have to spend quite a bit of time getting the data ready for analysis, so you need to build in time for that. The focus groups had to be transcribed, and I didn't get any admin support or resources for that: that was me, and actually transcribing everything took a month. That was a month I didn't anticipate, which is stupid because I should have thought about it.

As far as possible, prepare your data as you collect it.

Although it is time consuming, data preparation is one of the research tasks that can easily be done in small, bite-sized chunks. Even five spare minutes can be usefully spent in collating figures, entering data onto a spreadsheet, transcribing audio data or scanning pictures. Also, data preparation is one of the most boring parts of any research project, so setting aside a whole day for it can leave you feeling ready to jump off the nearest cliff by lunchtime. Boredom leaves you vulnerable to making mistakes or poor decisions, so try to interleave your data preparation with more interesting tasks. And remember, the end result will be worth the effort.

> The transcribing was very difficult because it took so much time, but the thematic analysis was great because it all made sense then.

One short cut could be to outsource the preparation of your data, to get someone else to input the data from your questionnaires or transcribe the data from your interviews. However, I would advise against this. The process of data preparation, although tedious, does help to familiarise you with your data.

> It's the going back over the interviews when you're listening to them that really helps. That's when you start to pick up on the connections, the differences or similarities, the further questions you want to ask – so in the end it helps to make it quite interesting.

> Be prepared to transcribe the data yourself. It is time consuming but you will understand the breadth and depth of what is being studied.

It is essential to be meticulous about the accuracy of your data preparation. To err is human, so it is worth putting in place some safeguards. However you prepare your data, you need an easy way to trace your collated or transcribed data back to the source. One implication of this is the need to preserve your original data, in its original form, at least until your research project is finished. Then, when you are analysing your data, if you think you may have found an error, you can go back to the original data and check. Of course how you do this will depend on the type of data you have collected. For example, if you have questionnaires, number each one before you start collating your data, and make sure each entry in your handwritten lists or spreadsheet rows is linked to the number of the individual questionnaire. Alternatively, if you are transcribing audio data, it is helpful to make a note in the transcript, at regular intervals, say every one or two minutes, of the amount of the recording you have transcribed, so that if you need to check for accuracy, you can find the relevant section of the recording quickly and easily.

It can also be helpful to be aware of the types of error you might make. Some common errors that occur when preparing data are:

- errors of omission – leaving something out;
- errors of commission – putting something in that shouldn't be there;
- errors of transposition – putting two numbers, letters, or words in the wrong order;
- misreading errors – reading something incorrectly;
- substitution errors – writing something incorrectly;
- typographical errors – reading correctly and intending to write it correctly, but accidentally pressing a wrong key on the keyboard.

In an extreme scenario a single error could completely change your findings. For example, when working with numerical data, a misplaced zero can cause a factor of 10 error. Putting the decimal point in the wrong place can also be a very big mistake. With handwritten numbers, it can be easy to confuse a 1 with a 7; with typewritten numbers, it can be easy to misread, say, 78332 as 78832.

When working with textual data, the substitution of just one letter can cause a dramatic change of meaning. Consider this interview excerpt:

"I told my precious wife I loved her."

An error could be made here by misreading, or substitution, or through a 'typo' as the character C is next to the V on a QWERTY keyboard:

"I told my previous wife I loved her."

Or:

"I was only kidding him."

The D is next to the S…

"I was only kissing him."

And of course these kinds of errors will not be detected by a computer spell-checker. Similar errors can easily be made with handwriting, too, especially when you're reading writing that isn't clear, or if you're writing in a hurry yourself (or if your handwriting, like mine, resembles the scrawl of a demented gibbon).

Take great care to be accurate when preparing your data – it will save you time in the end.

Because data preparation is so boring and therefore prone to errors, it is worth proactively checking a selection of your data for errors when you have finished the preparation. You can do this by taking a random selection of your original data and checking that it has all been entered correctly. If you find no errors, you can be reasonably confident that the whole dataset is error free. If you find a few errors, correct them as you go and keep checking until you are sure you have found them all. If you find a lot of errors, you will need to start again and re-enter the data, being much more careful this time around.

Quantitative data coding

When you are working with quantitative data, coding happens very early in the process. For example, if you are entering questionnaire data into a spreadsheet, you need to convert data into codes before you begin. Let's say your first question was about someone's marital status. The categories you offered were:

- Unmarried
- Married
- Living with partner
- Divorced
- Widowed

A simple way to code these categories is with their initial letters: U, M, L, D and W. So on your spreadsheet, the first row will be numbered 1 to correspond with the first questionnaire, and the first column will be labelled 'Marital status'. You look at your first questionnaire and the participant has indicated that they are living with their partner, so you enter an L in the first cell of your spreadsheet. Another option is to code the categories numerically from 1 to 5. Some people prefer numbers; some prefer letters; either enables you to sort your spreadsheet, so it doesn't matter which you use.

Some quantitative data doesn't need converting into codes. The answers to questions such as, 'How many children do you have?', or rating scales where the participant is asked to circle a number from 1 to 7, can be transferred directly onto a spreadsheet as they stand. But most data will need to be coded for ease of analysis.

You may also need to specify a code for missing data, such as XXX, 99999 or –42, or you may choose to leave cells blank where data is missing. There are two kinds of missing data. The first kind is where a participant, whether accidentally or deliberately, has not answered one or more questions. The second kind is where a question is structured such that the participant is unlikely to give all the possible answers. For example, consider this question:

Which of these beverages do you drink every day? Please tick all that apply.

☐ Tea   ☐ Other fruit drinks
☐ Coffee   ☐ Wine
☐ Hot chocolate   ☐ Beer/lager/ale
☐ Water   ☐ Spirits
☐ Fresh fruit juice   ☐ Liqueurs

It is very unlikely that anyone would drink all of those every day, so there will be some 'missing data' in the answers to this question.

As there are two kinds of missing data, you may choose two different codes, one for each kind. For example, you could leave a cell blank for a non-answer to an option in a question like this one, and use the code 99999 where a participant has not answered a question at all.

Qualitative data coding

Qualitative data coding is done at a later stage, after all the data has been prepared. A code, or label, may be applied to a chunk of data of any size from a single word to an entire file or document. With qualitative data, as with quantitative data, you decide what the codes will be, and this can feel quite daunting (Rapley, 2011: 280). There may be almost unlimited ways to code any section of qualitative data. However, many systems have been devised for dealing with this, and two seem particularly useful.

One approach is to devise a 'coding frame' or a set of words and phrases to guide your coding of the data. For example, if I were doing a piece of research to evaluate the effectiveness of a partnership service, I might decide to use this simple coding frame:

• Partnership working pros (PWP)
• Partnership working cons (PWC)
• Partnership working barriers (PWB)
• Partnership working enablers (PWE)
• Service effective (SE)
• Service effective reasons (SER)
• Service ineffective (SI)
• Service ineffective reasons (SIR)
• Suggestions for improvement (SFI)

Then, as I was coding the data, I would pay attention only to data that related to one of the points in my coding frame. This doesn't mean I would use the wording in the coding frame as my codes, although I would probably use the initials of the coding frame descriptions – PWP, PWC and so on – to link the chosen codes to the coding frame.

To show you how this works in practice, here's a piece of interview data:

> At operational level, we work together well. We know all the social workers and they know us, so we can sort problems quickly. But sometimes, you know you have to go higher for a decision. That slows it down, because the managers, they don't talk to each other.

Using my simple coding frame, I might code this data as shown in Figure 8.2.

Figure 8.2: Example of a simple coding frame

Data	Code(s)
At operational level, we work together well.	SE operational level
We know all the social workers and they know us,	SER operational level PWE communication
so we can sort problems quickly.	PWE time SE time
But sometimes, you know you have to go higher for a decision.	PWB decision-making level
That slows it down	PWB time SI time
because the managers, they don't talk to each other.	SIR strategic level PWB communication

I have added explanatory notes that will be used again, where appropriate, as I work through my data.

Where possible, it is best to devise a coding frame in conjunction with others, such as managers, tutors, commissioners, and/or service users.

Where you have to devise a coding frame alone, use background literature to help you identify relevant points to include.

This may look like fairly thorough coding, and indeed it is. But the coding of this piece of data might look very different if I used a different system. The other approach that many people find particularly useful is known as 'emergent coding', or whatever the researcher perceives to be of interest in the data. With this system there is no prior plan. Using this approach, the coding of the same piece of data might look as shown in Figure 8.3.

Figure 8.3: Example of emergent coding

Data	Code
At operational level	Front line
we work together well	Solidarity
We know all the social workers and they know us	Solidarity Reciprocity Us and them
social workers	Social workers
so we can sort problems	Problem solving
quickly.	Speed Time
But sometimes, you know you have to go higher	Hierarchy
for a decision	Decision making Problem solving
That slows it down,	Speed Time
because the managers, they don't talk to each other.	Hierarchy Communication Us and them
managers	Managers

I expect you have noticed some differences between this emergent coding and the previous version using the coding frame. With emergent coding, there will be more codes; the coding is denser. Also, the codes are more abstract and exploratory. You may have noticed that on two occasions, I have coded small segments of data using the same word or phrase for the codes as in the data itself: 'social workers' and 'managers'. This is known as 'in-vivo coding' and is useful where there are particular categories that you might want to review at the analysis stage.

Table 8.1 summarises the pros and cons of both types of coding.

I don't think either type of coding is better than the other. The point is to use the type of coding that is most appropriate for the research you're doing within the time-scale you have.

I find it easiest to code qualitative data using a software application called NVivo, which is widely used in social research worldwide and is often available through universities. There are other qualitative data-analysis computer applications, including free, open source software such as CAT and Compendium, proprietary software such as Atlas.ti and Framework, and web-based software such as Dedoose and CAT.

Table 8.1: Pros and cons of two kinds of coding

Coding frame	Emergent coding
Quick, efficient, targeted.	Takes longer, but more thorough.
Restrictions may cause researcher to miss points of interest.	Researcher should be able to include everything they are able to perceive.
Two people coding the same data should produce similar findings.	Two people coding the same data may produce quite different findings.
Can be seen as more 'valid' or 'reliable' from some standpoints.	Can be seen as more 'reflexive' or 'inclusive' from some standpoints.

> Now that I know how to use NVivo, which I only learned towards the end of doing my PhD, I would start by understanding a data management package and I would use that from the beginning because I think being systematic about what you're reading, thinking, collecting, it's all part of the same project isn't it? I don't think we often talk to people about it, we say, "You do your reading and then you collect your data," but actually they should be completely intertwined and I do think the software can help you do that.

Whichever application you choose will take time to learn to use and, if not free, open source software, will be expensive if you have to buy it yourself. There are other ways of coding data. For example, coding can be done in word processing software, using tables like those shown earlier, or by using coloured highlighting, comment functions or any combination of these and other features that you wish to devise. Coding can also be done by hand on print-outs of your data. If you prefer to use this method, I would recommend setting up your data to print out double-spaced, on one side of the paper only, and with wide margins at each side and top and bottom. This will leave you plenty of room to insert codes. I would not recommend coding qualitative data by hand if you have more than a few pages, because although the coding itself is manageable, the analysis can become very difficult (see later in this chapter for more on this).

When you have finished coding, the next step is to establish how many times you have used each code. The codes that are used most often will give you an initial idea of the major themes in your data – and can often be surprising. The codes that are used least often will need to be checked to see whether they are genuinely rare or whether they are examples of unclear thinking and should be combined with other codes. Box 8.1 shows an edited excerpt from the methodology chapter of my PhD thesis that illustrates how this can work in practice.

Box 8.1: Example of a review of coded data

The codes were reviewed. First, each code that had been used only once or twice was checked, to assess whether it was truly a single or double instance of something in the data, or whether it was a subject that had been coded in another way elsewhere in the data so that the coding needed revision. For example, in the first coding frame the word 'objectives' had been given a single-word coding once. A text search established that the word did indeed only appear once in the data. Then the paragraph in which it appeared was studied, and showed that it appeared in the phrase 'targets and objectives'. 'Targets' had also been given a single-word coding, which appeared ten times in five stories/discussions. The decision was made to change the coding so that the phrase 'targets and objectives' was coded with 'targets', as the phrase in its context was tautologous, and the code 'objectives' was deleted.

Another example came from the second coding frame. The code 'trapped' had been used twice in two stories/discussions. The code 'constrained' had been used 13 times in six stories/discussions. This led me to wonder whether the text coded as 'trapped' could legitimately be combined with the text coded as 'constrained'. All the text coded with both was carefully re-examined, and I concluded that combining them would detract from their meaning, as the text coded as 'trapped' expressed more helplessness than the text coded as 'constrained'. So in this case the coding was left unchanged.

In NVivo you can find out how many times you have used each code with just a couple of clicks of your mouse. Using word processing software, you can save your data in a new document and then copy and paste each instance of each code onto a separate page to make them easy to count. If you are working by hand, you will have to count and record each code in turn.

Whether you use a coding frame or emergent coding, or any other system, qualitative data coding is a laborious task. You will usually need to go through all your data at least twice to ensure that you haven't missed anything. This can take a long time and feel very onerous, but it will make your analysis much easier and give you more confidence in your findings.

> I didn't like going through the coding, but I liked reading it after the coding, especially because I found an unexpected theme. I got a fizzy feeling! I'd read about 300 documents and it hadn't come up in any of them. That was incredibly exciting. If I'd skipped it or been half-hearted because I had so much data – it is worth keeping going with the same level of detail, it does pay.

Quantitative data analysis

As we saw in Chapter Three, when you are working with numerical data, your analytic methods will be partly determined by the sampling technique you use. For any kind of sample, you can use descriptive statistics, such as percentages, averages, medians, and ranges, to communicate your findings. If you have used a truly random sample, you can also use inferential statistics, such as t-tests, analyses of variance, factor analyses, or regression analyses. These kinds of calculations enable you to draw conclusions about the population from which your sample is drawn, and to assess how likely or unlikely it is that those conclusions could have arisen by chance alone.

If you are mathematically eager, you may find this an exciting prospect and long to discover more. Conversely, if you are mathematically timid, you may find the prospect alarming. Either way, I have help for you.

I'm not going to go into detail about how to do statistical calculations. There are numerous textbooks on the subject, some of which are in the bibliography at the end of this book, and there is also a good deal of advice on the World Wide Web. If you enjoy mathematical activity, you can do the calculations yourself. If you don't, there is software available to do it for you, such as Microsoft Excel – which has the facility to do many statistical calculations – or SPSS (aka Statistical Package for Social Scientists), which is a specialist piece of software widely used for quantitative data analysis in research and available in most universities (Greasley, 2008: 2). Another option is StatsDirect, which does most of the same things as SPSS but is significantly cheaper, and easier to use (Davis, 2010).

One interviewee shared their experience of both SPSS and Excel.

> I love playing with data. I loved looking at SPSS and seeing what we could get out of it. We asked the question "would you prefer a same-sex service?" and we found out that most women would prefer a same-sex worker and most men would prefer a woman. That was quite interesting and unexpected. With SPSS you can play with things like that, gender, sexuality. We did have a monitoring section at the end of our questionnaire so we could cross-reference things, and use SPSS to do a bit of the data crunching, also at the same time learning about SPSS. One thing for this is, I wouldn't specialise too much on SPSS, it's a very expensive package, and with training I think programs like Excel can do just as much work. SPSS can be about £1,000 a licence; Excel, especially if you're a charity, you can pay £20. Obviously you need training but it can do most of the same things. We only had 80 participants, SPSS was like a sledgehammer to crack a walnut in some ways.

One thing I would add to this is that you don't even need to pay £20 for Excel. Also, it is a Microsoft Windows application, so cannot be used by everyone. If you want spreadsheet capabilities, check out OpenOffice, which is free cross-platform software. OpenOffice includes a spreadsheet application that is very similar to, and compatible with, Excel. And the open source option for full statistical analysis is The R Project for Statistical Computing, commonly known as R.

Although you don't need to be able to do the calculations yourself, in order to analyse your data effectively, you will need to know which calculations are appropriate for your kind(s) of sample, and the rationale behind each calculation (Bryman and Cramer, 2009: 69). Further, when you write up your research, you will need to explain the justification for using the calculations you chose. I will give a brief introductory overview here, but if you are intending to analyse quantitative data and you are not already statistically literate, you will need to read more widely to ensure that you understand what you are doing well enough to explain it to others.

Descriptive statistics

Whatever kind of sample you use, you will need to describe your data for your readers. Descriptive statistics, which can be used for any sample, include ways to summarise parts of your data. For single variables, these are known as 'univariate' statistics (Bryman and Cramer, 2009: 68), and include frequency distributions, measures of central tendency, and measures of variability.

Frequency distributions show how many times a particular variable has occurred, of itself and in relation to other variables. These are usually in the form of tables, graphs, or pie charts. Figures 8.4a, b, and c show an example.

Figure 8.4: Examples for frequency distribution in (a) a table, (b) a graph and (c) a pie chart

(a)

Marital status	Percentage
Unmarried	10
Married	25
Living with partner	32
Divorced	28
Widowed	3
Missing	2
Total	**100**

(b)

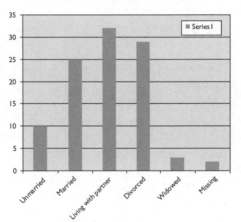

(c)

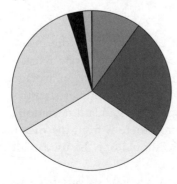

Measures of **central tendency** include mode, median, and mean or average. The mode is the value occurring most commonly, so in this dataset it would be 'living with partner' at 32%. The median is the middle value in a dataset after it has been ranked in order (or, if there are an even number of values, the average of the two middle ones). This is usually used for ordinal data, and is useful when there are a few extreme scores or the data is skewed. The mean, or average, is the total of all the values divided by the number of values. The mode and the median can be used with any type of data, but because the mean involves calculation, it should be used only with interval data.

Let's say you have a dataset of test scores. Your subjects scored 23, 47, 32, 46, 37, 36, 42, 33, 46, 29 and 41. To work out the median, you need to put these scores in order, to find the central score:

23 29 32 33 36 37 41 42 46 46 47

The median score is 37. The mode is 46, because it occurs most frequently, but in this dataset that's not very useful because it is so close to the top score. Data like this, where the mode is close to one end of the ranked data, is called 'skewed' data.

We can calculate the mean for this dataset, as test scores are an example of interval data. If we add all the scores together, we find that the total is 412. Then we can divide this by the number of scores, that is, 11:

$$412 \div 11 = 37.5$$

The mean of the dataset is 37.5. This is very close to the median, which is often the case.

Measures of **variability** show how values vary around the central tendency, and include range and variance. Range is the difference between the smallest and largest values, and can be used with any type of data. So the range for this dataset can be calculated as follows:

$$47 - 23 = 24$$

The range of the dataset is 24.

Variance is an estimate of the average distance of each value from the mean. To calculate this, you first need to work out the mean, then how far away each value is from the mean (ignoring any negative signs), and then take an average of those scores. This is known as the 'average deviation'. Computer statistics software will calculate this for you, or its close relative, the 'standard deviation', which is another way of showing how much variation there is from the mean. Like the mean itself, variance involves calculation, so should only be used with interval data.

As we know the mean of our small dataset, we can calculate its variance. In order, each score's distance from the mean is:

14.5 8.5 5.5 4.5 1.5 0.5 3.5 4.5 8.5 8.5 9.5

If we add all these together, we find that the total is 69.5. Then we divide this by the number of scores, that is, 11:

69.5 ÷ 11 = 6.3

The variance of the dataset is 6.3.

There are also descriptive statistics that can be used to describe the relationship between two variables, or **'bivariate' statistics** (Bryman and Cramer, 2009: 68). There are two main kinds of these relationships.

The first is known as **'covariant'**, which means the variables change in accordance with each other. An example of this might be a baby's age and weight in its first year of life – weight should increase quite steadily as age increases. Variables are also covariant if one increases as the other decreases. For example, as an adult's food intake increases above the necessary level, their quality of health decreases, so these variables are again covariant.

The second kind of relationship between variables is known as **'independent'**, which means the variables change independently of each other. So, for example, a researcher might hypothesise that women are more left wing than men, but find that the same number of women and men are left wing and right wing, that is, that political affiliation is independent of gender.

As with univariate statistics, bivariate statistics include graphs, tables, and statistical calculations. These are scattergraphs, frequency tables, correlation coefficients, and the chi-squared test.

Scattergraphs give an overview of the relationship between two variables by constructing a graph with one variable on each axis and plotting each piece of data as a dot or an 'x'. If there is a relationship between the variables, the scattergraph should enable you to identify its direction and its strength. To help with this, you can sometimes draw a line of best fit or 'regression line', with an equal number of dots or 'x's above and below. If the line is diagonal from bottom left to top right (or thereabouts), there is a positive relationship between your variables; if it is diagonal from somewhere in the top left to somewhere in the bottom right, there is a negative relationship. Where all the dots or 'x's are close to the line, the relationship is a strong one; if they are widely scattered throughout the graph, the relationship is weak. If the dots or 'x's are so widely scattered within the graph that your line is horizontal, the variables are independent. Figure 8.5 is an example of a scattergraph with a strong positive relationship between the variables.

Bivariate frequency tables have one variable in a column and the other in rows. So, for example, you could construct a bivariate frequency table to help you look at the relationship between marital status and income. It might look as shown in Figure 8.6.

Figure 8.5: Scattergraph

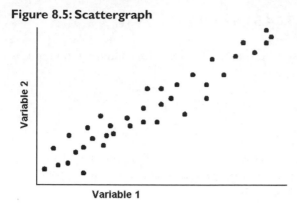

Figure 8.6: Bivariate frequency table

Income	Under £15,000	£15,000 to £29,999	£30,000 to £44,999	£45,000 to £59,999	£60,000 and over
Unmarried					
Married					
Living with partner					
Divorced					
Widowed					

You can enter your data into the table, simply in terms of the number of participants who fall into each category. When all the data has been entered, you will be able to see whether there is any kind of relationship.

Scattergraphs and bivariate frequency tables can be used with any type of data, and are useful for summarising data and giving the overall picture, but they give only a flavour of the relationship between the variables. For a more precise description, you need to use more complex calculations.

The **correlation coefficient** is similar to variance, giving an estimate of the average distance of each point on a scattergraph from the regression line. Like variance, it should be used only with interval data. All computer statistics software offer ways of calculating correlation coefficients, such as Pearson's r, Spearman's rho, and the phi coefficient. The closer the result of the calculation is to 1, the stronger is the correlation between the two variables. However, it is important to note that a correlation does not indicate cause and effect. Think of the baby in its first year of life. It does not gain weight because it increases in age, or vice versa. It gains weight because it is fed; it increases in age because time passes. The variables have a positive relationship but one does not cause the other; the causes of each increase lie outside the relationship between the two variables.

The **chi-squared test**, written as χ^2, gives us more detail about the relationship between the variables in a bivariate frequency table. It does this by showing whether and how the values differ from those that would exist if the two variables were independent. This calculation yields a probability figure, and the smaller this is, the less likely it is that the values in the table could have occurred by chance. So, for example, if the probability figure is $p < 0.05$, there is only a 5% risk that it could have occurred by chance; if the probability figure is $p < 0.01$, there is only a 1% risk that it could have occurred by chance. Because it is based on a bivariate frequency table, which can contain any type of data, the chi-squared test may also be used with any type of data.

Inferential statistics

Apart from descriptive statistics, the other main type of statistics is known as inferential statistics. These calculations allow us to infer something about a population from a sample. This is where you need a random sample that is large enough, or (in statistical terminology) has the 'power', to allow us to make these inferences. As we saw in Chapter Three, this raises the question, 'How large is large enough?' There are a number of online web pages that offer calculators of statistical power to determine the answer to this question, which is worth doing at an early stage to ensure that you are planning a sample that will give a firm basis to your calculations (Myers, Well and Lorch, 2010: 15).

Even with sufficient statistical power, inferential statistics are not fool proof. An inference may have a robust rationale, accurate calculations, and still be wrong. As with the chi-squared test, inferential statistics use probability figures to estimate how likely it is that the result could have occurred by chance. A convention in inferential statistics is to say that if $p < 0.05$, the result is 'statistically significant'. This is an unfortunate use of vocabulary, because people confuse statistical significance with practical and social significance, but in fact it means only that the result has a very low risk of having occurred by chance (Bryman and Cramer, 2009: 128).

To confuse things further, some descriptive statistics, such as the mean, correlation coefficient, and chi-squared test, can also be used as inferential statistics in contexts where they enable us to infer something about the population.

Perhaps the most commonly used inferential statistics are the t-test, F-test, analysis of variance (ANOVA), cluster analysis, factor analysis and regression analysis. These should be used only with interval data.

The **t-test** is used to compare the means of two different groups. Ideally, you need equal sample sizes, although this is not essential. There are two main kinds of t-test. The first is the 'dependent samples t-test' or 'paired two-group t-test', where the scores are linked in some way, such as having been provided by the same person before and after an intervention. The second is the 'independent samples t-test' or 'unpaired two-group t-test', where the scores are not linked, such as having been provided by an experimental and control group.

The **F-test**, also called the 'variance-ratio test', compares the variability of the scores around the mean across two groups. It is often a helpful calculation to use alongside a t-test, as two groups may have the same mean but different levels of variability.

ANOVA enables the comparison of the variability of the scores around the mean across more than two groups. The simplest kind of ANOVA involves just one independent and one dependent variable. There are more complex ANOVA calculations available for research with more than one independent variable. These are known as 'multivariate' tests.

Cluster analysis, factor analysis and regression analysis are also multivariate tests. **Cluster analysis** helps to sort data into categories, and is particularly useful where you have a number of variables and you want to find out whether some kind of classification system can be produced from your data. **Factor analysis** helps to identify factors that influence the relationships between variables. **Regression analysis** helps to show how the dependent variable changes as one independent variable changes (while the others are held constant).

All the inferential statistics described in this chapter are parametric, which means that the result of a calculation on the basis of a sample allows us to make an inference about the parameters of the population. They each have non-parametric equivalents, which don't make the same probability-based assumptions as the parametric statistics. These are shown in Table 8.2.

Table 8.2: Parametric tests and non-parametric equivalents

Parametric test	Non-parametric test
Paired two-group t-test	Wilcoxon signed-rank test
Unpaired two-group t-test	Mann-Whitney U test
ANOVA (one independent variable)	Kruskal-Wallis test
ANOVA (more than one independent variable)	Friedman test

There are also non-parametric versions of cluster analysis, factor analysis, and regression analysis.

 If you want to know more about statistics, there are lots of free advice and a variety of interactive web pages and calculators at http://statpages.org/.

This chapter merely skims the surface of statistics. There are many more descriptive and inferential, parametric, and non-parametric tests available for you to understand and use if you wish. In order to give a critical reading to reports of research including quantitative analysis, you do need to be able to understand the terms used here well enough to be able to use them yourself in conversation and writing. If you are new to statistics, this will almost certainly mean you have to read more widely to deepen your understanding.

Qualitative data analysis

There are a range of approaches to qualitative data analysis (Robson, 2011: 467), but in my experience, two kinds are predominantly used by researchers working in public services: content analysis, and thematic analysis.

In **content analysis**, you need to define categories (or codes) and count the number of instances within each category or code (Silverman, 2001: 123). This is an interesting example of quantitative-meets-qualitative that is useful in some contexts but can be quite superficial. Content analysis can be used with textual or visual data (Rose, 2012: 81–104). It is done for me by the computer software application NVivo 9 that I use to code and analyse qualitative data, but it is easy enough to do by hand with small datasets.

For **thematic analysis**, you need to identify themes within your coded data. You do this by extracting all the data coded with each code in turn (Robson, 2011: 467), which is sometimes known as 'slicing' the data, and reading each 'slice' to see what it seems to be telling you. It is sensible to make notes of what you find as you go. Don't worry if your notes seem disjointed; as long as you're getting everything down you can make sense of them later on. My approach is to use the findings of my content analysis to start from the code that has been used most often and work through the codes until I reach the one that has been used least often. You may find that you want to add new codes during this process.

Other kinds of qualitative data analysis include:

- narrative analysis, which focuses on stories, such as stories told by participants, or stories told about people or events or experiences;
- conversation analysis, which, despite its name, focuses on both the verbal and non-verbal content of everyday interactions – and in some detail, for example assessing the unwritten and unspoken rules by which people know when to take turns in a conversation;
- discourse analysis, which looks at patterns of speech and interaction in quite a detailed and sometimes quite quantitative way, for example measuring the length of pauses, or counting the amount of time taken up by each person in a group discussion;
- phenomenological analysis, based on the ways in which participants and the researcher experience the world and the meanings they find within, or construct from, their experiences.

For more information about these and other methods, please consult references such as those listed in the bibliography at the end of this book.

A real-life example of qualitative data analysis

Data analysis is one of the hardest parts of research to explain, which is probably why it is one of the hardest parts to do. A real–life example may help. For my PhD, I coded all the data three times in three different ways. First I used emergent coding. Then I devised a coding frame from both the literature on partnership working and the literature on emotion, combined. After that, as I had collected data in the form of stories, I decided that a second coding frame should be based on the literature on narrative analysis. Box 8.2 gives an edited explanation, from my thesis, which shows how I used my coding to work through my analysis.

Box 8.2: Example of qualitative data analysis

The codes that appeared most frequently were used to 'slice' through the data, extracting segments from all the documents where that code had been used. For example, in the first coding frame, the code 'power' had been used 128 times and had appeared in all 12 stories/discussions; the code 'identification' (where an apparently unconscious change of grammatical tense denotes a participant identifying with the story character being discussed) had been used 31 times and had appeared in 11 stories/discussions; and the code 'complexity' had been used 36 times and had appeared in 10 stories/discussions. The data coded with each code was extracted and reviewed to establish what light it could shed on the research questions. This is a constant process of asking questions and finding answers. For example, in the initial consideration of the code 'power', my internal dialogue went something like this:

"The 'power' code was used in each story/discussion. Hmmm, that's interesting. I wonder how many other codes were used in every story/discussion? Let's check … oh, OK, just 'amusement' and 'curiosity'. I wonder whether I should change 'curiosity' to 'questioning', I'm not sure the name of the code describes accurately enough what's going on there. That's not about power, though, so to save going off at a tangent I'll just make a note. There we are. Now, what kind of power are we talking about? Let's extract the data and have a look. Here we go. Well, it seems to be all about hierarchical power-over. Now that's interesting, too, because I would have said that my participants didn't have a zero-sum approach to power. But maybe they do. Let's read some more. Yes, it is all about power-over. I'd better write something about that in the 'findings' chapter, I'll just make a note of that. Now, I wonder whether something else will demonstrate that the participants don't see power as finite. Or maybe they do; perhaps I just want to believe that they don't because that's the way I think myself. Could I create that in the data just by looking for it? That may be a bit far fetched, and anyway it's a discussion for the reflexivity section, so I'll just make another note and come back to it at a later date. There. Now, about this 'power' code. I wonder whether the emergent coding could shed any light on it. I remember the code 'control' was high up in that one. I'll go and have a look, and see where that gets me."

This process of 'interrogating the data' went on until no new findings were being drawn from the questioning. Writing about the findings took place concurrently, mostly in disjointed sentences and paragraphs. All codes were double-checked to ensure that they had been considered.

When you are analysing qualitative data, you need to:

* be curious;
* be systematic;
* be open-minded, willing to use ideas from any source;
* follow hunches and gut feelings;
* take frustration in your stride;
* write down all your thoughts during the process;
* explore all the ideas you generate while working with the data.
  (Rapley, 2011: 279–80)

Geographic information systems[1]

Geographic Information Systems, or GIS, refers to working with data that contains location or place information, and plotting it on a map or doing calculations related to its position on the Earth. A great deal of secondary data contains locations, and so can be analysed spatially. One example is government administrative or statistical data, which, in the UK, is produced at various geographic resolutions from census output areas to wards to local authorities to government office regions. Map and boundary data to be used with GIS software can be obtained from EDINA (with an academic licence) or for free from Ordnance Survey Open Data. When you collect primary data, you may choose to include location information, such as postcodes, that can then be plotted on maps. Data with coordinates can also be plotted, such as readings from a GPS device or tweets from location-enabled devices.

GIS can be a useful tool when working with primary or secondary data, because it can enable you to communicate your data visually in a very powerful way. In recent history, mapping research data was limited to GIS 'geeks' and practitioners working with expensive software. However, recent developments online mean

---

[1] I am indebted to John Kaye, Lead Curator of e-social science at the British Library, for the first draft of this section.

that anyone familiar with spreadsheets and the Web can create basic maps online for little or no cost.

Online mapping software is developing fast. The easiest way to create a basic map online is to use Google Fusion Tables. To do this, upload your data with locations into a Google spreadsheet. Once it is loaded, click on 'Visualise' and choose 'Map' for a point map, and 'Intensity map' for a thematic map of a data value if you have boundary names or codes in your data (for example local authority). This method can yield usable mapping results in minutes. Google Fusion also allows you to export the map data as a KML (Keyhole Markup Language) file that can be opened in Google Earth on or off line.

There may already be online tools available to map the data you are looking for. A good example of this is the London Profiler Website created by UCL's CASA at www.londonprofiler.org, which contains a great deal of socioeconomic data for London that is ready to map on a user-friendly web-based interface. You can also load your own KML files into the website. CASA has also developed MapTube at www.maptube.org, where GIS analysts have deposited various mapping layers for others to reuse on a Google Maps interface.

These online tools offer easy ways of creating basic maps, but to carry out more advanced spatial analysis or to deal with a high volume of mapping, then GIS software may be required. Specialist training in this software is recommended, and the main applications used are: ESRI ArcGIS, MapInfo, and Quantum GIS (a user-friendly open source GIS platform). These systems give the user a lot more functionality and flexibility than the free online tools. Spatial statistics are available within these packages: these are formal techniques that analyse entities within data along their geographic properties. The statistical tests include spatial versions of the statistical methods outlined earlier in this chapter, and concern the distribution or 'complete spatial randomness' across a geographic area, or the correlation of variables in the data across that area.

If you want to work with large amounts of data, or on projects where a large number of maps need to be created, you are likely to need specialist GIS software. This software can be automated using programming code to create a large number of maps, or calculations and processes can be easily repeated. There are a number of open source GIS software systems available, as well as several proprietary systems (although these can be expensive), and you will find information about all of them on the Web.

If you want to use GIS software, take the time to identify the best option for your research.

Data synthesis

If you have collected data in different ways, it is likely to be easiest for you to analyse your datasets in different ways. For example, for a workplace evaluation, you might have:

- quantitative monitoring data;
- documents such as service plans and meeting minutes;
- questionnaire data with some quantitative and some qualitative elements;
- interview data;
- focus group data.

It would make sense to first analyse each of these separately, so that you can compare findings between methods. This would enable you to check whether any of your findings are specific to one method alone. Once you have done this, you will need to cross-analyse or synthesise your data. You can do this by looking at the results of each of the separate analyses and picking out any common threads and differences for discussion. This process can help you build answers to your research questions.

It is in the nature of research that answers often throw up more questions. This can feel frustrating and you can find yourself thinking, 'If only I'd known …'. The point here is that you couldn't have known, and if you had known, you wouldn't have needed to do the research in the first place. As individuals and collectively, the more we learn, the more we find out about what we don't know. If you take change into account, this seems likely to be an unstoppable process. So if your answers seem irritatingly partial, rather than satisfyingly complete, don't worry. As you write your research report, dissertation, or thesis, you will be able to identify what you have found out during the research and what still needs to be investigated. The process of doing that writing is the subject of the next chapter.

NINE

Writing up

Introduction

Although writing has a chapter all to itself in the second half of this book, it is not a discrete activity that happens late in the research process. Writing begins at the very beginning, with notes and plans and lists and, more formally, your written research proposal or plan. It continues throughout as you make records of literature and documents that you read, write a research journal, take notes, and code data. And it doesn't finish when your report, dissertation or thesis is complete, because you will continue to write your research as part of presenting your findings at a meeting, conference, viva or other event, or in a newsletter or journal article, or on a web page.

Myths about writing

This chapter aims to debunk some of the main myths about writing. The first myth is that writing happens in the same sequence as reading, that is, you start with the words 'Chapter 1', carry on until you get to 'The End', and then stop.

Actually there is plenty of reading that doesn't happen like that either; I'll bet most of the people who use this book don't read from the first page all the way through to the last. But some books are read as linear narratives, particularly fiction, and that is probably where the myth developed.

A second myth is that writing is easy and anyone can write if they feel in the mood. In fact writing is hard graft.

> Writing it all up, that was hard.

Like long-distance running, playing the piano, or riding a horse, you need a lot of practice before you can be good at writing. Unlike those activities, though, nobody can say to you, "Look at me, I'll show you how." Most writing is a solitary, private activity, much of which happens inside the writer's head. If you watched me writing, all you would see was my fingers tapping on the computer keyboard while I stared at the screen, interspersed with times where my fingers were still and I stared out of the window. Your observations wouldn't tell you anything about how to write yourself.

I suspect the myth that writing is easy arose because people see only the finished product (Becker, 2007: xiii). Because people don't see the process of producing what they read, it seems to have appeared as if by magic. But anyone who writes well will have done lots and lots of practice, just like anyone who is good at sport or music. As with sports players and musicians, different strategies work for different writers. You need to try out different strategies to find out what works for you. While you do that, be aware of the possibility of kidding yourself. If you feel that you have to clean the house for an hour before you can start writing, is that really because the house cleaning provides essential thinking time that helps your writing when you get going, or is it in fact a delaying tactic? Only you can know the answer, so be analytical and critical about your own practice.

A third myth is that you need huge chunks of free time to be able to write effectively. For some people, this may be true at some stages of the process.

> How it worked best was when I could carve out weeks at a time – this was in the writing-up stage – I really struggled when I couldn't take chunks of time like that, so it didn't work for me when I was doing a few hours every couple of evenings a week, it didn't allow me to build enough momentum. I needed my employer to be flexible with me so I could work a week on and a week off, but it was obviously difficult to get many of those so I ended up using holiday.

However, most inexperienced writers find large chunks of free time more useful for procrastination than for actual writing. More experienced writers know that it's more helpful to 'snack' than to 'binge' (Murray, 2011b: 9). It can help to break down your writing work into specific tasks and give each task a specific time. For example, you could decide to write two paragraphs about the research methods you used, and give yourself half an hour to do that, after dinner and before watching TV. Don't fall into the trap of thinking there's no point writing just two paragraphs. If you write two paragraphs, that's two paragraphs, probably 200–300 words, that you didn't have before.

> Trying to write it up I found laborious. In my head I'd already done it. You don't get taught how to do it. The books are there, but you almost need someone to sit down and go through a structure. I got quite phobic about the red pen, you'd go in and it would be, 'That's great, but …' so there was a bit of regression back to school days, which wasn't comfortable or necessary.

One helpful strategy here is to use Raymond Chandler's technique of The Nothing Alternative (Baumeister and Tierney, 2012: 254). To do this, you set time aside in which you allow yourself either to write or to do nothing. No tidying up or checking e-mail, real nothing. It can be useful, particularly if you're sitting at your computer with your mobile phone by your side, to switch off the sound on both devices. Internet addicts may also benefit from apps such as 'Anti-Social', which blocks loads of social networking sites like Twitter and Facebook as well as free e-mail sites like Gmail and Yahoo!, or Freedom, which blocks the entire Internet (although that's less helpful if you need to do online research as you write). During periods of time when you can only write or do nothing, you are likely to write more to stave off boredom.

A fourth myth is that all writing requires the same kind of skill. This is of course true to an extent, because all writing consists of combining words to make meaning. But writing a novel, or copy for the back of a cereal packet, or instructions in a technical manual, or a ghost-written celebrity memoir, each requires some very different skills. And writing for research is different again, which can make life even more complicated, particularly for people who are schooled in yet another way of writing.

> The police have this thing of writing, Accuracy Brevity and Clarity, so if you can write everything very briefly – within the police they have a research forecast, but a paper to the police is something that cuts to the chase and isn't wrapped up in any of the references or proof. You would have to read something, understand it, then write it in one-and-a-half or two pages so that it was understandable to everybody. It's overcoming this very prescribed way of writing that I think a lot of police find a problem.

Some of the myths about writing that have been regularly expressed to me by practitioners and research students are set out in Table 9.1, together with the essence of my responses.

Table 9.1: Regularly expressed myths about writing, with my responses

Expressed myth	Response
I'll write when I feel like it.	You'll get nothing done.
One day I'll be in the right mood for writing.	You don't know that for sure, you just have to get on with it.
I'll start writing when I know what I want to say.	You'll know what you want to say when you've written enough to work it out.
My writing will never be good enough.	It will if you practise writing.
I need to start at the beginning and write through to the end.	You need to start in the middle and write in chunks, move sections around, experiment.
I must write so well that my work won't need editing.	That's impossible, even for experienced professional writers; your work will need to go through several drafts.
I can't write unless I have a clear morning/afternoon/day.	In just five minutes, you can write 150 words in longhand, or 300 on a keyboard.
Everything I write is rubbish.	No it's not – although doubtless it can be improved. But so can the work of many published writers.
Writing is too hard for me; I can't do it.	When did you last write an e-mail? A text message? A status update or comment on a social networking site? They're all writing. You can write. All you have to do is keep going.

The good news is that writing is something almost anyone can learn to do, and to do well. This chapter will provide some pointers to help you. If you want to find out more after reading it, there are many excellent how-to books on writing, some of which are in the bibliography at the end of this book. And if you would prefer to learn from a teacher, there are a number of writing courses available on the open market.

The writing process

Many people, including very experienced writers, find it quite daunting to start a new piece of writing.

> It's the blank sheet of paper. I think the actual sitting down to start writing and the having a blank sheet of paper, it was almost like the piece of paper got bigger and bigger and bigger and bigger, it was almost like a flip chart rather than something on a screen.

 *Don't wait for the muse. She won't turn up.*

It may help you to know that writing often starts in the middle. I began writing this book with part of the chapter on data collection. As I draft this chapter, I have written probably two-thirds of the introduction and Chapters Three and Seven, one third of Chapters Four and Five, and one quarter of Chapter Eight. I didn't write them in that order. I'm avoiding Chapter Six because I'm scared of it, and I haven't thought much about the rest. I'm writing this section now because it's the bit I feel like writing now – I'm away from home, and I can begin drafting this section without access to my reference books or interview data. These kinds of things are, for me, what dictate which part I write next – not the order that the book will finally take.

> I had to start writing it, and I thought, I don't know how to do this. I think I thought I'd got to write it all as a continuous stream of narrative, but actually it was pointed out to me that you could break it up and talk about the various categories you'd found, and what you thought the significance of these was in relation to one another, and any reading or literature you'd got. Once I'd realised that, it was fine.

Breaking the work down into chunks makes a daunting prospect feel much more manageable.

> I do it by breaking it down into small, manageable tasks, so not thinking "OMG I've got to do a 20,000 word literature review", but thinking "What are the points I've got to make?" Then writing a section at a time, seeing the small things that will ultimately build into the bigger. Stop thinking about the bigger picture and start looking for the smaller take, whether it's themes or codes, and just keep your eye on the small key points and then write around those and look for the links.

Taking the approach of writing whichever section you feel most inclined to write can help to overcome anxiety. So can letting go of perfectionism. Freewriting can be useful here (Murray, 2011a: 101): set yourself a prompt related to your project, and write for 10 minutes (or five if you can type fast) without stopping or censoring yourself. This can be used to problem-solve or just to get you going. The kinds of prompts I use are along these lines:

- The main features of my method are …
- I want my data analysis to …
- I don't want to write because …
- I would like my research to achieve …

During the freewriting period, if I find my fingers flagging, I rewrite the prompt and carry on. I recommend trying freewriting if you've never had a go; as well as being helpful for getting your writing under way, it often yields surprisingly useful nuggets that you can transfer to your actual write-up. But if freewriting doesn't work for you, don't worry; the most important thing is to get words down on the page in whatever form comes most easily.

> I went back and wrote something that my supervisor, she said she just splurges, writes anything that's to do with whatever it is to get going, get into the flow of putting something on paper. If you don't use it again that's fine, if you do it's great. I used bullet points, wrote lists of bullet points, or I'd deconstruct a quote to work out what I thought about it, and that got me going again.

The best time-saving tip for writing is: write. Just write it down. Anything relevant, in any order. You can sort out the structure later on.

Writing, however haphazardly, will help you to clarify your thoughts and develop your ideas. Conversely, not writing when you need to write will increase anxiety and reduce self-confidence. My own first-draft writing is full of question marks where I can't think of the word or simile that I want, and stern reminders to myself in capitals that say things like WRITE MORE HERE or LINK THIS SECTION TO THE NEXT. That's fine. One thing I do find is that when I start to feel stuck during the actual process of writing, there's no point trying to get unstuck. It's like the classic scenario of the person who is mired in mud, and struggling only gets them in deeper. The best thing to do is make a note and move on. When I come back another day to the part that says WRITE MORE HERE, I often find I know what I want to write, when previously my mind had been as blank as the page in front of me. And when I reach LINK THIS SECTION TO THE NEXT, suddenly I can see how to make that link.

Set yourself a daily or weekly word count – and stick to it.

Make a commitment to yourself that each day, or each week, you will write a certain number of words. That number doesn't have to be very high. If you write 500 words per day, you will have written the first draft of a 15,000-word dissertation in a month. Five hundred words is not very many; it's about a page of

A4 typed in 12-point Arial. When I started writing seriously, I found 500 words per day was manageable. These days I find weekly goals easier, and my weekly goal for the first draft of this book was 5,000 words (which is equivalent to 715 words per day, so not that much more).

Do not try to edit your work while you are writing the first draft.

Being a researcher requires you to have shape-changing abilities. While working with literature and documents, you need meticulous recording skills. When you are collecting primary data, you are likely to need a high level of interpersonal skills, as well as a nerdy love of accurate recording. When you are coding data, you need geek-level thoroughness. But all this perfectionism is no use to you as a writer of research. Of course you need to write as accurately as possible and report your findings carefully and honestly. But when it comes to the actual art of writing, perfectionism is not an option.

We began to touch on the reason for this in Chapter Five, which explained about the richness of the English language and the range of synonyms available to writers. It is possible to agonise for hours, even days, about whether a sentence should use the word 'outstanding' or the alternative 'exceptional'. This is a monumental waste of time because there can never be a perfect piece of writing. As with doing research, there are lots of ways to write badly, but also lots of ways to write well.

One way to write well is to keep your reader in mind (Becker, 2007: 18). What does a reader of research need to know? Essentially, they need to know *what you did, why you did it, how you did it, and what you found* as a result (Clark–Carter, 2010: 392). In academic terms, they need you to help them understand your 'argument'. The word 'argument' has a slightly different meaning for researchers than for other people. It doesn't mean a quarrel, it means one side of an intellectual debate that is well reasoned and based on evidence (Jesson, Matheson and Lacey, 2011: 66). Readers need this conveyed to them in clear, readable English, within a structure that is easy for them to navigate.

Work out who your readers are and keep them in mind as you write. What do they need to know? What is the simplest way you can tell them?

The Plain English Campaign advises all writers to:

- be concise;
- use short words where possible;
- vary sentence length, but aim for an average of 15–20 words;
- avoid jargon;
- if you need to use technical terms, give an explanation of each one;
- use active rather than passive verbs (for example 'she collected the data' rather than 'the data was collected by her');
- write as if you are speaking to your reader;
- make sure your writing is helpful and polite.

If you want more information about writing in plain English, the Plain English Campaign has a good website with a number of free resources.

In some ways, with writing, it's easier to be specific about what you should *not* do than about what you should do. So here are some things to avoid.

Poor spelling, grammar, punctuation and so on. If you have difficulty with this, ask someone to check your writing for errors. Also, there is loads of advice on the World Wide Web, so anything you're not sure about, look up. (We all have blind spots. I've lost count of the times I've checked the difference between 'practise' and 'practice'. I'm still not sure, without looking first.)

Unhelpful structure. It's worth thinking about ways in which your report can be made easy for readers to navigate. Page numbers, headings, chapter titles, the contents list and an index all help readers to find their way around your work. The structures for workplace research or evaluation reports, and for academic dissertations or theses, are not so very different. The standard sections of these structures, and the purpose of each section, are outlined in Table 9.2. These aren't hard-and-fast rules, but in practice, most reports, dissertations, and theses follow a similar structure.

Long sentences. The Plain English Campaign advises using no more than 25 words per sentence. Don't worry about this when you're writing your first draft, but it's useful to keep in mind when editing.

Long words. Of course you need to use long words at times, but always choose shorter ones if you can. Some people think the use of longer words demonstrates their sophistication and cleverness and makes for impressive writing. In fact they are likely to make your reader want to stop reading. The word 'sesquipedalian' is a useful example: I'm sure most readers would prefer 'someone who tends to use long words' – which is what 'sesquipedalian' means. It is more difficult to produce clear and concise writing than to be obscure and verbose, but your readers will much prefer the former.

Table 9.2: Structures for research reports, dissertations, and theses

Workplace research/evaluation report structure	Purpose of section	Academic dissertation/ thesis structure	Purpose of section
Executive summary	To tell people about your work in as few words as possible	Abstract	To tell people about your work in as few words as possible
Introduction	Introducing your research and why you're doing it	Introduction	Introducing your research and why you're doing it
Document review	Putting your research into context (optional – otherwise context may be covered in introduction)	Literature review	Putting your research into context
Method	How you did your research	Method	How you did your research
Findings	What you found out	Results	What you found out
Discussion	The implications of your research for practice (may be linked with theory; may include recommendations)	Discussion	What your findings mean – link with theory and, if relevant, practice
Conclusion	Next steps	Conclusion	The implications of your research
Appendices	Relevant supplementary information	Appendices	Relevant supplementary information

Research reports, dissertations, or theses that are longer than they need to be. There is a famous quotation, which has been attributed to all sorts of people from Pliny the Younger to Mark Twain, that reads: 'I'm sorry I didn't have time to write you a short letter, so I wrote this long one instead.' In academic research you will have a word count, but it's a maximum rather than a target. You won't lose any marks for saying everything you need to say in fewer words, and you will always gain marks for clarity. This is also good practice in workplace research.

Unedited work. However skilled you are in using the English language, you will always have to edit your writing if you are going to make it as good as it can be.

Use of jargon or technical terms. In some cases there may be no alternative, in which case make sure you also include a clear definition of the word.

Clichés. Avoid these like the plague, because familiarity breeds contempt. More to the point, a cliché doesn't have the impact that a fresh turn of phrase will bring to your work.

Repetition. There are times where you need to reiterate something, for example a point made in the introduction to a lengthy research report or thesis, of which you wish to remind the reader when you reach the conclusion. Reiteration is effective writing to help the reader understand your argument. Repetition, on the other hand, is annoying for readers and should be avoided.

Trying to write and edit at the same time. The first draft and the final draft require different skills. To begin with, just get the words down in a way that makes sense to you. At this stage, don't worry about whether they will make sense to anyone else. As the well-known novelist Elmore Leonard said: "The first draft is always shit." This also applies to non-fiction.

Trying to edit as soon as you finish writing. This won't work. You need to leave your draft alone for a good chunk of time so you can come back to it with fresh eyes. A month is good; six weeks is better. If you have only a week, then take a week.

Proof-reading your own work. It's notoriously difficult to spot your own errors. And it's fine to get someone else to proof-read your work, even for an academic qualification, as long as they're only looking for things like typos, grammatical mistakes, numerical errors, and omitted references.

Leaving your writing to the last minute. Writing is an iterative process and you need to give it time if you're going to do it well. Most good writing goes through at least three drafts: the first draft, where you churn out the words; the second, where you knock it into shape; and the third, where you review your word choices, grammar, and structure. You need to rest your draft between each stage. So leaving your writing to the last minute is a really, really bad idea.

Another reason why it's a good idea to do your writing with plenty of time to spare is that then you can ask someone to give you feedback on your work. Writing is always improved by feedback, but the process may not be easy or comfortable, particularly if you haven't had much – or any – experience of this. It's important not to be protective about your writing, as you need to be willing to accept and use constructive criticism if you're going to produce your best work. Feedback is an invaluable opportunity to learn. There is more about dealing with feedback in the section on editing later in this chapter.

 Always read your work out loud before you decide it's finished. It's amazing how many typos, grammatical errors, and clunky sentences you discover when reading out loud that you couldn't see on the page.

Structure

As shown in Table 9.2, most research reports, whether workplace or academic, have a similar overarching structure, which is something like: introduction, methods, findings, discussion, conclusions/recommendations, appendices. Within this, the writer needs to use sub-headings that enable the reader to find their way around the report. These should be in a logical order. Ideally, if you listed all the sub-headings with none of the text, the reader should be able to understand how the information you wish to communicate flows through the report. Doing this as an exercise at intervals, as you write the report, can help you to identify gaps, overlaps, and inconsistencies.

Another potentially useful exercise, particularly for dissertations and theses, is to pull out the first and last paragraph of each chapter. Again, the information being conveyed should flow smoothly through these sections of your writing. As with the sub-headings, doing this exercise can help you to identify omissions, repetitions, and other structural errors.

A contents list will be helpful for your readers, and this is easy to produce with most word processing software. An index is also helpful, but this is more complicated to produce. Word processing software will often create a basic index, but compiling a full index that will be most helpful to readers is a specialist job and therefore costs money. A good compromise may be to generate a basic index using your software, and then have a quick check through to see if there's anything that might be useful to readers that you can add to the basic index. It's not possible for an inexperienced indexer to foresee every item that a reader might wish to look up, but it's still worth doing what you can to improve on the basic index.

Remember to number your pages.

Some people, perhaps particularly inexperienced writers, need to write first and create their structure later. Others are more comfortable starting with the structure.

> I sit down and construct a framework and then backfill it with references, so you get the idea of what you're going to write. You construct a framework, go and do your reading, and it's just like building a big jigsaw.

If you are going to start with the structure, you either need enough understanding of the subject area to know the main issues that are likely to arise, or enough flexibility to amend your structure as necessary in response to unexpected ideas or connections.

Plagiarism

Plagiarism means presenting someone else's ideas or words as your own original work (Murray, 2011a: 135). This is a form of theft, because – in the Western world – original ideas and words are regarded as the 'intellectual property' of the person who created them. Plagiarism is also a form of fraud because the plagiariser is lying about the origins of the ideas and/or words they have used. It is a serious academic offence, with various penalties for students, ranging from the plagiariser's receiving a zero mark for the piece of work concerned to expulsion from the entire course. Plagiarism is not a crime in law, although it may involve copyright infringement, if the original source is copyrighted. In most countries copyright infringement is a legal offence that can land the offender in a court of law to face the full might of the judicial system.

Luckily, plagiarism is easy to avoid. Knowing the reasons for plagiarism will help. It is unlikely that many people set out to plagiarise, but some may be tempted, due to factors such as:

- pressure, from managers, tutors, families, friends, and so on, to do well in studies or workplace research;
- peer pressure from other researchers who think plagiarism is a short cut to success;
- feelings of inadequacy leading the researcher to feel that they can never produce anything as good as the work of others;
- looming deadlines leaving insufficient time for the careful reading, interpretation, and analysis that are essential for good-quality research.

Plagiarism may also occur by accident due to factors such as:

- inadequate record keeping, which can make it difficult or impossible to find information when it's needed for a reference list or citation;
- errors in paraphrasing, which can lead to someone else's work being interpreted incorrectly, in such a way that plagiarism results;
- incorrect citation methods, such as using a quote from someone else's work but forgetting to use quotation marks, or paraphrasing and failing to include the citation.

Even if plagiarism occurs by accident, it is still highly unethical. Remember that accidents can be prevented. As a researcher, 'I didn't mean to' or 'I didn't notice' are not defences against plagiarism. It is your responsibility to do research to high ethical standards. To avoid plagiarism, you need to cite others' work correctly. This means that you must make sure that you have enough time to do your research work thoroughly, and you must keep your records accurate and up to date.

You also need to be able to paraphrase, that is, to restate an idea or argument in your own words. This is a skill that is rarely taught, even on research-methods courses. And it's not easy. To paraphrase effectively, you need a clear understanding of what you have read, and a good command of English to be able to restate it clearly and accurately in your own words. This also, inevitably, means using a different structure from that chosen by the original author.

Some novice researchers find paraphrasing quite daunting and decide to rely almost entirely on quotes from other people's work. This is understandable, but not a good move, especially in academic research, where your tutor or examiner will want to see evidence that you have developed skills in interpreting and analysing text. Paraphrasing is a good way to develop and demonstrate these skills.

Let's look at an example. We'll assume that I am working on a review of the literature about the role of emotion in paid work. I have found an excerpt of text that is relevant:

> For about one in three of all British workers, exhaustion, stress or both have become an inescapable part of their working lives. That is a shocking failure of our imagination and our will to devise a work culture that sustains human well-being rather than erodes it. A job that demands a huge proportion of an individual's energy, time and emotional resources is a job that is unsustainable; it passes the cost on to the worker in terms of their health, and to his or her partner, children, friends and community.(Bunting, 2004: 177)

Here is an inappropriate paraphrase, with the words I have changed in bold:

> Bunting (2004: 177) says that for **1 in 3** workers **in the UK**, exhaustion **and** stress **are** an **inevitable** part of their **work**. **It is** shocking **that we cannot create** a work culture that **supports people's** well-being **rather than damaging it**. **If work** demands **most of someone's** energy, time and emotional resources **then that is** unsustainable **because it will damage the worker's** health **and put pressure on** his or her **family and** friends **as well as the wider** community.

This paraphrase is inappropriate because all I have done is change some words and phrases for other, synonymous words and phrases. The structure of the paraphrase is identical to that of the original, and I have not restated the passage in my own words. This is one form of plagiarism.

Here is a more appropriate paraphrase.

> According to Bunting (2004: 177), exhaustion and stress are an inevitable part of the work of as many as one-third of British workers. Her view is that this is unsustainable because of the damage it causes, not only to the health of those workers, but also in the knock-on effects for their families, their friends, and the wider community.

Here I am crediting Bunting for the fact in the first sentence of the paraphrase, and for the opinion in the second sentence. It is also an appropriate paraphrase because I have departed from the structure of the original. I have chosen not to include the more journalistic opinion from the second sentence of the original text because, having read Bunting's work carefully, I don't think leaving it out changes the meaning of her argument. I have restructured the quote and restated it in my own words to give my picture of Bunting's argument, which demonstrates that I can analyse and interpret text written by someone else. Therefore this is not plagiarism.

You will notice that I have included only the author's surname, year of publication and page number within my own text. This enables the reader to turn to my bibliography, which is in alphabetical order for ease of navigation, and find the full reference:

> Bunting, M. (2004) *Willing slaves: How the overwork culture is ruling our lives*, London: HarperCollins.

Citation

'Citation' means stating the details of the source of an idea, fact, or opinion that you draw on in your research. 'Source' could be many things: book, article, website, video, dataset, radio programme, personal communication, and so on. In your citation, you should give enough information to enable the reader to track down and read your source if they wish to do so – and if that is possible. In some cases, such as personal communications, tweets, or broadcast media, it may not be possible. However, this is no excuse for sloppy citation. All details should be given wherever possible, such as dates, names, and page numbers. If you give a web page address or URL as part of a citation, you should also give the date when you looked at the web page, because the content and/or URLs of web pages frequently change. As discussed in Chapter Six, the move towards using DOIs may help to resolve this problem, for some sources, in time.

You do not have to cite sources for every single point you make. If you are referring to common phenomena that are widely known, such as that more men than women are convicted of criminal offences, or that dementia occurs more frequently in older than younger people, you do not have to cite a source. A good rule of thumb is: if in doubt, cite a source.

If you're new to referencing or struggling to understand the principles of citation or paraphrasing, I recommend *Cite Them Right* by Richard Pears and Graham Shields, published by Palgrave in 2010 (8th edition).

Broadly, there are two methods of citation: the 'bracket' method and the 'note' method. The bracket method is the one used in this book, where the name of the author(s), the year of publication and sometimes the page number are included within the text in brackets. The full reference is then given in a reference list or bibliography, usually at the end of the document and listed in alphabetical order. This system is sometimes known as Harvard referencing. The note method uses consecutive numerical superscript references[1] to the references in the bibliography, which are then listed in order of citation. This system is sometimes known as Vancouver referencing. In either system, each reference is only listed once in the bibliography, no matter how many times it is cited in the text.

There are guides to these systems online, as well as some established referencing systems to choose from, such as those of the American Psychological Association and the Modern Humanities Research Association. Whatever system you use, it is essential that you use it consistently; you should not mix and match different referencing systems within the same piece of research work.

If you are doing workplace research, you can probably make up your own mind about the referencing system you prefer. Universities usually have a system that their researchers are required to use, so if you're doing academic research, ask your tutor about this or check your university's website.

Citations also allow you to frame your own ideas. So, for example, I might add to the paraphrase given earlier as follows:

> According to Bunting (2004: 177), exhaustion and stress are an inevitable part of the work of as many as one-third of British workers. Her view is that this is unsustainable because of the damage it causes, not only to the health of those workers, but also in the knock-on effects for their families, their friends, and the wider community. On 16 May 2011, a press release from the mental health charity Mind stated that it had commissioned a professional research organisation to survey over 2,000 workers in England and Wales, and it had found that 41% were 'stressed or very stressed in their jobs'. So it seems that workplace stress may be on the increase in the UK.

---

[1] Like this.

This includes a second citation (the Mind press release) and a final sentence giving my own idea. You will notice that I have worded it carefully, saying 'it seems that workplace stress may be on the increase' rather than 'workplace stress is on the increase'. This is for two reasons. First, despite careful reading, I'm not sure where Bunting got her figure of 'about one in three' workers, so I don't want to rely on it too heavily. Second, Bunting's figure refers to 'British workers', that is, including those in Northern Ireland and Scotland as well as the workers in England and Wales who were surveyed for the Mind research. It may be that workers in Northern Ireland and Scotland experience much less workplace stress than do those in England and Wales, which would explain the differences in the figures. My own opinion is that this is unlikely, but I must acknowledge the possibility, hence my cautious wording.

All research is part of a massive worldwide expression of humankind's thirst for knowledge. Your research builds on the knowledge created by others, and it generates knowledge for use by those coming afterwards. The proper use of citations demonstrates this in two ways. First, citations acknowledge and show respect for the work of authors who have gone before you. Second, citations show care for the researchers who come behind you, by enabling readers to follow your thought processes back to their sources, if they wish to do so.

Findings versus recommendations

Findings are simply what you have found out through doing the research. In most academic and some workplace research, a discussion of your findings is all that is needed, although there may be recommendations for future research. In other research, particularly evaluation research, you need to write recommendations for future action. These recommendations should be unmistakably rooted in your findings, and should also be possible to implement (Robson, 2011: 507). This requires a good working knowledge of the real-world context for the research. So, for example, an evaluation of an outreach service provided by a statutory organisation may find that service users want twice as much of the service as they get. It might seem that a sensible recommendation in this case would be for the service users to get twice as much of the service as they do at present. However, the statutory organisation has neither the capacity nor the funding to provide more of the service. So recommendations might include: seeking other sources of funding; increasing the capacity of the service, perhaps through secondments or restructuring; looking at services provided by the third sector to see whether some of the service users' needs could be met by other services; and so on. Writing recommendations can require quite a bit of lateral thinking, and sometimes some last-minute research into feasibility. It is all worthwhile, though, when you see the fruits of your labours in the form of improved provision for service users.

Editing

When your first draft is complete, celebrate! Yes, it's messy and full of holes – but it's also your raw material, the ingredients from which you can craft a perfectly cooked report or thesis. It's a massive milestone reached, and you deserve a reward. Leave the draft alone for a while – at least a week, longer if time allows. You need to be able to read it with fresh eyes. It is really hard to edit your own work effectively, so feedback from others on the readability of your writing is useful at this stage.

Accepting feedback on writing can be difficult when you've sweated and wept your way to the point you've reached (Becker, 2007: 6). Even very constructive criticism can hurt and leave you feeling defensive. Try to get feedback in writing, and take time to digest and consider it before responding. Remember that the person giving the feedback has voluntarily contributed their time and skills to your project, and aim to respond with your head rather than your heart.

The ability to accept feedback gracefully is essential for a researcher, because your conclusions or recommendations are likely to receive criticism even if your writing is beyond compare. So it helps to start acquiring this skill at the writing stage.

If you are doing workplace research, you will have to decide whether to ask for feedback from a colleague who knows a lot about your work or from one who knows a little. Each approach has advantages and disadvantages. Someone who knows a lot about your work may be able to give more detailed feedback, but may also want to influence your research more than you are comfortable with. Someone who knows a little about your work may be able to give a more balanced perspective on your research, but may not have the in-depth knowledge necessary to give a more thorough response. Only you can decide which will be best, in the light of your needs and the individual personalities involved.

While you can ask for very detailed feedback on workplace research if you wish, the situation is rather different with academic research. Here it is much more important that the work is entirely yours. This does not mean that it is inappropriate to ask for and use feedback from others, but those giving feedback should restrict themselves to commenting on the quality of your writing rather than engaging with the arguments you make. This can be a fine line. For example, where a point is unclear, this may be because of insufficient writing skill or because the subject hasn't been fully thought through. Therefore the person giving feedback should confine themselves to pointing out the lack of clarity, and leave it to you to find a way to solve the problem.

When you have your feedback, consider each point carefully. The points made will fall into three categories:

1. The no-brainer, which you will want to implement immediately. Typographical, grammatical and spelling errors fall into this category, as do

any more complex suggestions that make immediate sense to you, for example for simplifying the structure of part or all of your work.

2.   The no-thanks, which you will never want to implement. These often occur when the person giving the feedback hasn't entirely grasped the point you're trying to make and thinks the problem lies with the writing. However, these pieces of feedback can be a useful indication that a careful review of the relevant section would be a good idea.

3.   The in-betweener. These require more thought. They may occur because the person giving feedback has identified a problem (which you agree with) but has been unable to come up with a solution. They may also occur when you agree with the problem but are not so comfortable with a suggested solution. In either case, you need to find a solution yourself, hence the need for thought.

When you have received and digested your feedback, re-read your draft and make a list of the points you need to address. Then work through the list, systematically, until you have completed all the editing tasks. Now you are ready to polish your writing, and at this stage it is again a good idea to leave it alone for a week or more before starting on the next phase of the work.

Polishing your writing

Polishing involves making sure every detail of your writing is correct. First, you should review the structure of your work at every level: overall document, chapter or section, paragraph, and sentence. It may help to repeat the editing exercises of pulling out all the headings and looking through them to make sure the flow of information is logical and complete, and then pulling out all the first and last paragraphs of each chapter or section and reading them in order, for the same purpose.

When you are happy with the structure, you need to go through your work line by line, checking your grammar, word choices, spelling, and punctuation. As you do this, you can also check that all the references you have cited in the text are in your reference list. I do this by printing out a fresh copy of my reference list and ticking off the references on the list as I go through my writing. This also means that, at the end, I can check that every reference in the list has a tick – if any do not, they should be deleted, as it is not good research etiquette to list references in your reference list if they have not been cited in your writing.

Finally, give your work one last read-through out loud, to pick up any clunky sentences your eyes may have missed.

Polishing is a tedious process but worth doing. You'll be surprised by how many errors and inconsistencies you will pick up. It's best if you can correct these yourself, rather than leaving them for your readers to find.

$$\overline{\text{TEN}}$$

Dissemination

Introduction

The point of disseminating your research is to share the knowledge you have gained through the process. Etymologically, the word 'dissemination' means 'to scatter seeds in every direction'. As gardeners know, not every seed will germinate and take root, but it's important to provide the conditions that will give them the best chance of growth. The same applies with disseminating research.

Dissemination is not easy, and there are usually barriers to overcome. Nevertheless, it is really important, because dissemination is where theory, research, and practice meet. Doing research is a vital way of gathering evidence about a subject, but there's no point gathering all that lovely evidence if you don't tell people what you discovered. Your research is not just for you to learn from, it's for other people too.

Summarising research

Most research outputs are in the form of written reports, dissertations, or theses. These are necessary so that research commissioners, managers, tutors, and examiners can gain a thorough understanding of what has been done, why and how it has been done, and what the findings are. However, these written outputs are usually long and, even when clearly and concisely written, can be difficult to digest. So, for effective dissemination, the researcher needs to produce a summary, sometimes using a different medium.

The classic types of summary are an 'executive summary' for workplace research, which is usually between one and four pages long, or an 'abstract' for academic research, usually 250–500 words long. An executive summary or an abstract should give a distillation of the rationale, method, and findings of the research. These are not easy to write, and will probably take several drafts, but they are useful for two reasons. First, the process will help you to clarify your own understanding of the key points of the research. Second, they are powerful tools for dissemination. Many more people will be prepared to read an executive summary or an abstract than a whole research report, dissertation, or thesis.

Executive summaries and abstracts are quite dry, and there are many other ways to disseminate research. Academic research may be disseminated through such media as journal articles, conference papers and posters, and book chapters. Workplace research may be disseminated through a variety of methods, including meetings, newsletters, exhibitions, and websites. There is a movement among some qualitative and mixed-method researchers, both in the workplace and in academia, towards more creative methods of dissemination, using techniques such as poetry, song, video, and story-telling.[1]

> I'm just coming to the end of a really interesting research dissemination exercise I've been involved in, it was well funded. They wanted a small sub-study filming people about their experiences of having a joint crisis plan, three times over a year and a half, so I've been working with a film-maker to do this work and it's been really fascinating, a really good way forward.

Barriers to dissemination

Dissemination is subject to the same restraints of cost and time as other aspects of research. Also, dissemination involves more work, often at the point when you may be feeling you've had quite enough of your research project. You may have to: rewrite your research for different audiences; produce summaries in different media, such as posters or Microsoft PowerPoint presentations; attend meetings and sound enthusiastic about the findings of a project that is, as far as you're concerned, in the past. And even if you can disseminate your work using only your existing summary or abstract, you may well face other barriers to the process.

---

[1] Personal communication from delegates and organisers at several Qualitative Research conferences hosted by the Centre for Qualitative Research, Bournemouth University.

If you produce research in the course of your work, your employer is likely to hold the copyright to your research report, and will therefore have the right to decide what is done with the findings. Copyright laws vary in different countries. In the UK, the writer of any document holds the copyright to that document unless they have signed some kind of agreement to relinquish their rights over their 'intellectual property' (as creative output is known in legal circles). Research commissioners often demand the right to own the copyright of research that they have paid for, which seems reasonably justifiable. More worryingly, more and more universities are demanding the right to own the copyright of the work of their postgraduate students. The trouble with signing away your rights over your own research is that you lose the power to disseminate your findings. If someone else holds the copyright to your research, they may not disseminate the knowledge you have worked so hard to gain, and this can be enormously frustrating. This may be due to lack of time, will, or resources.

> People that do research for dissertation, they quite often end up choosing a topic that is work related but there isn't a proper forum for such work to be disseminated. If you gain access to the dissertation repositories of the different universities, I think that nationwide there would be a considerable amount of research that is done that is never built on or capitalised.

Also, research commissioners may choose to suppress findings they find unpalatable – which can be understandable in terms of managing political pressures, but is nevertheless highly unethical.

Here is an excerpt from a research brief I received as I was writing this chapter. The commissioning organisation is large, publicly funded, and has a good reputation. Its brief said:

> A report presenting an analysis of the research findings will be required from the successful supplier. However, it should be noted that [commissioning organisation] may publish a report under its own name in respect of this research and reserves the right to draw and add in its own conclusions and recommendations. Proper acknowledgement will be given to the supplier in any [commissioning organisation] report.
>
> [Commissioning organisation] may decide, for various reasons, to keep some of the research findings internal and not include them in the published report. This will be at [commissioning organisation's] discretion.

The organisation has every right to do this in law, and it is presumably seeking to maintain its good reputation. This is eminently sensible when outsourcing research to an as yet unknown supplier who will produce as yet unknown findings and draw as yet unknown conclusions. But my interpretation of its reasoning is also guesswork, as it doesn't say why it stipulates these conditions. The part I have most difficulty with is 'for various reasons', particularly as this comes from an organisation that trumpets its commitment to transparency, accountability, honesty, and openness all over its website. I think it should be transparent, honest, and open about what might cause it to keep some of the research findings internal, and why. The lack of transparency here is unhelpful, as it leads to inevitable but fruitless speculation – will the organisation suppress findings it doesn't like? Will it ignore findings if it doesn't like the *researcher*?

During my career as an independent researcher, I have had some interesting experiences with the ethics of dissemination. At times I have lost clients by holding fast to my ethical position. By contrast, other clients have told me that they value my input particularly because I work to a high ethical standard. This doesn't mean I'm perfect; in my research practice, I have done things that I would now, on reflection, judge as unethical. But I have always aimed to consider ethical issues as fully as possible at all stages of every research process, and to act wherever it seems necessary. I think that's all anyone can ask.

Universities may not have the resources or the will to disseminate all the research that is done by their postgraduate students, and may choose to focus on that which will best serve their purposes. This too is unethical. All knowledge gained should be shared, however unpleasant or unwelcome it may be. There may also be unethical barriers to dissemination of workplace research, as this interviewee explains:

> It's a real political issue, dissemination. We're going to be met with a lot of resistance about putting people's opinions on the website. People worry about what if they say something negative? The organisation censors itself very highly. It could be a department like press and marketing commenting on content and programmes because it wants to advertise or give a certain style of voice. I think it should be content led rather than style led, in a way, content should inform style. It would make me respect an organisation if they said what they could learn from this, because it would make me feel like they want to work with people, but if an institution is only blowing its trumpet, it doesn't feel like it's truly participating in a dialogue at all.

Dissemination methods

Dissemination is most effective when it's tailored to the needs of your various audiences (Robson, 2011: 495). For example, if you are carrying out an evaluation of a community-based service as part of your work, you might:

*   give a full written research report to your manager;
*   talk through your findings in a team meeting;
*   e-mail the executive summary to your colleagues in partner agencies;
*   hold a community event in which research participants help to present the findings to the wider community.

If you are doing doctoral research, you might:

- present your proposed method verbally at a departmental seminar;
- present initial findings through a Microsoft PowerPoint presentation at an academic conference;
- give your written thesis to examiners;
- publish your final conclusions in a peer-reviewed academic journal article.

Dissemination doesn't only happen when the research is completely finished. Sometimes it's useful to disseminate interim findings.

> I did lots of little dissemination exercises that didn't take much but kept them in the loop.

It is also good practice to check findings with participants before finalising research, especially in the workplace. As we saw in Chapter Two, this is ethically sound and can improve the quality of research findings. Disseminating research to participants is also helpful more broadly, in demonstrating the value of participation and the reasons for doing the research.

> There are so many people asking for information, and so little of it is fed back, that people get research fatigue and won't want to get involved.

Sometimes, however, disseminating research to participants can be difficult or impossible. For example, if your participants are itinerant homeless people, or people in police custody, they may not be contactable again at a later stage. But where it does work, it has a number of practical and ethical advantages, as this interviewee found:

> We held a feedback session for the patients that took part and invited every single one of them. We presented it to them first, before anyone had seen anything. We asked them if it was an accurate reflection of what had been said, told them what was going to form the recommendations. "What do you think about these? Are they workable? Have you got any better suggestions?" Then we formed our final. I don't think it happens very often. Most of the patients that were involved, a lot of them had been involved with other things before, there were a significant number that expressed surprise at being invited to come in again at that stage. Most of them said, "We're an afterthought." If you're doing research in the community, they shouldn't be an afterthought.

There are a wide range of possible methods for disseminating research, each of which has its pros and cons. The pros and cons of the most commonly used methods are summarised in Table 10.1.

Table 10.1: Pros and cons of different dissemination methods

Method	Pros	Cons
Written report, dissertation or thesis	Can include full details of the research	Too long for most people to read
Executive summary or abstract	Short length makes it accessible; helps people decide whether to read more	Gives only an overview
Informal presentation at a meeting or seminar	Can be useful for reaching a small group of interested people	May get lost or side-lined if other agenda items take precedence
Formal presentation at a meeting or conference	Can be useful for reaching a larger group of people who may be interested	Nerve racking for some researchers; time consuming; may involve travel and other costs
Peer-reviewed academic journal article	Good for reaching interested academics; career-enhancing for academics and people wanting to be academics	Researcher has no control over reviewer or editorial input; limited audience, especially if not an open access journal
Article in non-peer-reviewed academic journal or professional journal	Should be easier to achieve than peer-reviewed publication; may reach a wider audience of interested people	Not regarded as highly as publication in peer-reviewed journals by some people
E-mail	Can reach a lot of people; cheap/free	Recipients may not read it; won't reach everyone
World Wide Web	Can in theory reach most of the people in the world; cheap/free	Often used as a box-ticking dissemination exercise rather than as part of a well thought-out strategy
Community event	Good way to include research participants; good for local publicity; can be lots of fun	Time consuming and resource intensive
Creative methods (film, art exhibition, drama, and so on)	Unusual, so can attract attention	Time consuming; you need suitable skills
Mass media (newspapers, magazines, radio, TV, and so on)	Can reach a lot of people	Research findings may be misrepresented or taken out of context

When you start thinking about dissemination – which, ideally, should be at an early stage of your research project – you need to consider questions such as:

- Whom do I have to tell about my findings?
- Whom do I want to tell about my findings?
- Who else might find my research useful?

In the same way that research questions help you to identify suitable research methods, the answers to these 'who' questions can help you to work out how best to disseminate your research. When you have answers to these questions, you will know who your potential audiences are. When you know who your audiences are, you can decide which method or methods are likely to be most effective for each audience.

With audiences from your own profession or academic discipline, you can use professional or academic language, without the need to censor or define relevant jargon. With professionals from partner agencies or academics from different disciplines, you can use a fair amount of professional or academic language, with perhaps a definition here and there as you see fit. With professionals from other agencies or non-academics, you will need to keep jargon to a minimum and define any technical terms that you can't avoid using. And with the general public, you will need to use plain English (Clark-Carter, 2010: 392).

The language and structure you use will be different if you are presenting your research in writing than if you are giving a spoken presentation. Everyone uses language and grammar differently in speech than in writing. This is natural, and unconsciously understood, which explains why two of the biggest blunders you can make are to read a verbal presentation from a written script, or to read your PowerPoint slides word for word. Either of these approaches will come across as stilted and unnatural, and will at best bore, and at worst alienate, your audience.

If you need to give a spoken presentation, the key is thorough preparation. Write a full script for your presentation if you like; the process of writing will help to clarify your thoughts, and producing a full script can be a confidence-boosting exercise. But once you have a script, you need to find a way to commit it to memory. I don't mean learning it word for word, although you can if you like, but that would be very time consuming for most people and I believe there are better ways, as recitation is almost as boring as being read to. (I once went to a fringe theatre show in which an actor recited one of the books of Milton's *Paradise Lost*. It was an admirable feat of memory, but not in itself very interesting or entertaining; I'm ashamed to admit that my main remembrance of the event was my amusement at the incongruous sounds from the Morris dancing that was taking place just outside the window.)

My own approach to any verbal presentation is to summarise the presentation as a narrative, whether from a full script or from the ideas in my head. I try to reduce it to around five key elements that I can write on a single index card. So, for example, if I were going to present the story of Little Red Riding Hood, this is what I might write on the card:

- Little girl lives in forest with mother.
- Girl needs to visit sick grandmother but is in danger from big bad wolf.
- Girl makes it to grandmother's, BUT …
- Sick grandmother turns out to be big bad wolf in disguise, eek!
- Little girl saved at last minute by hunter. Phew.

With that index card in my hand, I could spend several minutes telling the story, with embellishment, description, and drama, to bring it to life and entertain my listeners.

> In teaching, I illustrate with stories, and the students respond, it makes sense, it's clear. I use a lot of case studies in assignments and class activities, all of them are from my experience, obviously anonymised but they're real, this is what you're faced with. The feedback I get is that it helps them understand, it makes it real.

The same applies to research. It is often possible to talk about and present research in a story-like way, which is a good idea as people enjoy, remember, and learn from stories (Gabriel, 2000: 1).

Disseminating workplace research

The most common ways in which workplace research are disseminated are:

- by verbal presentation at a meeting or conference;
- by written presentation in a newsletter;
- by e-mail to colleagues;
- on a website.

Verbal presentations can be nerve-racking, particularly if you're presenting interim findings, when you may be less confident in your research than at final presentation stage. Remember, though, that people attending interim presentations may give feedback or make suggestions that will prove invaluable to your research and that you couldn't receive in any other way. Of course this is not guaranteed to happen, but by presenting you are creating a new opportunity for your research to improve, which is good research practice.

Do your preparation carefully and make sure you know what you want to say.

Don't read from a script.

Make a page of bullet-point notes at most; they should be in big print and well spaced to make them easy to read. Some people prefer to use index cards, which are easier to hold unobtrusively. If you wish, or are required, to use PowerPoint, again, don't read what you've put on your slides. Try to use pictures rather than words where possible, so the audience can look at the pictures while they listen to your words.

Google Images is a great source of pictures for PowerPoint presentations, but do avoid any that are subject to copyright.

Try to make your words into stories. As well as the benefits for your audience outlined earlier in this chapter, creating stories will help you to remember what it is that you want to say.

As you present your work, aim to relax as much as possible, and take your time.

Invite the audience to question you as you go along if they want you to clarify anything. The prospect of taking questions may seem terrifying, but you need to have confidence in your research and in your own knowledge of your research. The most likely outcome is that the audience will be interested in what you have to say, and will ask questions that you can answer easily. If anyone asks you something you can't answer straight away, say so, get their contact details if you don't already have them, and tell them you will find an answer for them.

It can be helpful to give people a short hand-out with the key points from your research. This should include your contact details so that people can get in touch with you later if they think of something else they would like to ask or contribute.

A written presentation, whether for a newsletter, an e-mail circular to colleagues, or a website, should be clear and concise. Again, it should include your contact details, so that people can get back to you if they have any questions.

There are more creative ways to disseminate workplace research, such as through a drama performance or an art exhibition. Some workplaces take more readily to these than others, schools and museums being two of the main ones in my experience. Using creative methods can stimulate interest from people where it might not otherwise exist. However, it is important not to let the method of dissemination obscure the messages you want to communicate.

Dissemination of research findings is often a low priority in busy public service organisations.

> To be honest, unless it's a major project and there's been a catastrophe, there doesn't seem to be anywhere that the findings go to, from my department.

This is both unfortunate and unethical, because it prevents the learning from that research being shared.

Even where the conditions for dissemination are good, colleagues may be dismissive of research that they feel is telling them something they already know. This happens most often with evaluation research. 'What's the point of doing all that research,' they may say, 'to tell us what we knew already?' The answer is that there is now evidence for their assertions (Oliver, 2010b: 134), evidence that may be useful as a lever in making necessary changes to the service or obtaining funding. Sometimes 'what everybody knows' is actually wrong. At other times, the conclusion is correct, but the reasoning is incorrect. For example, providers of a service that is in great demand may conclude that their service is well used because it is of good quality. A service evaluation may show that there are many ways in which the quality of the service could be improved, and it is only well used because there is no other similar service within easy reach. This is why managers, funders, and so on are reluctant to make decisions on the basis of 'what everyone knows' and much prefer to base their reasoning on evidence.

Disseminating academic research

The most common ways in which academic research is disseminated are:

1. Through a verbal presentation at a seminar, workshop or conference, often known as 'giving a paper' – the written version may be published in conference proceedings.
2. Through a poster at a conference.
3. As an article in an academic journal.
4. As a chapter in an academic book.

There are two important differences between workplace and academic conference presentations. First, you have to apply to give a presentation at an academic conference, usually by sending an abstract or summary of your paper – which can be difficult when you haven't written the paper yet because the conference is six months away and you're still in the middle of collecting data. Second, if you are accepted for an academic presentation, you need to write a fully referenced paper, similar to a journal article.

Traditionally you would have been expected to read the paper to the audience. These days this is less often the case, and I think there are two reasons for this. First, people rarely speak faster than 150 words per minute, which means that a 20-minute presentation can only be 2,500 words long – and that is a very short space in which to put forward a rounded and well-reasoned argument (and much shorter than most journal articles, which usually weigh in at around

6,000–9,000 words). Second, listening to an inexperienced and unskilled reader can be unbelievably boring, which makes it hard to engage with their argument.

The best way to give an academic paper is to write the paper and then prepare and deliver a presentation, following the advice on workplace presentations given earlier in this chapter. You should provide hand-outs: either a full copy of your written paper, or a summary of the key points, with your e-mail address so that anyone who wants the full paper can get it from you by e-mail.

Academic conferences often have space for posters to be displayed, and these are intended to present a summary of research findings. Like verbal presentations, posters can cover interim or final findings. They are usually large in size, like a flip-chart sheet or even larger. Visual learners often enjoy making and looking at posters, while others may view the prospect with dread. If you are planning to make a poster, here are a few tips:

Find out the size of poster preferred by the event organisers, and what kind of fixings they intend to use.

Don't use large areas of dense text.

Do use attention-grabbing visuals such as headings, pictures, graphs, cartoons, and so on.

Don't make it too busy – keep it simple to get your messages across more effectively.

Do include your contact details.

Make two copies and transport them separately (ideally in suitably sized cardboard tubes) in case one gets damaged.

Academics, too, may be open to more creative methods of dissemination. I have been to conferences and seminars where research findings have been communicated through song, poetry, story-telling, and multimedia presentations.

The advice on writing in Chapter Nine will help if you are aiming at publication in an academic journal or book. However, writing up all or part of your work for professional publication involves some different and specific skills. If you want to write for a journal, you need to decide which journal is most appropriate, and then research that journal to find out as much as you can about its criteria for publication, how its articles are structured, their length, and so on (Murray, 2009: 47). You also need to be prepared to receive and deal with detailed feedback from reviewers, which you may disagree with and which may even be destructive (Murray, 2009: 193). Writing a chapter in an academic book can be an easier process, but you can't simply decide to write a chapter, you need to wait for someone who is editing a book to ask you to become involved.

Dissemination of research findings is a higher priority in academic research than in other workplaces. This doesn't mean it's easier. Competition for places to present at conferences can be fierce. Also, conference presentations are often concurrent, which means there may be several taking place at the same time, and conference delegates can choose which to attend. It can feel dispiriting when you have worked hard for months to reach the point of presenting your work, and you are faced with six people scattered around a room that could hold 80. But don't be discouraged: those are the six people who are really interested in your work, and may well have useful contributions to offer, both during your presentation and later in the conference as you meet over coffee or lunch.

Dissemination ethics

Disseminating research is an ethical act in itself, but only if the research is presented accurately, fully, and accessibly, to the right people. The question of who 'the right people' are can sometimes be a tricky one to answer. Generally speaking, it is held to be good practice to include all your research participants. However, this can be difficult if your participants are, for example, itinerant homeless people or terminally ill people. It can also cause anxiety for the researcher, as this interviewee shows:

> For me, when I do a piece of research, I send it out to all the people who took part in it, and that's daunting in case you've misrepresented them.

As well as participants, your dissemination should ideally include everyone else who has an interest in the research. This includes funders, commissioners, tutors, supervisors, people who helped you along the way, people who work with your research participants, and so on. It is not always easy to know how best to approach your potential audiences. Simply putting your research on the Web does not make it accessible unless you tell people where it is. It is equally pointless to send a fat research report to everyone you can think of, because that would be expensive and most of them wouldn't read it. You need a strategy somewhere in between the two options.

Put both a summary and the full report on the Web, and send people a short e-mail describing your research, with links they can click on if they want to read more.

Closing the dissemination loop

There's not much point banging on about the importance of disseminating research without some acknowledgement that it's also important to be receptive to research disseminated by others. Whether you ever want to do any more research yourself or not, your experience of conducting research should make you a more discerning reader of other people's research. As a minimum, you should read the journal that is most relevant to your practice. However, achieving even this minimum standard isn't always easy.

> We often joke, can you imagine if you're sitting at your desk in a busy social work office reading the *British Journal of Social Work* and the manager comes out and says, "What are you doing, we've got 12 cases that need assessment here?" It's flippant, but there is a real link. If you want practitioners that are evidence based you've got to have time to do it, to read, to keep up to date.

Research into practice

As we saw in Chapter Two, there are a number of barriers that can make it difficult to use the knowledge gained by research to improve your practice. Practitioners, particularly those who become involved in research, often find these barriers intensely frustrating. This is because they can see how theory and research could benefit their service users in practice, and therefore improve society as a whole.

There's a belief that research is done by academics, uni people. We need to be bringing that more to the workplace, that's where I see bridging the gap between the theory and practice.

There are a lot of jobs within the police where research as a function could revolutionise the way policing is done. The growth in analysts, that's very interesting. What the analysts do is look at crime intelligence and look at patterns. It's a type of profiling, but it can go deeper than that. If they could learn to be sophisticated enough to use different sociological theories, based on a sample of live data that they have, they would be able to come up with explanations and action plans for how to address crime in that particular area.

I wish that more nurses, midwives and health visitors would embrace research and audit to improve their practice and develop the professions. It is a fascinating experience, an achievement, and skills that are transferable in a number of practical ways.

What I'd like to see is a real valuing of research in practice and that's got to come from practitioners and employers as well.

The good news is that practitioners who undertake research are in a position to help break down these barriers. Practitioners may not have the power to change commissioning or management practices, but practitioners can use their research findings to inform and develop their work (Bloor, 2011: 413).

During the MA process I learned that you can generate your own theory, and I think that is something you have to learn, because – particularly in my bit of the world – you are presented with *the* theories about child development, how children learn, staff training and development, and you think, "Ooh, all these famous people have done all this." And actually you can generate your own, and it is valid if you've got the data to back it up, and you can talk about the way you've analysed it, and why you've done it like you have. It's something about how your confidence grows as you're doing it.

Research conducted by practitioners often addresses real-world, front-line problems. Doing research well, and disseminating it thoroughly, can help to demystify research and increase people's confidence in the process.

ELEVEN

Conclusion

One interviewee for this book, a researcher who is also an experienced tutor and supervisor of practitioners undertaking research, gave me her views about what she thought practitioners coming to research for the first time would find most challenging.

> I think the thing with practitioners is, there are certain things that are straightforward and others that are mystical and magical and difficult. They can formulate really good research questions that are really meaningful in practice, they've got all the skills to make research work: engage people quickly, good communication skills, can explain research in lay terms, they can use all of those personal skills that they've got but the theoretical stuff and the analysis that goes around it tends to be more difficult. It's interesting and relates to everything they do, so finding the focus is the hardest bit, especially finding a very small and contained research question that means it's manageable and leads to a small piece of analysis is often the trick. The students who don't do very well often fail to find that focus adequately, they think they've got it going in but it gets a bit flaky when it comes to analysis. They do bring a lot of strengths to the research process, they have to manage the identity of a researcher rather than a practitioner, but it's really the theoretical and analytic bits where they need the input.

Judging by the input from other interviewees, this is an accurate summary of the situation. Another part of the work that has proved to be difficult for beginner researchers is learning to have confidence in your own work and your knowledge. This also applies to both workplace and academic research.

> There is another researcher that works for the organisation and she was available for me to pick brains and she read through things and made comments and stuff. Interestingly, we clashed over a couple of things, and one of my learning points has been to trust my instincts. I went against my instincts because she has more experience than I do, I deferred to her knowledge and in hindsight I shouldn't have. It meant some of our data couldn't be used. If I was giving people advice, I'd say, "Do listen to what people say that have been involved in research before, but it's your research. If it doesn't sit well with you, take it on board but make your own decision, and don't automatically assume that they will be right just because they have more experience."

> I wish someone had said this to me, you've really got to take responsibility from day one. You've not got to expect the supervisors to have the answers or think other people know better. In that first year you've got to work at developing your own confidence in the field so that you believe the stuff that you're thinking. I do think that was my biggest downfall, not standing up for myself against supervisors.

One essential research skill is the ability to change focus rapidly and frequently. It's a bit like having a zoom lens in your brain. We saw in Chapter Three that you need to narrow the focus of your research topic as you plan your research. The focus changes I'm talking about here are the ones you need to make as you carry out your research project. You need to be able to shift focus from close up (for example, to scrutinise one small piece of data, or to write a single paragraph) to mid-range (for example, to review your tasks for completion in the next week or fortnight) to a wide-angle view of the whole project.

Having said that, I wouldn't recommend using the wide-angle view more than you have to, because it can be so daunting. As soon as you've planned and prioritised, you shouldn't need to look at the project as a whole until you're well under way with writing, except briefly from time to time to make sure you're still on track. Keep it in the back of your mind, and focus from mid-range to close-up.

Let's recap the key points made in this book. First, more and more practitioners in public services are being required to carry out research on top of their day jobs. To do research well, you need to:

- plan early, plan thoroughly;
- read, write, and think, critically, throughout the research process;
- find people you can talk to about your research;
- stay focused on the likely positive outcomes of your research;
- understand the broad paradigms of quantitative, qualitative, mixed-method, and value-based research;

- make sure that research ethics underpin all stages of the process;
- look after yourself as well as everyone else;
- accept support from others;
- remember that research, theory, and practice are closely linked;
- choose your research topic carefully: keep it small, keep it simple;
- write a proposal or plan at an early stage;
- organise your work – including time for breaks;
- manage your time;
- keep meticulous records;
- collect only as much data as you need;
- prepare your data accurately;
- code your data carefully;
- write clearly and concisely;
- disseminate your work widely and effectively;
- reward yourself when you achieve key milestones.

At times, practitioners may feel that their research is so small and local as to be pointless. There is certainly some odd research in the world, such as that celebrated by the Ig Nobel awards, which includes research into why woodpeckers don't get headaches, how to grow diamonds from tequila, or how far penguins can poo (note: I did not make these up). But I think any research that aims to improve conditions for fellow human beings is worth doing, however small and local it may be.

Doing, and using, research is on the increase in public services, so it makes sense to learn the techniques so that you can understand and make effective use of research in your work, even if you don't want to conduct research.

> I say as a practitioner, if you're doing an intervention with someone you need to be able to say why, and the answer, "Because I think it might help," won't cut it. You might be doing it because law or policy dictates, or because it's the procedure of your agency, but that will be because research tells us it works. Or if you're in a commissioning agency, and tasked with commissioning a service for drug and alcohol users, and someone comes to you and says, "We do this because the research shows it works," and someone else says, "We do this because we think it helps," it's pretty clear who you're going to give your money to.

Research is an uncomfortable business. As a researcher, you're giving the unknown and the uncertain a large role in your life. Most people are not willing to do this because it can make you feel so uncomfortable. Console yourself with this: if you don't feel very comfortable when you're doing research, you're probably doing it right.

I wish you the very best of luck.

Job titles of interviewees

All interviewees worked in the public and/or third sectors in at least one of their jobs. I asked interviewees to give me their job title(s) in a form that they thought best represented what they did, not necessarily in the form that was used by their employer(s). I was also concerned to protect the anonymity of interviewees, so I have removed any details that might have identified them, such as locations.

1. Marketing and Communications Manager (third sector, cultural)
2. Head of Early Years and Childcare (local authority, children's services, education, social care)
3. Local Involvement Network (LINk) Community Researcher (health)
4. Shared Service Manager (local authority customer services)
5. Management and Training Consultant, Associate Tutor, and Honorary Senior Research Fellow (private sector, criminal justice academic)
6. Head of Bereavement Care (health)
7. Health Protection Team-Project Lead, and Midwifery Lecturer (health, higher education)
8. Third Sector Programme Manager (third sector)
9. University lecturer and tutor, and director of a community-interest company (higher education, third sector)
10. Freelance well-being and mental health consultant (third sector, private sector)
11. Probation officer and Open University Associate Lecturer (criminal justice, higher education)
12. Senior Development Manager: Children and Families Commissioner (NHS) (health)
13. Senior Lecturer and Researcher in Education (higher education, education)
14. Museum Outreach Officer (third sector, cultural)
15. Mental Health User Consultant (private sector, health)
16. Social worker and social work academic (social care, higher education)
17. Reader in Entrepreneurship (criminal justice, higher education)
18. Counsellor and trainer in private practice, and acting project manager in the voluntary sector (private sector, third sector, social care)
19. Senior Lecturer – School of Health and Social Services (higher education, health, social care)
20. Middle management in a further education college (further education)

Sample record-keeping grid

This is a grid used by one of the interviewees for this book, who has left in one reference so you can see how the grid was used.

Author/date/ publisher	Title	Quote/page	Why significant	Where potentially useful
Adair, J., 1988 Pan Books, London	*Effective Leadership*	'There can be no success without working on the edge of failure.' p 142	Risk of 'failure' does this inhibit innovative leadership?	Section on leadership modes

APPENDIX 3

Exchanging information electronically[1]

Modern computer and information systems provide useful scope for people to share information. However, people attempting such sharing sometimes fall foul of the specific mechanisms they choose to use. When trying to share any kind of computerised information with others, it is essential to bear in mind that not everyone uses the same software and data formats. Furthermore, it is often the case that non-technical users do not understand this fact, or how to manage its implications.

The best way to share effectively with even the most non-technical people is to be pre-emptive, and to equip yourself with as much knowledge and understanding as you can about the problems of different computer types and data formats. Ideally, this will enable you to do two things:

1. Make effective use of information that others send to you;
2. Send information to others in a format that they can use in whatever way they need to.

Caveat 1: While this appendix should provide you with some useful general information, it will not provide an exhaustive guide to every possible permutation of data and file formats and exchange mechanisms. While it's a good idea to follow some basic ground rules that will be explained here, ultimately the best way to guarantee effective information sharing is to communicate effectively with the people with whom you are sharing.

Caveat 2: This appendix was written in early 2012, and the information in it went out of date the moment it was sent off for publication. But while the specific versions and brands of software come and go, the basic principles of effective collaboration are fairly constant.

Knowing your software 1: computer operating systems

For a long time, most personal computers (PCs) sold in the UK have been equipped with Microsoft's Windows operating system. If you don't know what kind of operating system your computer has, it's probably Windows.

---

[1] I am indebted to Nik Holmes, Managing Director of Creative Technology Ltd, for the first draft of this appendix.

In some specific areas (for example the education sector in North America or France, or the professional design and graphics sectors worldwide), Apple Mac computers are just as common, and in recent years they have become more popular as general-purpose PCs in the UK. The Apple Mac's operating system is usually known as 'Mac OS' or 'OSX'.

There is a third class of operating system that is still quite rare in the desktop computer world, but that is becoming more popular because of its adoption in the mobile phone and tablet computer industries. It is not commercial, and thus not controlled by any single company for purely commercial reasons in the way that Microsoft controls Windows and Apple controls the Mac OS. Rather, it is a general-purpose framework that is usually provided at no cost to the end-user, and its core elements are maintained and developed by volunteers who choose to make their work available for free.

This operating system is most commonly known as Linux, but you may also encounter specific branded or customised versions of it under other names, such as Ubuntu or Android. Across the world, various versions of Linux are increasingly widely used on desktop PCs, and although it is still perceived as somewhat geeky in the UK, other countries, including China and Germany, have adopted it as a standard for some of their public sector IT systems. Since Linux is free, it is an increasingly popular choice for very low-cost computers.

Knowing your software 2: software applications (sometimes called programs or apps)

If you want to minimise collaboration problems, you need to be aware of exactly what you're using to create and work with your data – not just what operating system, but also which 'application'. For example you may have Microsoft's Office suite of applications, which includes Word (the word-processor application), Excel (the spreadsheet application), and sometimes other applications like PowerPoint or Publisher. If you have a Mac, you may have the iWork suite, which includes the Pages word-processor application and the Numbers spreadsheet application.

Knowing what application you are using is only half the story. You also need to know what version you have, as newer versions will provide more options for saving and opening documents in different file formats. You should also be able to use the 'Save As' or 'Export' feature of your applications to save files in different formats – if you are not sure how to do this, have a look at your application's Help file or manual.

Effective collaboration

The purpose of getting to grips with these technicalities is effective collaboration, so you should also take note of what your collaborators are using. The simplest way to achieve effective collaboration is to use the same applications to work on your data, but if that is not an option, you can often work well with different applications as long as they use the same file formats.

Option 1: use the same applications

The simplest solution to compatibility problems is to equip all collaborators with the same software, ensuring that everyone can work with the same data. In a typical organisation staff will probably already be using the same software – but collaborative working between different organisations or across different computer types can mean that it's not practical to use the same software. If everyone involved with your project has the same version of the same software already, you probably won't have any problems sharing data – but if you do have problems with conflicting application versions or data incompatibilities, the notes below may be useful.

One quite new approach to this problem is to bypass your computer's physical operating system altogether, by working 'in the cloud'. The term 'cloud' is fairly new and, like most pieces of IT terminology, is used by different people to mean very different things – but for our purposes, it means that instead of installing a software application on your computer, you just log in to a website (such as Google's Docs, Microsoft's Skydrive, or Apple's iCloud). You can then create, edit, store, and, in many cases, share documents and files of many types using the tools on these websites, and the only software you need to have installed on your own computer is the web browser, that is, the application you already use to look at and interact with websites.

The editing tools you can use with these online systems are sometimes called 'web apps', with the term 'cloud' more commonly being applied to the storage and sharing mechanism – but all of this terminology is new, and the meanings of specific terms are not standardised across different providers and systems.

Cloud computing provides some excellent new possibilities for collaborative working, but it has one key drawback: you can use it only while you have access to the Internet. As soon as you go offline or your connection fails, you cannot access any of your files or data – and even if this isn't a problem for you, you may find that you cannot collaborate effectively with others because of their Internet connection situation.

Another potential issue with keeping your data 'in the cloud' is confidentiality. It is hard to be sure that your data is secure and unreadable by anyone else if that data is stored on a computer that you do not control. The 'cloud' is just a large number of computers located in data centres and connected to the Internet, and these computers are owned and operated by commercial providers – so there is a theoretical risk that anything stored there could be accessed by unauthorised people or hackers. If you use personal or confidential data, this may present a problem.

If the practicalities make cloud-based information sharing unworkable for a particular project, another option is to use software that is available free and operates on any PC running Windows, Mac OS, or Linux. You may be surprised to learn that such software exists, is widely used around the world, and you can download it from the Internet. The Linux operating system described above is an example of this type of software, which is known generically as 'FOSS', or 'Free and Open Source'.

FOSS applications are available for all sorts of computer work, and one of the most popular is the suite developed as a free alternative to Microsoft's Office suite. This is available in two versions: OpenOffice, the original version, and LibreOffice, a recent variant created by the programming community in response to concerns that OpenOffice may not be supported indefinitely by new owners. The suites can be downloaded free from www.openoffice.org and www.libreoffice. org respectively.

But while the option of using the same software works well for collaboration within an organisation, or where users have some choice about what software they use, in some situations it is simply not practical because users do not control which computers and software they can use. Or they may already be perfectly happy using a familiar word-processing or spreadsheet application, and be unwilling to try a different one. In these situations, the better option is to use a common file format for sharing documents.

Option 2: use the same file types and formats

Most software applications have their own preferred file formats, but there are a number of general-purpose formats that are supported to a greater or lesser extent by most applications for a particular data type. For example, Microsoft Excel 2010 will by default save its files in a native format indicated by a file-name ending in '.xlsx' – but if you choose to save your spreadsheet using options provided under Excel's 'Save As' command, you can choose a different format to suit your purposes. Options include formats that are compatible with earlier versions of Excel (usually '.xls'), and options that almost all spreadsheet applications can use (such as '.csv', which stands for 'comma-separated values').

Similarly, while Microsoft Word will normally save documents in its own 'native' format that may not be readable by a different word-processing application (or by an earlier version of Word), it can also save documents in formats that are compatible with older Word versions, or in a more general-purpose format such as RTF (Rich Text Format). The RTF format does not necessarily support all the features of a word-processor document, and implementations of RTF vary widely between different word-processing applications, but it is still a useful way of sharing simple, formatted textual information.

However, most common data formats (including RTF and CSV) suffer from a significant disadvantage – they work as simplified data-exchange formats, which means that they do not contain all the information that is stored in a proper word-processor document or spreadsheet file. For example, an RTF document saved from Word may not include any automatic paragraph numbers or index markers, and a CSV spreadsheet saved from Excel will not include any colour-coding of cells, or cross-referenced data from different worksheets.

A more effective solution is to use Open Document Format, or ODF. ODF is supported by the International Organization for Standardization (ISO) and is the default file format system used by the OpenOffice and LibreOffice application suites. It is also fully supported in Windows versions of Microsoft Office after 2007 – though it may not be supported in earlier Office versions, or in the Mac version. At the time of writing, ODF is not supported by any of the Mac OS iWork application suite.

Check the Web for up-to-date information on ODF support, and more generally for information on file-format handling in particular applications. File converters for ODF are widely available as free downloads, so even if your preferred application does not support ODF itself, you should be able to find a way of converting between the ODF formats and your application's own file formats.

One possible issue with using different applications to work with the same file formats is that different applications will sometimes vary in how comprehensively they support advanced features in specific document formats. For example, transferring ODF files between different word-processor applications might result in page breaks occurring in different places, because of small differences in how the applications handle the page layout. Likewise some spreadsheet applications may not format or present the same data in exactly the same way. In general, not all applications that can import files of a particular format necessarily support all the features that those files can contain, so if you are using advanced application features (such as cross-references between different spreadsheets, or automatic paragraph numbering in a word-processor document), it is better if all collaborators use the same applications.

Other types of data

It is also important to note that not all data exists in the form of spreadsheets, word-processor documents, and presentations. Photographs, graphic images, video, and sound are all types of information that can cause compatibility problems when shared between different computer systems, and there are far too many other types to list them all here. If you need to work collaboratively with data that is not handled by general-purpose office software, you need to conduct some initial tests with your collaborator(s) to establish what works well and what doesn't, and once you have found an effective combination of applications and file formats, stick to using those.

As a general point, if cost is an issue for you or your collaborators, it's worth searching the web to see if FOSS applications are available for the type of work you are doing. If so, this means that everyone can download and install the same applications for working with the data, at no cost. Some FOSS software can be complicated to install and configure, but applications like the OpenOffice suite, which has been around for a long time and is a mature product, are very user friendly and simple to install.

Glossary

This glossary contains definitions of words and phrases as they are used in this book. You need to bear in mind that research terms are not always used in the same way by everyone.

Words and phrases in italics are defined within this glossary.

abstract: summary of *academic research*, usually 250–500 words long

academic research: *research* conducted for an academic qualification, such as a diploma, Master's degree or PhD, or in support of an academic career

action research: an iterative process of reflection and problem solving in groups or communities

analysis: see *data analysis*

application programming interface (API): a piece of source code that is being used to release some *open data* in such a way that external programs can communicate with it and access or exchange *data*

average: see *mean*

background research: part of a *research* project designed to give context to the *research question*, which may be in the form of a *document review* – for *workplace research*; or a *literature review* – for *academic research*

bibliography: a list at the end of a book or other written *document* containing *references*, some of which are cited in the text and some of which are not but may be useful to readers

bivariate statistics: *descriptive statistics* which describe the relationship between two *variables*

case study: a *research method* in which a single 'case' (person, organisation, country and so on) is studied in depth

citation: giving the details of the source of an idea, fact or opinion which you draw on in your *research*

closed question: a question with predefined answers to choose from

code: a label for a piece of *quantitative data* or *qualitative data*

coding: labelling *quantitative data* or *qualitative data* to facilitate *data analysis*

coding frame: a set of words or phrases to guide your *coding* of *qualitative data*

content analysis: a method of analysing *qualitative data* where you count the number of instances of each *code*

convenience sample: a *sample* where you choose the first *participants* you can find who are willing to help

copyright: the legal right of control over original written (or musical or artistic) work

correlation co-efficient: a statistical calculation that gives an estimate of the average distance of each point on a *scattergraph* from the regression line

covariant relationship: a relationship where two *variables* change in accordance with one another

cross-analysis of data: see *data synthesis*

data: information collected for *research*

data analysis: methods of analysing *data* to find out what it can tell you

data collection: methods of collecting *data* for *research*

data mashup: a mixture of *data* from two or more *APIs*

data preparation: methods of preparing data for *coding* and *analysis*

data repository: a place where *data* is kept, usually on the World Wide Web

data synthesis: comparing and contrasting the *findings* of different segments of *data analysis* within the same piece of *research*. Sometimes called *cross-analysis* of data

dependent variable: a measurable characteristic which stays constant in the course of the *research*

descriptive statistics: *statistics* which enable us to summarise and describe numerical *data*

dissemination: sharing knowledge gained through *research*

dissertation: the write-up of a piece of *academic research* conducted for a qualification such as a Master's degree

document review: a review of relevant *documents* to provide context for *workplace research*

documents: pieces of text which may be used for *background research* or as *data*

doi: Digital Object Identifier, used to uniquely identify *electronic resources*

draft: an unfinished piece of writing

edit: work to improve a *draft*

emancipatory research: see *value-based research*

emergent coding: *coding* based on whatever the researcher perceives to be of interest in *qualitative data*

ephemera: text and/or images that are not designed to be kept, but may be useful as *data*, such as advertising leaflets and social media updates

ethics: the rules of conduct for a particular activity

ethnography: a time-consuming *research method*, used in *qualitative research*, from the discipline of anthropology

evaluation: a type of applied *research* used to assess the effectiveness of services or interventions, and make *recommendations* for improvement

Excel: computer software by Microsoft designed for spreadsheets and with the ability to perform statistical calculations

executive summary: summary of *workplace research*, usually 1–4 pages long

findings: the results of *research*

focus group: a *data-collection* technique in *qualitative research* that usually involves one or two *researchers* and several *participants*

formal theory: a way of making sense of an aspect or aspects of the world around us, based primarily on thought

freewriting: a technique to help writers overcome blocks or solve problems

frequency distribution: a way of showing how many times a particular *variable* has occurred, both of itself and in relation to other variables

generalisability: the extent to which the *findings* of *research* apply in situations beyond that in which the research was conducted

geographic information system: a way of working with *data* that contains location or place information, and plotting it on a map or doing calculations related to its position on the Earth

graph: a diagram to show changes in one *variable* or the relationship between two variables

grey literature: *documents* that are not formally published, but that may be available in hard copy and/or electronic formats from individuals, organisations, or governments

grid: a table designed for keeping records, for example of *documents* or *literature*, or making notes, for example of *observations*, for the purposes of *research*

hypothesis: a hunch, guess, or suspicion about something unknown

independent relationship: a relationship where two *variables* change independently of one another

independent researcher: a researcher who is not part of an academic or other institution

independent variable: a measurable characteristic that changes in the course of the *research*

inferential statistics: *statistics* that enable us to infer something about a *population* from a *sample*

informal theory: a way of making sense of an aspect or aspects of the world around us, based primarily on experience

instrument: see *measuring devices*

intellectual property: original ideas or words, which are held to belong to the person who created them

interval data: *quantitative data* in ranks with a defined numerical distance between them, such as age in years

interview: a *data-collection* technique in *qualitative research* that usually involves one *researcher* and one or two *participants*

inventory: see *measuring devices*

literature: academic texts that may be used for *background research*

literature review: a review of relevant *literature* to provide context for *academic research*

location: a researcher's position, which may be geographical, political, theoretical and so on

mashup tool: a technological tool for combining *data* from different APIs (*application programming interfaces*)

mean: a statistical calculation for *quantitative data* in which the total of all values is divided by the number of values. Also known as the *average*

measuring devices: scales, tools, instruments or inventories designed to measure human characteristics and conditions

median: the middle value in a set of *quantitative data* after it has been ranked in order

meta-analysis: similar to a *systematic review*, but also includes a statistical summary of *findings* from *quantitative research*

metadata records: *data* about *data*, such as grids designed for recording data during *observation* or for coding *visual data*

mixed-method research: *research* drawing on both *quantitative data* and *qualitative data*

mode: the value occurring most commonly in a set of *quantitative data*

nominal data: *data* in categories with labels, such as categories of ethnicity

non-probability sample: a *sample* in which every member of the *population* does not have an equal chance of becoming a member of the *sample*

NVivo: computer software designed to support the *coding* and *analysis* of *qualitative data* including text, audio, and images

observation: a *data-collection* technique in *qualitative research* that usually involves one *researcher* and many *participants*

open access: free access for everyone, for example to academic journal articles

open data: *data* collected by governments and made freely available to everyone

open question: a question with no predefined answers

OpenOffice: freely available software that is compatible with Microsoft Office, including Microsoft *Excel*, and that performs the same functions

ordinal data: *quantitative data* in ranks without a defined numerical distance between them, such as the first, second, and third places in a competition

participant: someone who participates in *research*, for example by completing a *questionnaire* or taking part in an *interview*

participant observation: a time-consuming method of collecting *data*, often used within *ethnography*

participatory action research: similar to *action research*, but with a slightly stronger emphasis on partnership

pie chart: a way to show how many times a particular *variable* has occurred, of itself and in relation to other variables

pilot: a test run of a *data-collection* method to assess its quality

plagiarism: presenting someone else's ideas or words as your own original work

polish: the final stage in the writing process, to remove any remaining errors and finalise structure, grammar, word choices and so on

population: all of the people you could, in theory, include as *participants* in a *research* project

practitioner: someone who works in *public services*, whether paid or unpaid

primary data: *data* collected specifically for your *research* project

probability sample: a sample in which every member of the *population* has an equal chance of becoming a member of the *sample*

public services: services run by society for society, such as health, social care, criminal justice, and education services from pre-school to university

purposive sample: a *sample* of people who, in the researcher's judgement, have most to contribute to the *research*

qualitative data: *data* in the form of words, images, sound, or anything except numbers

qualitative research: *research* based on *qualitative data*

quantitative data: *data* in the form of numbers

quantitative research: *research* based on *quantitative data*

questionnaire: a *data-collection* instrument for *quantitative research*

quota sample: the *population* is divided into segments on the basis of characteristics (for example gender, age, geographical location) and then a different type of *sample*, such as a *convenience sample* or *purposive sample*, is taken from each segment

random sample: a *sample* where random numbers are used to select *participants*

range: the difference between the smallest and largest values in a set of *quantitative data*

recommendations: suggestions for how *workplace research* can be put into practice

reference: the full details of a *document* or piece of *literature*, signposted by a *citation*

reference list: a list at the end of a research report, dissertation, or thesis, containing *references*, all of which are cited in the text

reliability: the extent to which a *research method* will produce the same results when used in different situations

research: systematic investigation, using a predefined *research method*, to gather information with the aim of answering a predefined *research question*

research commissioner: someone who holds a budget for a piece of *research*

research method: system for conducting *research*

research plan: similar to a *research proposal*, most commonly used in *workplace research* to inform people such as research commissioners, managers, and colleagues

research proposal: a written explanation of what you intend to *research* and why, and how you intend to carry out the research, to inform people such as potential funders or PhD supervisors, most commonly used in *academic research*

research question: the stated question which a piece of *research* aims to answer

research report: the write-up of a piece of *workplace research*

research topic: the subject area of a piece of *research*

researcher: a person who does *research*

sample: the people you include as *participants* in a *research* project, drawn from a *population*

scale: see *measuring devices*

scattergraph: a *graph* that gives an overview of the relationship between two *variables*

secondary data: *data* that was not collected specifically for your *research* project, but that you can use in your research

service user: a user of *public services*

snowball sample: a *sample* where one or more *participants* help the researcher to find other participants

SPSS: Statistical Package for Social Scientists, computer software designed to perform statistical calculations

standpoint: a person's own position from which they view or judge things

statistics: a branch of mathematics that enables the *analysis* and interpretation of numerical *data*

stratified random sample: a sample where the *population* is divided into segments on the basis of characteristics such as gender, age, or geographical location, and then a *random sample* is taken from each segment of the population

stratified sample: a *sample* where you use one number generated at random to select the first *participant*, then choose other participants at regular intervals, for example every third or every tenth person

survey: a piece of *research*, often large-scale, to investigate people's experiences, attitudes, behaviours, judgements, beliefs and so on

systematic review: a review of all the *research* previously conducted around a specific *research question*

thematic analysis: a method for identifying themes within coded *data*

theory: a way of making sense of an aspect or aspects of the world around us. See also *formal theory* and *informal theory*

thesis: the write-up of a piece of *academic research* conducted for a qualification such as a PhD

third sector: organisations and groups that provide *public services* and are neither state-funded nor run purely for profit, such as charities, social enterprises and community groups

tool: see *measuring devices*

transcribe: to convert *data* from audio to text

univariate statistics: *descriptive statistics* that describe a single *variable*

URL: Uniform Resource Locator; that is, the address of a web page

validity: the extent to which a *research method* does what it claims to do

value-based research: *research* intended to effect positive change, sometimes called *emancipatory research*

variable: a measurable characteristic

variance: in *quantitative data*, an estimate of the average distance of each value from the *mean*

visual data: *qualitative data* in the form of images, such as photographs, paintings, drawings, collage, video

viva: an oral examination for *academic research* such as a PhD

workplace research: *research* conducted to support professional work, such as *evaluation* research, skills audit, training needs analysis

Bibliography

Alaszewski, A. (2006) *Using diaries for social research*, London: Sage.

Barber, R., Boote, J., Glenys, P., Cooper, C. and Yeeles, P. (2011) 'Evaluating the impact of public involvement on research', in M. Barnes and P. Cotterell (eds) *Critical perspective on user involvement*, Bristol: The Policy Press, pp 217–23.

Barnes, M. and Cotterell, P. (eds) *Critical perspective on user involvement*, Bristol: The Policy Press.

Baumeister, R. and Tierney, J. (2011) *Willpower: Rediscovering our greatest strength*, London: Allen Lane.

Becker, H. (2007) *Writing for social scientists: How to start and finish your thesis, book or article*, Chicago: Chicago University Press.

Bell, J. (2010) *Doing your research project: A guide for first-time researchers in education, health and social science* (5th edn), Buckingham: Open University Press.

Bhana, A. (2006) 'Participatory action research: a practical guide for realistic radicals', in M. Terre Blanche, K. Durrheim and D. Painter (eds) *Research in practice: Applied methods for the social sciences* (2nd edn), Cape Town: University of Cape Town Press Ltd, pp 429–42.

Björk, B-C., Welling, P., Laakso, M., Majlender, P., Hedlund, T. et al (2010) 'Open access to the scientific journal literature: situation 2009', *PLoS ONE*, vol 5, no 6, p e11273. doi:10.1371/journal.pone.0011273.

Bloor, M. (2011) 'Addressing social problems through qualitative research', in D. Silverman (ed) *Qualitative research: Issues of theory, method and practice*, London: Sage, pp 399–415.

Bourgois, P. (2002) *In search of respect: Selling crack in El Barrio* (2nd edn), Cambridge: Cambridge University Press.

Bowen, G. (2009) 'Document analysis as a qualitative research method', *Qualitative Research Journal*, vol 9, no 2, pp 27–40.

Branfield, F. (2009) *Developing user involvement in social work education*, Workforce Development Report 29, London: Social Care Institute for Excellence.

British Library (n.d.) 'Quantitative methods in social research', British Library Social Science Collection Guide: Topical Bibliography, http://www.bl.uk/reshelp/findhelpsubject/socsci/topbib/quantmethods/quantitative.pdf. (Lists lots of useful websites, journals, and other helpful information and resources.)

Bryman, A. (2011) *Social research methods* (4th edn), Oxford: Oxford University Press.

Bryman, A. and Cramer, D. (2009) *Quantitative data analysis with SPSS 14, 15 and 16: A guide for social scientists*, London: Routledge.

Bunting, M. (2004) *Willing slaves: How the overwork culture is ruling our lives*, London: HarperCollins.

Clark–Carter, D. (2010) *Quantitative psychological research: A student's handbook* (3rd edn), Hove: Psychology Press.
(This is a readable and comprehensive book on quantitative methods with many worked examples. It is potentially useful for anyone interested in quantitative research, not just psychology students or professionals.)

Cottrell, S. (2005) *Critical thinking skills: Developing effective analysis and argument*, Basingstoke: Palgrave Macmillan.

Creswell, J. (2007) *Qualitative inquiry and research design: Choosing among five approaches* (2nd edn), London: Sage.
(The five approaches are: narrative research, phenomenology, grounded theory, ethnography, and case study. The book is well written and worth reading, whether or not you intend to use one of these approaches.)

Dahlberg, L. and McCaig, C. (eds) (2010) *Practical research and evaluation: A start-to-finish guide for practitioners*, London: Sage.

Davies (2007) *Doing a successful research project using qualitative or quantitative methods*, Basingstoke: Palgrave Macmillan.

Davis, C. (2010) *Statistical testing in practice with StatsDirect*, Tamarac, FL: Lumina Press.

Diamond, S. (2010) *Getting more*, London: Penguin.

Dryden, W. (2009) *Self-discipline*, London: Sheldon Press.

Etheridge, D. (2007) *Excel 2007 data analysis*, Hoboken, NJ: Wiley.

Ethical Code for Socio-Economic Research in Europe, www.respectproject.org/code/index.php.

Ethical Code of the American Psychological Association, www.apa.org/ethics/code/index.aspx.

Ethical Code of the British Psychological Society www.bps.org.uk/sites/default/files/documents/code_of_ethics_and_conduct.pdf.

Faulkner, A. (2004) *The ethics of survivor research: Guidelines for the ethical conduct of research carried out by mental health service users and survivors*, Bristol: The Policy Press.

Fox, M., Martin, P. and Green, G. (2007) *Doing practitioner research*, London: Sage.

Gabriel, Y. (2000) *Storytelling in organizations: Facts, fictions and fantasies*, Oxford: Oxford University Press.

Gillham, B. (2000) *Developing a questionnaire*, London: Continuum.

Glasby, J. (2011) 'From evidence-based to knowledge-based policy and practice', in J. Glasby (ed) *Evidence, policy and practice: critical perspectives in health and social care*, pp 85–98. Bristol: The Policy Press.

Goldacre, B. (2008) *Bad science*, London: Fourth Estate.

Greasley, P. (2008) *Quantitative data analysis using SPSS: An introduction for health and social science*, Maidenhead: Open University Press.

Hart, C. (1998) *Doing a literature review*, London: Sage.

Hart, C. (2001) *Doing a literature search*, London: Sage.

Hayes, C. (2011) *A review of service user involvement in prisons and probation trusts*, London: Clinks.

Hine, C. (2005) *Virtual methods: Issues in social research on the Internet*, Oxford: Berg.

Jesson, J., Matheson, L. and Lacey, F. (2011) *Doing your literature review: Traditional and systematic techniques*, London: Sage.

Kahneman, D. (2011) *Thinking, fast and slow*, London: Allen Lane.

Kemshall, H. and Littlechild, R. (eds) (2000) *User involvement and participation in social care: Research informing practice*, London: Jessica Kingsley Publishers.

Krueger, R. and Casey, M. (2009) *Focus groups: A practical guide for applied research* (4th edn), London: Sage.

Kumar, R. (2005) *Research methodology: A step-by-step guide for beginners*, London: Sage.

Laakso, M., Welling, P., Bukvova, H., Nyman, L., Björk, B-C. et al (2011) 'The development of open access journal publishing from 1993 to 2009', *PLoS ONE*, vol 6, no 6, p e20961. doi:10.1371/journal.pone.0020961.

Langdridge, D. and Hagger-Johnson (2009) *Introduction to research methods and data analysis in psychology* (2nd edn), Harlow: Pearson Education.

Markham A. (2011) 'Internet research', in D. Silverman (ed) *Qualitative research: Issues of theory, method and practice*, London: Sage, pp 110–27.

Mason, J. (2002) *Qualitative researching* (2nd edn), London: Sage.

Murray, R. (2009) *Writing for academic journals* (2nd edn), Maidenhead: Open University Press.

Murray, R. (2011a) *How to write a thesis* (3rd edn), Buckingham: Open University Press.

Murray, R. (2011b) 'Developing a community of research practice', *British Educational Research Journal*. doi:10.1080/01411926.2011.583635.

Myers, J., Well, A. and Lorch, R. (2010) *Research design and statistical analysis* (3rd edn), London: Routledge.

Oliver, P. (2010a) *The student's guide to research ethics*, Maidenhead: Open University Press.

Oliver, P. (2010b) *Understanding the research process*, London: Sage.

Pallant, J. (2010) *SPSS survival manual: A step by step guide to data analysis using SPSS* (4th edn), Maidenhead: Open University Press.

Pears, R. and Shields, G. (2010) *Cite them right* (8th edn), Basingstoke: Palgrave.

Petticrew, M. and Roberts, H. (2005) *Systematic reviews in the social sciences: A practical guide*, Oxford: Blackwell.

Poynter, R. (2010) *The handbook of online and social media research: tools and techniques for market researchers*, Chichester: John Wiley & Sons Ltd.

Prior, L. (2011) 'Using documents in social research', in D. Silverman (ed) *Qualitative research: Issues of theory, method and practice*, London: Sage, pp 93–110.

Prosser J. and Schwartz, D. (1998) 'Photographs within the sociological research process', in J. Prosser (ed) *Image-based research: A sourcebook for qualitative researchers*, London: RoutledgeFalmer, pp 115–30.

Punch, K. (2000) *Developing effective research proposals*, London: Sage.

Rapley, T. (2011) 'Some pragmatics of data analysis', in D. Silverman (ed) *Qualitative research: Issues of theory, method and practice*, London: Sage, pp 274–90.

Rapport, N. (2008) *Of orderlies and men: Hospital porters achieving wellness at work*, Durham, NC: Carolina Academic Press.

Robson, C. (2011) *Real world research* (3rd edn), Chichester: John Wiley, pp 495–513.

Rose, G. (2012) *Visual methodologies* (3rd edn), London: Sage.

Silverman, D. (2001) *Interpreting qualitative data: Methods for analysing talk, text and interaction* (2nd edn), London: Sage.

Silverman, D. and Marvasti, A. (2008) *Doing qualitative research: A comprehensive guide*, London: Sage.

Stein, S. (1995) *Solutions for writers: Practical craft techniques for fiction and non-fiction*, London: Souvenir Press.

Streiner, D. and Norman, G. (2008) *Health measurement scales: A practical guide to their development and use*, Oxford: Oxford University Press.
(This book focuses on psychological testing. It provides a good introduction to measurement devices, signposts some of the existing devices, and offers advice for anyone who wants to develop a new device.)

Thomas, G. (2011) *How to do your case study: A guide for students and researchers*, London: Sage.

Turner, M. and Beresford, P. (2005) *User controlled research: Its meanings and potential*, Final report, Shaping Our Lives and the Centre for Citizen Participation, Brunel University.

Westmarland, L. (2011) *Researching crime and justice: Tales from the field*, London: Routledge.

Wetton, N. and McWhirter, J. (1998) 'Images and curriculum development in health education', in J. Prosser (ed) *Image-based research: A sourcebook for qualitative researchers*, London: RoutledgeFalmer, pp 263–83.

Whitelaw, S., Beattie, A., Balogh, R. and Watson, J. (2003) *A review of the nature of action research*, Sustainable Health Action Research Programme, Cardiff: Welsh Assembly Government.

Index

Note: The letter t following a page number indicates a table.